D1797512

THE ROYAL NAVY
SINCE 1945
Its Transition to the Nuclear Age

The Royal Navy Since 1945

Its Transition to the Nuclear Age

A. CECIL HAMPSHIRE

With a foreword by
Admiral of the Fleet Sir Peter Hill-Norton, GCB,
Chairman of the Military Committee of NATO

BOOK CLUB EDITION

This edition published by
Purnell Book Services Limited
St. Giles House, 49/50 Poland Street, W1A 2LG
by arrangement with William Kimber Limited

© A. Cecil Hampshire, 1975
ISBN 0 7183 0034 3

Made and printed in Great Britain by
The Garden City Press Limited
Letchworth, Hertfordshire SG6 1JS

Contents

List of Illustrations

Between pages 82 and 83

Naval clearance divers at work
Amphibious warfare group   *Crown copyright*
Tribal class frigate   *Crown copyright*

Between pages 114 and 115

HMS *Hampshire* firing Sea Slug   *Crown copyright*
Loading the Seacat guided weapon
Limbo anti-submarine mortar   *Crown copyright*
HMS *Dreadnought*   *Crown copyright*
Replenishment at sea
Buccaneer aircraft over Aden   *Imperial War Museum*
Guided missile destroyer replenishing from RFA *Olwen*
                              Photo: Angus McNee
The *Leander* class frigate *Andromeda*   *Crown copyright*
The Polaris submarine *Resolution*   *Crown copyright*
Helicopter support ship *Engadine*

Between pages 146 and 147

Oceanographical survey ship *Hecla*   *Crown copyright*
Board of Admiralty in session   *Imperial War Museum*
The aircraft carrier *Ark Royal*
One of her engine rooms   *Crown copyright*
Main engine controls in a guided missile destroyer
                              Crown copyright
Control room of nuclear fleet submarine   *Crown copyright*
Wasp helicopter landing on board a frigate
The helicopter cruiser HMS *Tiger*   *Crown copyright*
Wessex helicopter refuelling from a *Rothesay* class frigate

Between pages 178 and 179

'Ton' class coastal minesweeper at speed   *Crown copyright*
SRN 5 Hovercraft in Sarawak   *Imperial War Museum*
Fast patrol boats   *Imperial War Museum*
HMS *Bristol* firing a Sea Dart
The Ikara anti-submarine missile   *Crown copyright*
Skynet communications system   *Crown copyright*

Foreword

Admiral of the Fleet Sir Peter Hill-Norton, GCB,
Chairman of the Military Committee of NATO
Formerly First Sea Lord and Chief of the Naval Staff,
and Chief of the Defence Staff

I am particularly pleased to have been invited to introduce this book because it deals with a period covering much of my Naval Service. In fact, many of the decisions taken, and changes introduced, in the 1960's and early 1970's occurred during my time in office either as a member of the Admiralty Board or as Chief of the Defence Staff.

The wind of change inevitably buffeted the Royal Navy in much the same way as it did many of our other historic and valued institutions, and this book chronicles the impact of the change on the international balance of power, and of the influence of national sociological, economic and scientific developments on the structure, organisation and capability of the Royal Navy in the years from 1945 to 1975.

Virtually every aspect of Naval activity has been faithfully, factually and dispassionately recorded with a wealth of detail which never becomes boring. I found it an eminently readable and fascinating account of the contemporary history of my profession, and of the Service in which I have been fortunate enough to spend most of my life. It does indeed go further, and there is much to be learned, in passing, of the Royal Navy in earlier days.

Pax Britannica is in the past and the British Sailor today has grown up in the knowledge that allegiance to collective security in the form of the North Atlantic Treaty Organisation is the best way to serve his country. In all ranks and ratings he has had to acquire a range of new and demanding skills, and the rapidity and success with which he has done so is a recurring feature of what must be the most dynamic years of Naval history.

Conversely, it seems inconceivable that long overdue reforms in conditions of service should have taken so long to set in motion. Not until ten years after the end of the Second World War was the two to three year commission away from families reduced to twelve months, and then, much later, to nine months. Married Quarters, tolerable living conditions ashore and afloat, and many other amenities long and properly taken for granted by the other two Services, took many years to become a reality. And despite all the dire forebodings, rum, the curse of the Navy in the second half of the twentieth century, was abolished with scarcely a murmur; but not until 1970.

For the most part we are left to draw our own conclusions as to why a particular course was chosen, and here I would suggest that it needs to be kept constantly in mind that in matters of major policy it is Her Majesty's Government which takes the ultimate decisions. The Admiralty Board and the Chiefs of Staff Committee, which are not autonomous, are there to advise before such decisions, and to implement them once taken.

I believe that this very comprehensive work will do much to further a better understanding of what the Navy has been doing during the past thirty years. The accent, and rightly, is on change—change of attitudes, change of hardware, change of shape and of size, change of methods, of promotion and entry systems, of pay and even of uniform, and of discipline. An evolution, for which dramatic is not too strong a word, has taken place in thirty years. What has not changed, and Mr. Hampshire does well to say so, is the wholly admirable sense of duty and pride in their Service of the officers and men of the Royal Navy, the Royal Fleet Auxiliary, and the civilians who support them.

P. J. Hill-Norton, A. of F.

'The progress of science and the development of new weapons increases rather than diminishes the basic uses of sea-power because its principles of mobility, flexibility and ubiquity remain unchanged.'

J. L. SULLIVAN, US Under-Secretary for the Navy,
speaking on American Navy Day, 1946.

CHAPTER ONE

Rundown

When, on 2nd September 1945, Japanese envoys signed the instrument of unconditional surrender on board the American battleship *Missouri* in Tokyo Bay, thus officially bringing to an end the Second World War, the Royal Navy had grown to a size greater than at any period in its long history.

It included 15 battleships, four of them among the newest and most powerful in the world; 52 aircraft carriers; 63 cruisers; 257 destroyers; 137 submarines; 542 sloops, frigates and corvettes; 1,069 minesweeping and anti-submarine vessels; 1,389 motor torpedo-boats, motor and steam gunboats, patrol boats and motor launches; 4,986 landing craft of all types, and some 430 miscellaneous auxiliary vessels, ranging from repair and supply ships and tankers to tugs and salvage craft. Fleet Air Arm aircraft totalled 1,336 front line machines alone, formed into more than 70 strike and fighter squadrons. Serving personnel numbered 790,000 officers and men and 74,000 WRNS.

The British Pacific Fleet, which had been created towards the end of the war in Europe to take part with the Americans in the main operations against Japan, was itself a vast armada, more numerous and powerful than any previously detached British naval force. Under the command of Admiral Sir Bruce Fraser, it totalled more than 200 warships of all classes, from battleships to minesweepers. To maintain this formidable array of fighting ships, operating many hundreds of miles from its nearest base, were nearly 100 auxiliaries, including storeships, tankers and water-carriers. This 'Fleet Train', as it was called, was commanded by an admiral, and even boasted an 'amenities ship', whose star attraction was a brewery known appropriately as 'Davy Jones's' which produced some 250 barrels of 'English mild ale' weekly.

Yet the vastly expanded Navy of Britain was completely overshadowed by the enormous and still growing size of the United States fleet. In August 1945 the Americans were deploying in the Pacific theatre of war alone 23 battleships, 89 aircraft carriers, 67 cruisers, 759 destroyers and destroyer escorts, and 238 submarines. In addition it was planned that by the end of the year these would be joined by another 1,300 warships of all types, including a number of 'super' aircraft carriers. Thus the surrender ceremony on board the USS *Missouri* marked not only the end of the greatest conflict in history, but the end also of Britain's centuries-long reign as Mistress of the Seas. The days of *Pax Britannica* were over, and Britannia's trident would pass to the United States, which had now reached the pinnacle of maritime power.

But this significant aspect of history passed almost unnoticed amidst the prevailing atmosphere of relief and rejoicing. If strategists gave any thought to the shape of things to come it was that the appearance of the atom bomb had rendered both navies and armies obsolete.

Barely a month after the end of the war in Europe, demobilisation of Britain's armed forces began, release being effected under a group system. For the Navy this rundown of manpower was easier of accomplishment than had been the case at the end of the First World War. During that conflict the personnel of the Fleet had risen from just under 150,000 to almost half a million, regular Navy entrants having been expanded along with those of the Reserves. But in the Second World War expansion had been confined to the Reserves only.

Nevertheless, demobilisation imposed a considerable strain on the Fleet because of immediate post-war commitments. These included provision of a share of the forces needed to ensure the execution by the defeated Powers of the terms of surrender; the liquidation of Japanese occupying forces in South-East Asia and the repatriation of hundreds of thousands of Allied prisoners of war and internees; the reduction of garrisons and the maintenance of internal security and the restoration of settled conditions throughout the Empire; the safeguarding of communications and the upkeep of bases. Probably the most important and immediate task was to clear the seas of the enormous number of mines sown by the belligerents during six years of war.

Some hint of the size of Britain's post-war Fleet was given in the Navy Estimates of March 1946. The first to be presented in detail since the outbreak of war, during which all Votes had been for a token £100, they totalled £255,075,000. But only £29 million of this sum was allocated to new construction. The building programme originally planned for the financial year had been drastically cut when the war in Europe ended, and now included only two escort vessels, one submarine, two surveying ships, six small floating docks and a number of miscellaneous small craft.

One battleship, HMS *Vanguard*, which had been laid down in 1941 and launched in November 1944, was, however, to be completed. The largest ever built in this country, her standard displacement was 42,500 tons, and she embodied all the experience human ingenuity could devise, gained in the war at sea which had introduced homing torpedoes, magnetic and acoustic mines, and radio-controlled aerial bombs. It was claimed that if she was not unsinkable she would take a lot of sinking. Exclusive of guns and mountings, her total cost was £9 million, more than three times as much as her immediate predecessors of the *King George V* class.

Since VE-Day no fewer than 727 projected vessels, from fleet carrier downwards, had been cancelled. Thousands of wartime vessels were to be sold or scrapped, a large number of them small craft for which there would be no place in the peacetime Navy. The size of the Reserve Fleet was fixed at a total of 400 ships of all types, to be maintained in the highest degree of material readiness at minimum cost and with maximum economy in manpower by means of a new method of preservation known as cocooning or 'mothballing'.

(This process involved sealing a ship's armament inside cocoons built of a wood and webbing structure, covered with fish netting, sprayed with a lacquer and coated with a latex compound and finished off with layers of plastic, a desiccant being put inside to absorb moisture. Cathodic protection helped to preserve the underwater hull; dehumidification the internal compartments; and packaging and sealing the main and auxiliary machinery and boilers, electrical and radio equipment. Vessels so protected could be re-activated at short notice.)

Peacetime seagoing commands were to be reinstituted, but to the alarm of naval strategists who foresaw dire results of this oft-repeated policy in our past history, they would be smaller in numbers and less powerful than before. The reasons, however, could scarcely be argued with. The country's economy had been seriously weakened as a result of the war, and Britain's position as a World Power diminished by the rise of the United States and Soviet Russia. As Winston Churchill had remarked after the dropping of the atom bombs on Hiroshima and Nagasaki, 'Henceforward most of the accepted theories of strategy were seen to be out of date and a new and undreamt of balance of power was created, a balance based on the ownership of the means of mutual extermination.'

Up to the outbreak of the war the Navy's two largest seagoing commands had been maintained in home waters and the Mediterranean. In 1938 the Home Fleet had comprised six battleships, two aircraft carriers, five cruisers, three destroyer flotillas and one submarine flotilla. In the Mediterranean were three battleships and a battle cruiser, one aircraft carrier, five cruisers, four flotillas of destroyers, a submarine flotilla and a number of minor war vessels. The China Squadron, next in importance of overseas stations, comprised five cruisers, an aircraft carrier, one destroyer flotilla, fifteen submarines and some forty smaller craft, which included a number of river gunboats. The East Indies Squadron, which was also required to provide warships for patrolling the Persian Gulf, consisted of two cruisers and six escort vessels. At the Cape of Good Hope were one cruiser and four escort vessels; and on the America and West Indies station four cruisers and an escort vessel.

The new commands again included a Home Fleet, but this time it would comprise only one battleship, as Fleet flagship, one or more aircraft carriers, a cruiser squadron and two destroyer flotillas. The Mediterranean Fleet was to consist of one or two aircraft carriers, a cruiser squadron and one destroyer flotilla. The East Indies station would comprise one cruiser squadron; the Pacific Fleet one or more aircraft carriers, a cruiser squadron and a flotilla of submarines. A cruiser squadron would be maintained in the South Atlantic based on the Cape, and another on the America and West Indies station.

In order to preserve long-standing associations which individual squadrons and flotillas had formed with local British communities in various parts of the world in peacetime, and because most of the fleet trophies and mementoes were inscribed with pre-war numbers, the post-war cruiser squadrons and destroyer flotillas reverted as far as possible to their previous nomenclature.

But one old-time division of an overseas naval station was not re-established. This was the gunboat patrol of the Yangtse and West Rivers which for many years had constituted an important adjunct to the Royal Navy's peacetime China Station. As far back as 1858 the Treaty of Tientsin had enacted that 'British ships of war, coming for no hostile purpose or being engaged in the pursuit of pirates, shall be at liberty to visit all ports within the dominions of the Emperor of China'. This right had been carried over into the twentieth century after China became a republic. During the Second World War, however, as a gesture of goodwill to our Chinese allies in the struggle against Japan, this and other extraterritorial privileges had been finally abrogated.

After the outbreak of war in 1939 the gunboats were gradually withdrawn, either for scrapping or service in other theatres, and now would never be replaced. The forebodings of those who deplored the weakening of our naval strength overseas were to be realised within four years when once again China found herself in the throes of a civil war which resulted in the final overthrow of the Nationalist Government of Chiang Kai-shek.

The main home commands reverted to the normal three—at the Nore, Portsmouth and Plymouth, the remnants of the famous wartime Western Approaches command at Liverpool being taken over by the Commander-in-Chief, Plymouth. But the wartime appointment of Flag Officer, Naval Air Stations, remained with headquarters at Lee-on-Solent. Future training was to be systemised and standardised. A School of Combined Operations Training was set up in north Devon under a senior Royal Marine officer, and a Joint Anti-Submarine School in Londonderry. HMS *Collingwood*, a boys' training establishment at Fareham, in Hampshire, became a combined Radar and Electrical Training School. In September the Dartmouth cadets returned to their own college from Eaton Hall, Cheshire, whence they had been evacuated in 1942.

New rates of pay were introduced, to come into force from 1st July 1946. Thus an Ordinary Seaman on entry would now receive four shillings (20p) a day, nearly twice the amount paid during the war; Able Seamen six shillings (30p); Leading Seamen seven shillings and sixpence (37$\frac{1}{2}$p); petty officers nine shillings (45p); and chief petty officers ten shillings and sixpence (52$\frac{1}{2}$p).

In addition there was trade pay for artificers, and a new increment system after two years' service. Good Conduct Badges, each worth two shillings and fourpence (11$\frac{1}{2}$p) weekly would be awarded after four, eight and twelve years man's service; the grading of marriage allowances according to the number of children was discontinued, and a flat rate of one pound fifteen shillings (£1.75) a week introduced, with higher rates for senior ratings. Children were to be eligible for family allowances, and a new basic scale of pensions introduced common to all three Services on completion of twenty-two years' service from the age of 18 which would be considerably higher than the old rates. These new rates similarly applied to the Royal Marines.

Officers' pay had already been increased a few months earlier, but with a common scale for all branches, and specialist pay abolished. Thus a midshipman's pay went up from six shillings and ninepence (34p) a day to seven shillings and sixpence (37½p); lieutenants by sixpence (2½p) to seventeen shillings (85p) on promotion, and by increased amounts according to seniority; commanders by thirteen shillings (65p) to two pounds seven shillings and sixpence (£2.37½) daily; captains from two pounds twelve shillings and fourpence (£2.61½) to three pounds five shillings (£3.25); while that of an admiral of the fleet went up from seven pounds four shillings and tenpence (£7.24) daily to nine pounds.

Command Money varied from three shillings (15p) a day for a lieutenant to ten shillings (50p) daily for the captain of a major warship. Flying Pay and Submarine Pay continued at three shillings (15p) per diem; Marriage Allowance varied according to rank, but the qualifying age was reduced from 30 to 25. Unhappily the latter was now made taxable.

One interesting relic of past naval history remained to be disposed of. In December 1945 the First Lord of the Admiralty announced that prize money would be paid for the last time since, under modern conditions of warfare, it raised many anomalies and inconsistencies. In any future hostilities it would be assimilated into the normal grant of gratuities.

Prize money originated in remote history when the monarch, who usually had to build and equip the Navy himself, made private bargains with his captains and admirals as to the division of all captures. Thus Henry VIII claimed half of all money and valuables as well as the guns and rigging of all ships captured; and in the Elizabethan era there were many opportunities for fabulous sums to be made both by the Crown and naval commanders. In 1649 under the Commonwealth a Prize Court was established, and the half share previously claimed by the monarch went to the Navy Treasurer for charitable purposes.

A new Act regarding the disposal of prize money was introduced by Charles II in 1661, which was amended by Queen Anne when the Prize Fund was vested in the Crown and a substantial portion of it in the form of a grant made to the captors, for whom an exact ratio of shares was laid down. But large fortunes could still be made by individual commanders. Thus Admiral Anson received £125,000 for captures made during his voyage round the world; Admiral Saunders, under whose command the frigates *Active* and *Favourite* captured the Spanish treasure ship *Hermione* in 1762, received

£64,393 as his share of the prize money, every lieutenant concerned got £13,000, and each seaman and marine £485.

At the beginning of the First World War it was recognised that modern conditions made it unfair to adhere to the former rule of distributing prize money only to those who actually captured an enemy ship, and it was decided that all those serving in the Royal Navy at sea should be eligible to participate in a general share-out at the end of hostilities. But even this seemed to be unfair, for of the £14 million available for distribution in 1919 an admiral commanding-in-chief received 850 shares, while an ordinary seaman got only three. Thus Admiral Beatty received approximately £4,000, but an able seaman only £25.

In 1945, however, the total sum available as prize money amounted to only £5¼ million. The reason for this was that in the First World War the Germans took very little care to protect their merchant ships; thus a large number were captured. But in the recently ended conflict the enemy had seen to it that his ships were kept in port as far as possible. Those that did venture on to the high seas had orders to scuttle themselves immediately if capture appeared likely. The result was that fewer ships were captured, and therefore there was very much less to divide.

In previous wars ships had always been captured by other ships, but in the Second World War the Air Force came to play a considerable part in naval warfare, in particular Coastal Command which had a great deal to do with the capture of ships. Accordingly the sum of £1¼ million from the total Prize Fund was handed over to the Royal Air Force. This sum was not, however, distributed to individual members of that Service, but made available to charitable and welfare organisations associated with the RAF.

The remaining £4 million was distributed to all naval officers and ratings and Royal Marines and merchant seamen who had been subject to naval discipline, provided they had served at sea continuously for six months. The number of shares varied from ten for an admiral of the fleet to one for an ordinary seaman. The actual distribution, which worked out at approximately £60 for a senior flag officer to £6 for an ordinary seaman, was made two years later. Thus a fascinating link with British naval history, and a one-time recruiting incentive, was finally severed.

In October 1945 the Royal Naval Volunteer Reserve, entry into which on a permanent basis had been suspended since the outbreak of war, was reconstituted, with Divisions as before designated

'London', 'Sussex', 'Severn', 'Mersey', 'Clyde', 'Ulster', 'Forth', 'Tay', 'Tyne', 'Humber' and 'Solent'. Total strength was fixed at 10,000 officers and men. Since it was not possible to grant permanent commissions to all temporary officers entered during the war who wished to transfer to the permanent Reserve, the Admiralty re-established the Royal Naval Volunteer Supplementary Reserve. This Reserve consisted of a list of officers of all branches who had held temporary commissions in the RNVR during the war and were willing to be called up for service with the Navy on the issue of a Royal Proclamation calling out the Reserves. No training commitment was involved and no bounty or retaining fee paid; nor were officers required to provide themselves with uniform. Former 'Hostilities Only' ratings of most branches were also invited to join the new permanent RNVR.

Despite the continuance of National Service, which was found necessary in order to carry out smoothly the demobilisation programme, a recruiting campaign for regular engagements was launched for all three Services, the newly increased rates of pay and other measures being expected to go a long way towards providing the necessary incentives. Referring to the Navy's needs, the Parliamentary Secretary to the Admiralty told the Commons that whatever might be the future of conscription, National Servicemen could not provide crews for ships on foreign stations, nor the long experience and technical qualifications for higher ratings. The Navy must rely on long-term voluntary engagement.

Added inducements to recruiting included the introduction of a new four-year engagement with a bounty of £125 on completion, while men already serving who extended their engagements could qualify for a bounty and a gratuity for each completed year of extended service. Similar offers were made to certain regular and 'Hostilities Only' ratings who had already taken their discharge.

It was decided that the WRNS should not be completely disbanded as had been done after the end of the 1914–18 war, but remain as an integral part of the Navy not subject to the Naval Discipline Act and with its own separate disciplinary code. Service would be for periods of four years, and there would be twenty-four categories of rating, ranging from cooks and stewards, quarters and welfare workers, down to transport drivers, wireless operators, radar mechanics and naval airwomen. Temporary extended service was open to all officers and ratings of the WRNS who had completed one year's service, those accepted being eligible to apply for permanent service when this should be introduced.

In all new construction ships and those refitting, efforts were begun to improve living conditions for ships' companies along lines which were already commonplace in the US Navy. Thus galley and bakery equipment was to be modernised, and facilities for bathing and washing clothes improved. The principle of separating recreational spaces from messes where men ate and slept was to be adopted as far as possible. Other amenities included the provision of automatic refrigerators, soda fountains and ice cream machines, facilities for tailoring, boot repairing, dry cleaning and hairdressing. Labour-saving devices such as automatic chipping, scaling and paint-spraying machines would also be introduced. In larger ships such as the *Vanguard* a complete dining hall was provided. In some of the other large vessels cafeteria messing was introduced. Most ships, excepting the smallest, would be able to boast a fully equipped cinema theatre.

But there were limitations to the extent of such improvements in the older ships which were being retained because of the need to accommodate the mass of new technical equipment, such as radar and other electronic devices, coming into service, higher speeds and better protection. These necessitated increased complements with consequent overcrowding of living spaces. The effect was also to send up the tonnage of new ships in relation to armament. Thus, although the *Vanguard* mounted only eight 15-inch guns, she displaced 42,500 tons as compared with the *Nelson*'s 33,900 tons; yet the latter was armed with nine 16-inch guns and carried twenty-six smaller calibre weapons as secondary armament. New cruisers were 1,000 tons heavier than earlier vessels of comparable gunpower, and destroyers nearly 700 tons in excess of their wartime sisters.

Although the bulk of projected new construction was cancelled immediately after the end of the war because of financial stringency, the need to re-think naval policy in the light of new forms of offence, and to clear the slipways for the rebuilding of our merchant fleet, certain other warships as well as the *Vanguard* had become so far advanced that it was decided to complete them. Largest of the projected new aircraft carriers was the *Eagle*. Laid down in October 1942 in the Belfast yard of Harland and Wolff, she was launched in March 1946 by the then Princess Elizabeth. Her building had been retarded by other priorities and, in fact, another five years would elapse before she was finally completed. But this delay enabled many improvements to be incorporated. Originally to be named *Audacious*, she was the first of a new *Ark Royal* class of four fleet carriers. Two of these had been cancelled but the name ship was still on the stocks in Cammell Laird's yard at Birkenhead and would eventually take the water.

The last two of a class of seven 18,000-ton light fleet carriers were completed, and a third of a similar class named *Leviathan* was towed in an unfinished state from her building yard on the Tyne to Portsmouth to be completed in the Royal dockyard when possible. In the event she was never finished.

Of the smaller vessels under construction, sixteen destroyers were completed during the year, eight submarines, four sloops, a frigate and two despatch vessels. A new type of all-welded destroyer was also launched, the methods used in her construction which enabled much of the work to be completed under cover being subsequently adopted for other classes of warships.

Three of the old 'R' class battleships were turned into training ships, and the 9,850-ton cruiser *Devonshire* converted into a sea-going classroom for Dartmouth cadets by the removal of all but one of her 8-inch gun turrets. Of vessels regarded as superfluous to peace-time requirements many were transferred or sold to foreign Powers, and others to Commonwealth navies.

Among the vessels finally condemned to the scrapyard were the famous old battleship *Warspite*, which for much of the war had served as Mediterranean Fleet flagship, and the *Iron Duke*, Jellicoe's flagship at the battle of Jutland. Demilitarised to the status of gunnery training ship, and serving as base ship and floating defence battery at Scapa Flow in 1939, the *Iron Duke* had been severely damaged during a bombing raid early in the war, towed into shallow water and beached, but continued to serve as a base ship. Now she was re-floated and towed to the Gareloch for breaking up. The *Warspite*, however managed to cheat the breakers by going aground in Mount's Bay, in Cornwall, while on tow and was eventually left to the mercy of the elements.

Another historic vessel sent to the breaker's yard was the cruiser *Cardiff*. Completed in 1917, and formerly flagship of the Sixth Light Cruiser Squadron of the Grand Fleet, she had led the German High Sea Fleet to surrender in November 1918. Accompanying her to the scrapyard was the little destroyer *Scout*, oldest of her class and already a veteran at the outbreak of the Second World War, along with two of the Navy's last surviving 15-inch gun monitors, *Marshal Soult* and *Erebus*, which had performed distinguished service in two world wars.

Aimed at unifying control of the three Services, an important change was made in the nation's organisation for defence. During his wartime premiership Churchill had assumed the additional title of Minister of Defence, taking charge of the general direction of the war and consolidating the separate capacities of the individual Services into an effective whole by his supervision of the Chiefs of Staff Committee. With the return of peace it was felt that a separate Minister should relieve the Prime Minister of that part of his responsibility for national defence which was concerned with the inter-relation of the three Services, and formulate a unified defence policy. His duties would include the apportionment of available resources between the Services in accordance with the strategic policy laid down by the Defence Committee—to include research and development and the correlation of production programmes—questions of general administration involving a common policy for the three Services, and control of various inter-Service organisations such as Combined Headquarters.

The White Paper introducing the new Ministry stated that Britain's defence problems could not be viewed in isolation.

We must be ready to play our part in any measures of collective defence which may be organised under the aegis of the United Nations, and must maintain and develop our machinery for collaboration in defence of the British Commonwealth and Empire.

It was also emphasised that the security of the remaining Colonies rested mainly upon the maintenance by United Kingdom forces of command of the sea and air approaches to those Colonies, and freedom of lines of communication between different parts of the Commonwealth.

The first incumbent of the new office was Mr. A. V. (later Viscount) Alexander, who left the Admiralty where he had held the office of First Lord throughout much of the war, to take up his new duties in January 1947. But in fact, although a new procedure for presenting the annual Service Estimates in total heralded centralisation of control of the armed forces, a number of years were to elapse before this finally came about.

Early in June 1946 a great victory march was held in London. King George VI accompanied by members of the Royal Family took the salute in the Mall, and the parade included the Chiefs of Staff and Naval, Army and Air Force commanders. The Royal Navy was represented by amphibious jeeps, DUKWs, mobile wireless units, aircraft refuellers and mobile sick bays, along with contingents of seamen, engine room personnel, miscellaneous branches, Royal Marines and Reserves, QARNNS and WRNS. There were displays in a number of London parks, evening entertainments, illuminations and fireworks. Cruisers, destroyers, corvettes and minesweepers were berthed at Greenwich,, Woolwich, Deptford, and in the London docks, and were also illuminated at night. But there was a sombre background to these junketings.

'As war waged by a coalition draws to its end, political aspects have a mounting importance,' declared our most famous statesman. This now became evident as Russian influence began increasingly to dominate those countries which had been liberated by the Red Army. By the time the war ended with the Japanese surrender, territories under Soviet control included the Baltic provinces, Czechoslovakia, a large part of Austria, the whole of Yugoslavia, Albania, Hungary, Roumania and Bulgaria, and the Russian grip was tightening on Poland.

During a tour of the United States, undertaken at the invitation of President Truman, Britain's wartime leader drew the attention of the free world to the new danger. In a speech delivered at Westminster College, Fulton, in Missouri, Winston Churchill advocated a special relationship between the United States and the British Commonwealth and Empire, with a common study of political dangers, similarity of weapons and instruction, interchange of officers and cadets and the joint use of naval and air bases throughout the world; also for the United Nations to be equipped with an international armed force.

'A shadow has fallen upon the scenes so lately lighted by the Allied victory,' he went on. 'Nobody knows what Soviet Russia and its Communist international intends to do in the immediate future. From Stettin in the Baltic to Trieste in the Adriatic an iron curtain has descended across the Continent.' This 'curtain' was to divide the nations of the world into two opposing factions, the effect of which was all too soon to become apparent.

Although the origins of the United Nations Organisation are recorded in the appropriate reference books, they are worth briefly recalling here. In June 1945 the Charter of the Organisation was signed by fifteen nations in San Francisco. It was the outcome of an earlier conference which had been held at Dumbarton Oaks, near Washington, in the autumn of 1944 at which the United States, Great Britain, Russia and China proposed that all peace-loving States should join a new organisation to be called the United Nations pledged to maintain international peace and security. This would consist of a General Assembly and a Security Council. The Assembly, however, could only recommend and pass declarations but could take no executive action. It would be the task of the Security Council to investigate disputes between member States and settle them by force if this could not be done by peaceful means. The Council would comprise five permanent members, Britain, the United States, Russia, China and France; and six non-permanent members elected for a two-year term by a two-thirds majority of the General Assembly.

The United Nations Charter was founded on the assumptions that the five Powers on the Security Council would be able to reach lasting agreement on major matters, and that, apart from Russia's known claims on Japan which had been agreed as a condition of her entry into the war against that country, none of these Powers sought territorial aggrandisement. In the event neither of these assumptions proved correct.

The General Assembly of the United Nations met for the first time on 10th January 1946, in London. The first item on the agenda was Russia's claim for oil concessions in Persia, and for the incorporation of the whole of the Persian province of Azarbaijan into the Soviet Union. Pressure brought to bear by Britain and the United States enabled this claim to be resisted, although Soviet troops remained in that area until an oil agreement had been wrung from Persia's unwilling Prime Minister. But without teeth it seemed that the United Nations Organisation was likely to prove as ineffective in action as its discredited predecessor the League of Nations.

Meanwhile the world was given another demonstration of the fearsome new weapon which had brought the Second World War to an end. Early in July 1946, in a test appropriately titled 'Operation Crossroads', the fourth atom bomb (the first was an experimental one) was exploded by the American Navy over a specially assembled fleet of more than eighty target warships ranging from battleships to landing craft anchored in Bikini Atoll in the south Pacific. On board the ships were 200 pigs, 200 goats and 4,000 rats, some of which wore anti-flash clothing.

As a result of the explosion fifty-nine of the vessels suffered degrees of damage assessed as from heavy to negligible, while heat damage, even to ships lying distant from the centre of the explosion, showed that human survival would have been doubtful. Most of the animals were killed or died subsequently from the effects of radiation, although one pig was found swimming in the lagoon twenty-four hours after the ship in which it had been placed had sunk!

Three weeks later a fifth bomb was exploded in the anchorage, this time under water, which resulted in over four times more tonnage being sunk and heavier subsidiary damage. The general assessment of the experts on the results of the tests were that the bombs had damaged more ships than had ever before been damaged by a single explosion, and that they had provided adequate data for re-designing ships to minimise damage to superstructure and deck personnel. The tests were thus amply justified.

Amid the chorus of opinion that naval surface forces had had their day, British naval reaction to 'Operation Crossroads' was more cautious. 'Because an atom bomb has had great success against battle-ships anchored in a tropical lagoon for three or four months, do not let us think that has solved the problem,' declared the then First Sea Lord, Admiral Sir John Cunningham. 'It may be . . . that the safest place in the next war will be on board a ship. The atom bomb as we know it at present has still got to be carried to its target and dropped by an aircraft. In the problems of interception and attack of aircraft all three Services have attained considerable proficiency. Our hopes for peace are based on an effective United Nations. It is not clear what machinery of coercion the United Nations will have, but it is quite clear that there must be such machinery, and that it must possess dominant sea power.'

Four years later the Soviet Union had the atom bomb, and two years after that Britain exploded her own atomic weapon in the Montebello Islands, off the north-western coast of Australia. A new and deadly arms race had begun.

There were, however, more immediate post-war problems to be faced. As has been mentioned, the most important of these was mine-sweeping in order to re-open the ocean trade routes. In May 1945, immediately after the end of the war in Europe, an International Central Board for post-war mine clearance was set up in London under the presidency of a British flag officer to formulate plans for tackling this formidable undertaking.

Hundreds of captured or surrendered charts and documents as-sembled from enemy sources gave details of all enemy minefields. During the course of the war the Germans had laid nearly 126,000 mines and over 32,000 explosive sweep obstructors in the waters of north-west Europe, excluding the Baltic. Another 100,000 had been laid in the Mediterranean. British mines laid in north-west European waters and the Mediterranean totalled some 255,000. Of these about 20,000 had been swept and others accounted for. Thus something like 480,000 remained to be swept. Some of these were laid in mixed fields of moored and ground mines, including magnetic, acoustic and pressure, which would make sweeping difficult. In the Barents Sea, on the route of so many of the wartime convoys to Russia, and in the Baltic and Black Sea over 100,000 mines and 23,000 sweep obstructors had been laid. The number of these which might already have been swept was unknown.

Member States of the Central Mine Clearance Board included Britain, France, Russia and the United States, and they divided the areas to be cleared of mines into four main zones. These were in turn sub-divided into smaller areas of responsibility. Thus there was the East Atlantic zone, code-named 'Eastlanzon', the nations sharing responsibility for its clearance being Belgium, Denmark, France, Holland, Norway, the USSR, Britain and the United States, with Sweden sitting in as observer.

The Mediterranean zone, code-named 'Medzon', became the responsibility of France, Greece, the USSR, Britain, America, Yugoslavia and, later, Italy; the observer nation being Turkey. The Barents, Baltic and Black Seas, given the code name 'ThreeBzon', had as participating members, Denmark, Norway, Poland, Russia, Britain and, later, Finland, with Turkey and Sweden acting as observers. Lastly came the Kattegat, Baltic Straits and their approaches, which were code-named 'Kabazon'. Participating member States in the clearance of this area were Denmark, Norway, Russia and Britain, while the United States and Sweden provided observers.

As will be seen from these allocations the largest share of the work fell to the Royal Navy. Each zone had its own board of control, and a Central International Intelligence Office was set up in London through the agency of which information of channels and areas considered to be clear could be promulgated.

It was not possible, however, to bring the whole organisation into force at the same time. Thus 'Eastlanzon' began operations on 15th August 1945, 'Medzon' on 5th November, and 'ThreeBzon' and 'Kabazon' in February 1946. The order of priority fixed by the Mine Clearance Board was (a) the clearance of fishing grounds; (b) widening of channels for trade; (c) clearance of waters to enable ships to repair undersea cables which had been cut or destroyed during hostilities; (d) clearance of areas containing mines dangerous to surface shipping; and (e) the clearance of areas where deep anti-submarine mines had been laid.

At the outset the Royal Navy employed some 586 minesweeping vessels on this task which, during the first six months of operations, cleared more than 3,000 mines in the 'Eastlanzon', while in the Mediterranean area 211 British minesweepers alone cleared 666 mines and obstructors. British minesweepers were also loaned to foreign countries which lacked this type of vessel, and ex-enemy minesweepers manned by former German Navy personnel worked under British supervision to help in clearing the 'ThreeBzon' and 'Kabazon' areas.

Between May 1945 and the end of March 1946 over 20,000 mines of every type were swept in all zones for the loss of three British minesweepers sunk and one damaged. Despite the issue of routeing instructions, however, as areas were cleared and channels widened, a large number of merchant ships continued to be sunk or damaged. Most of these casualties occurred through ships sailing outside the specified channels and ignoring published advice. It also became clear that minesweeping would have to continue beyond the time limits at first calculated since the effective life of a magnetic mine could last for anything from eight to twelve years, depending on the age of its batteries.

The International Mine Clearance Organisation was ended by mutual agreement at the end of 1951, but the oceans were by no means completely free of the menace. Special sweeps were carried out from time to time by international minesweeping squadrons to clear areas in which shipping casualties had occurred; and representatives of the member nations continued to meet at intervals to report on further clearances.

In 1960 a new type of ahead-throwing asdic was developed in Britain which could locate and classify any mine-like object on the sea bed with an accuracy and range previously impossible. The set was fitted in a coastal minesweeper and tested both in Britain and the United States with great success. As a result a new breed of war-ship came into being known as the minehunter or mine counter-measures vessel.

It was indirectly due to the humanitarian task of cleansing the seas that the Navy's first post-war clash with a Communist State came about.

After having been occupied for most of the war, first by the Italians and then the Germans, Albania had been finally liberated in November 1944 by her own patriot forces, with Allied assistance, under

Colonel-General Enver Hoxha. Twelve months later his administration was recognised by Britain, America and Russia as the provisional government of the country on the understanding that free elections would be held at an early date in order that a truly representative government could be formed.

When these elections took place in December 1945, however, a Communist-controlled Assembly was returned, and the country proclaimed a People's Republic following the Soviet line. Because Hoxha had refused to allow independent observers to attend the elections, Britain and America broke off relations with Albania and subsequently vetoed her application for admission to the United Nations. Thus ill-feeling was engendered between Albania and the West.

British minesweepers had already cleared the Corfu Channel and the approaches to the chief Albanian ports, losing a minesweeper in the process, before the International Central Mine Clearance Board was set up. When the Mediterranean zone came into operation in November 1945, Britain accepted responsibility along with Greece and Yugoslavia for clearing the Adriatic, which had been thickly sown with mines. The official observer was Turkey, but Albania was not represented although the Russians had asked that she should be. But as the former possessed no navy and could not afford to pay her share of the costs the proposal was turned down. Albania was, however, provided with charts of the minefields and notices of safe channels as these were cleared, but her Communist government showed no disposition to co-operate. Then came the first indication of active hostility.

In May 1946 two British cruisers, the *Orion* and *Superb*, were steaming through the Corfu Channel when they were suddenly fired on by an Albanian coastal battery, fortunately without hitting either of the warships. When the British Government protested at this unfriendly act the Albanians claimed that the shooting had been an accident, and blamed the Greeks for committing acts of piracy. There was bad feeling between their two countries at the time because of Greek territorial claims against Albania, and Greek minesweepers were operating in the coastal waters of the southern Adriatic. But British cruisers could hardly have been mistaken for such small vessels.

After a demand by the Albanians that they should be informed whenever the Royal Navy wished to use the Corfu Channel was rejected by the British on the grounds that the channel constituted part of the high seas, Hoxha's government then announced that neither foreign warships nor merchantmen would be permitted to navigate within three miles of Albania's coastline. Such a ban was clearly unacceptable, and Albania was warned that if British warships were fired on again they would fire back. Both Russia and Yugoslavia, the latter now a fully Communist State, showed their inclination to side with Enver Hoxha, thus emphasising the growing gulf between East and West. There was more unpleasantness to come.

Later on that year the Mediterranean Fleet sailed from Malta on its regular autumn cruise. Corfu was among the scheduled places to be visited in the Levant before the ships assembled at Argostoli, in Cephalonia, where the fleet's regatta was to be held. The vessels detailed to visit the island were the cruisers *Mauritius* wearing the flag of Rear-Admiral Harold Kinahan who commanded the Fifteenth Cruiser Squadron, and *Leander*, accompanied by the destroyers *Saumarez* and *Volage*.

On 22nd October at the end of their visit the four ships left Corfu for Argostoli, intending to steam northabout and transit the Corfu Channel on their way south. The flagship led the way with the *Saumarez* astern. Following at an interval of about two miles came the *Leander* and *Volage*. In case Albanian coastal batteries should try to deny them passage by force, the warships' crews were closed up at action stations, but their guns were kept trained fore and aft.

Suddenly there was a violent explosion on the starboard side of the *Saumarez* and a fire at once broke out on board. She had struck a mine. With great difficulty due to the narrowness of the channel and the danger that more mines might be detonated, the stricken destroyer was finally taken in tow by the *Volage* which had by now come up, and the two ships began heading slowly back to Corfu. But after they had gone only part of the way the *Volage* herself struck a mine which blew her bows off. Although severely damaged she did not sink, and eventually the four warships safely reached harbour. Forty officers and men had been killed in the two destroyers and forty-three injured. The *Saumarez* was later towed to Malta where she was found to have been so badly damaged that she had to be scrapped.

While Albania protested to the United Nations of the unauthorised penetration by foreign warships into her waters, an intensive sweep of the Corfu Channel for mines, code-named 'Operation Retail', was carried out by the Fifth Minesweeping Flotilla of the Mediterranean Fleet who took with them an official observer from 'Medzon'. No less than twenty-two mines of German origin were swept up, all of which

HMS *Vanguard*

Inchon under bombardment during the Korean War

Submarine escape: 'Free Ascent' method—entering the escape chamber
Submarine escape: 'Built-in Breathing System' method—showing the escape trunk

HMS *Andrew*—'A' class submarine

appeared to have been recently laid. Evidence clearly indicated that the mines had in fact been deliberately sown in a formerly swept channel.

Britain's complaint against Albania was debated at length in the United Nations, and the matter eventually referred to the International Court at The Hague. Hoxha's government rejected the British accusations completely, but when the case was heard some years later the Court returned a verdict for Britain, and upheld her claim for financial compensation amounting to £843,947. Not a penny of this was ever to be paid. No further minesweeping was carried out in Albanian waters, but by then the Royal Navy had other troubles to cope with.

In the eastern Mediterranean British warships were at grips with one of the most unpleasant tasks they had been called upon to undertake—the prevention of illegal Jewish immigration into Palestine.

In 1922 Palestine had been entrusted to Britain under Mandate by the League of Nations with the threefold task of preserving the well-being and development of the people; to help establish a home for the Jews and assist their immigration; and to prepare the people for eventual self-government. In order to avoid creating an imbalance between Jews and Arabs, which would have been contrary to the spirit of the Mandate, the British Government decided in 1939 to limit Jewish immigration to 1,500 monthly. There were already 650,000 Jews in the country and their continued arrival was adversely affecting hopes of a general settlement being reached between Jews and Arabs.

But with the end of the war in Europe illegal immigration again began to increase. Thousands of the would-be entrants were displaced persons from Russia, Poland, Germany, Austria, Hungary, Roumania and Czechoslovakia who had spent years in Nazi concentration camps and wanted to find a home where they would be safe from wars and persecution. Supported by financial contributions from Zionist sources, a highly organised movement was set up to transport them to Palestine.

Ships were obtained from wherever they could be found, and groups of Jews secretly moved to ports in southern Europe from which the vessels sailed, to run themselves ashore anywhere along the Palestine coast. Most of the ships were in fact little more than floating slums, unseaworthy, lacking navigational aids and grossly overcrowded. Men, women and children, aged, sick and expectant mothers, were crammed into spaces where they scarcely had room to

move, without fresh water and adequate sanitary arrangements. The
ships flew the flags of many countries, Panamanian, French, Italian,
in fact any national colours they happened to carry. The filth on
board was appalling and the stench could be smelt for miles, which
thus often gave early warning of the proximity of an illegal immigrant
ship.

The Arab States bordering Palestine had all vowed to drive the Jews
already in that country into the sea, and terrorist organisations on
both sides were active. Somehow the traffic had to be stopped,
although in endeavouring faithfully to carry out the terms of the
League of Nations Mandate, Britain stood liable to be blamed by
both Arab and Jew and the rest of the world indiscriminately.

The British Army and the Palestine Police already had their hands
full in coping with the situation and, anyway, once the immigrants
had arrived it was too late to do anything. Destroyers from the
Mediterranean Fleet were accordingly detached to patrol the
Palestine coast and arrest the immigrant ships before they could
complete their voyages. A naval base was set up in Haifa under a
Commodore, and the 117-mile long coastline divided into twenty-mile
code-named patrol areas. An internment camp was opened at Fama-
gusta, in Cyprus, in which illegal immigrants could be held until
their future was decided. RAF aircraft patrolled up to 200 miles from
the coast to give early warning of the approach of suspected immigrant ships. Between May 1945 and May 1948 when the Mandate
was finally given up, seventy-eight ships tried to beat the blockade
and twenty-one of them were successful.

At first the immigrant vessels obediently stopped when ordered
and allowed the British destroyers to put boarding parties on board.
But as time went on this attitude changed and frequently desperate
resistance was offered. To avoid being boarded an immigrant ship
would make violent alterations of course, turn her boats out filled
with women and children, and even try to drop them on those of
the destroyer. Boarding parties were met with tear gas, smoke bombs,
steam hoses, fuel jets, bottles, axes and iron bars, and in the frequent
hand-to-hand battles sailors and Jews alike were injured and sometimes killed. But to the captains of the patrolling warships it was
always a matter of the utmost importance that no lives should be
lost.

To cope with the increasing violence they were encountering the
crews of destroyers on patrol had to be given special training in
close combat, and equipped with steel helmets, stomach protectors,

shields and coshes as well as revolvers; while two warships were found necessary to arrest an immigrant ship where formerly a single vessel had sufficed. Once the naval boarding party had gained a foothold, however, the Jews promptly sabotaged the main engines of their own vessel, smashed the steering gear, and threw all the navigational equipment overboard.

In the intervals between patrols the crews of the unfortunate British warships got very little rest. They had to remain alert against sabotage by swimmers with limpet mines and other explosive devices. The ship's waterline was kept illuminated at night, and small depth charges released at irregular intervals, thus depriving the men of their much needed sleep. Once a week they were allowed into Haifa to take on fuel and stores, and to have the ship's underwater hull examined by naval frogmen.

Finally, after the United Nations had agreed that the Mandate should be terminated and the country given its independence, the Navy's thankless task came to an end and the base at Haifa closed down, the environs of the port having to be defended to the last by Royal Marine Commandos.

When the post-war reorganisation of the armed forces was begun in 1946, all Army Commandos were disbanded and this role reverted exclusively to the Royal Marines as being one for which they were fully qualified by their long tradition and history. During the war the strength of this famous Corps had reached 80,000, its highest total. As always, Marines had fought both ashore and afloat in every theatre of war, from the River Plate action to the Dieppe landing, and from the invasion of Sicily to the assault on the Arakan, in Burma. On 6th June 1944, when the Allied Expeditionary Force landed in Normandy, no less than 10,000 Royal Marines went in. They included five Royal Marine Commandos, an Armoured Support Group, an Engineer Commando, Landing Craft Obstruction Clearance Units, signallers, drivers, provosts and guards. In addition, two-thirds of the assault landing craft were manned by Royal Marines.

Because of the many demands made on the Corps early in the war, Marines took no part in the initial activities of the Commandos, and these were then entirely Army formations. In 1942, however, the first Royal Marine Commando was formed. It was quickly followed by a second, and eventually by seven more, together with an anti-aircraft brigade, an armoured support group and crews for landing craft and beach organisations.

Of the four mixed Army and Royal Marine Commando Brigade Headquarters which existed in 1946, No. 3 Royal Marine Brigade at Hong Kong took over the new formation. The number of Commandos was reduced to three—Nos. 40, 42 and 45—all of which were eventually assembled in Hong Kong. There they performed many varied functions in the rehabilitation of the Colony after the Japanese occupation, when Hong Kong was placed under the temporary governorship of Admiral Sir Cecil Harcourt who had taken the enemy surrender.

After the re-institution of civilian government in April 1946, No. 3 Commando Brigade Headquarters continued to remain in the Colony, with the Commandos becoming part of the garrison. Forming the largest concentration of fighting men in the Corps, the Brigade could quickly be moved to any trouble spot by air, with its heavy equipment following by sea, or in landing craft and whatever ships and auxiliaries that could be made available. The Commandos were to see much active service in the years that lay ahead.

While the post-war policy of the Corps was thus being implemented, the administrative run-down of Royal Marine strength to a peacetime total of 15,000 all ranks was smoothly effected. In 1947 the old Royal Marine 'Grand Divisions' which had existed at the naval ports of Chatham, Portsmouth and Plymouth since their original formation in 1755, were abolished and replaced by geographical groups, each under a major-general. Thus the Chatham Group became responsible for pre-embarkation training; Portsmouth for sea training and gunnery; and Plymouth for infantry and amphibious training. The depot at Deal continued to train recruits and to house the Royal Naval School of Music, headquarters of the Royal Marine Band Service.

A centralised pay and record office was set up in Melville Barracks at Chatham in place of the old Home Base Ledger Office. Three years later, as an economy measure, the Chatham barracks were closed altogether, Divisional Colours being laid up in Rochester Cathedral. In 1960 the Pay and Record Office moved to Portsmouth where it was housed in the former Royal Marine Gunnery School. Thus the Corps severed a connection with Chatham which had lasted from 1779.

The School of Combined Operations had been established at Fremington, in Devon, and a Royal Marine general officer appointed

Chief of Combined Operations. Later this title was changed to Chief of Amphibious Warfare; the school was moved to Poole, in Dorset, combined with the Royal Marines Amphibious Warfare School and renamed Joint Services Amphibious Warfare Centre.

The importance of command of the air over the sea as an integral part of maritime power had been amply demonstrated during the war years. From being something of a Cinderella of the forces up to 1939, the Fleet Air Arm had come into its own during hostilities as a potent weapon of sea warfare. There was to be no going back. With the aim of ensuring an adequately manned and efficient air component for the post-war Navy, the Admiralty announced in 1946 that all officers of the executive branches, irrespective of their probable future employment in the Navy, were to be given the opportunity of gaining a pilot's 'A' licence as part of their naval training.

The aircraft carrier was gradually replacing the battleship as the capital ship of the Fleet, but since the need for economy would limit the amount of sea time these vessels would be able to put in, it was decided to retain a considerable number of wartime naval air stations both at home and abroad, thus accelerating and facilitating training. The term 'Fleet Air Arm' was superseded by 'Naval Aviation' in order that the Air Branch should not take on the characteristics of being a 'service within the Service'. Seven years later, however, the old title was reverted to, the Admiralty being influenced by the strong appeal of its glorious wartime association.

Like warships, naval aircraft were undergoing a period of transition. When the war ended the preponderance of Fleet Air Arm aircraft were American-built machines obtained under Lease-Lend arrangements. These included Wildcats, Avengers, Corsairs and Hellcats, which far outnumbered the British designed Seafires, Barracudas and Fireflies which had come into operational service towards the end of the war. By the close of 1946, however, practically all the American-built aircraft had been returned to the country of their origin.

New aircraft developed for the Fleet Air Arm since 1944 included the Hawker Sea Fury, a fast fleet fighter with a speed of over 400 mph; the De Havilland Sea Hornet, a twin-engined, long-range, single-seat fighter, with a range of over 2,000 miles, maximum level speed in excess of 450 mph, and a high rate of climb; the Seafire 47 with a maximum speed of 440 mph; Spearfish torpedo-dive-bomber, successor to the Barracuda; and the Short Sturgeon for target-towing. Trainers included the Oxford, Anson, Sea Mosquito, dual-controlled Firefly, Meteor 77, and the Percival Sea Prince. All of these were piston-engined.

The shape of things to come in naval aviation was foreshadowed when, in December 1945, Lieutenant-Commander 'Winkle' Brown, a naval test pilot, set up a world record by successfully landing a prototype jet-propelled, 540 mph Vampire—at that time the fastest aircraft in the world—on to the heaving flight deck of the light fleet carrier *Ocean*. Landing each time within 100 feet, he thrice repeated a faultless performance.

But the advent of jet aircraft brought with it special problems for naval aviation. For an important requirement of the seagoing aeroplane is that it must fit into severely limited shipboard hangar space with many others. Equally important is compensation for loss of performance due to the special requirements for take-offs and landings at sea. Essential fittings on a naval aircraft are a catapult launching hook and an arrester hook, both of which tend to reduce speed. The greatest weight penaliser, however, is a heavier undercarriage than a shore-based aircraft which is needed to absorb the shock of semi-stalled landings.

Rocket-Assisted Take-off Gear (RATOG), an external piece of equipment which was designed to extend the length of take-off run required by a heavily laden aircraft from a carrier's flight deck added to the load. The Navy, therefore, began experimenting with a flexible flight deck designed to reduce undercarriage weight. After preliminary trials at Farnborough, Lieutenant-Commander Brown successfully brought his special skid-fitted Vampire to rest on a new flexible flight deck which had been installed in the aircraft carrier *Warrior*.

While these were remarkable 'firsts' in any Navy, years were in fact to elapse before jet-propelled aircraft finally superseded their piston-engined counterparts afloat.

CHAPTER TWO

Contraction and Conversion

In February 1947 Viscount Hall, who had succeeded Alexander as First Lord of the Admiralty on the latter's translation to the newly created post of Minister of Defence, presented the Naval Estimates for the coming financial year. They totalled some £78 million less than for the previous year. In his explanatory statement the First Lord emphasised that the Navy was still undergoing a period of contraction and conversion, and outlined the progress that had been made.

Surplus ships and stores, including trawlers, drifters and other small craft formerly employed as minor war vessels had been sold for some £6.5 million. All requisitioned fishing vessels had been released to former ownership, some 4,500 merchant ships formerly in Admiralty service had been dispersed, and the release of all Merchant Navy personnel serving on special Admiralty agreements completed.

During the first full year of peace the Navy had been required to operate in support of the Allied forces of occupation and control in ex-enemy territories and other areas where the restoration of law and order and the maintenance of Allied authority was necessary.

In the British Zone of Germany the Royal Navy's primary task was the liquidation of the German fleet. A total of 116 U-boats had been destroyed and smaller warships either transferred to minesweeping or to other nations. German naval personnel had been finally disbanded, but as a temporary measure a small number of skilled ex-naval personnel were employed in minesweeping, disarmament and demolition. Thousands of tons of armament stores, including all types of explosives, had been destroyed, dumped at sea, or used in the demolition of coastal defences, anti-aircraft and other installations; ports had been demilitarised and handed over to the Control Commission.

A squadron of the British Pacific Fleet, including units of the Royal Australian and Royal Indian Navies, was based at Kure, in Japan, at which port a naval party was stationed as part of the British

Commonwealth Occupation Forces. Royal Naval units were co-operating with the US Navy in maintaining order in the Trieste area which had become the subject of dispute between Italy and Yugoslavia; there was a British Naval Mission serving in Greece, and there were Royal Naval parties in Austria. Cairo and Alexandria were being cleared of wartime naval stores, and the naval detachments which had been operating in Indonesia with Dutch forces had been withdrawn. The British Pacific Fleet was now based on Hong Kong instead of Australia, and had been reduced to two carriers, two cruisers, a flotilla of destroyers, five submarines and ten escort vessels.

Demobilisation was continuing satisfactorily, but was an intricate process since the reduction of naval personnel to a peacetime level needed careful adjustment in order not to remove from ships in commission too high a proportion of their crews as to render them inefficient as units. An elaborate system of reliefs for ships on foreign stations had been worked out so that they could be kept up to strength while releasing 'Hostilities Only' and time-expired personnel due for demobilisation in their various groups. National Service on the basis of eighteen months' service would therefore have to be retained for the interim period until this process had been completed.

But soon after this statement had been published, political pressure brought about a summary reduction of the period of National Service to twelve months. Justifying their change of heart, the Government declared that it was felt inevitable and right that the rehabilitation of the civil economy should increasingly absorb the country's efforts and resources. A balance had therefore to be struck between the country's defence and the urgent requirements of post-war national economy. This severely affected the Navy.

The carefully drawn-up scheme of commissions and warship movements had to be scrapped, and drastic reductions made in the strengths of squadrons on foreign stations. The Government's decision also meant practical abolition of the Home Fleet, the ships of which with the exception of one cruiser and four destroyers were reduced to nucleus crew status. Never since the end of the Napoleonic wars had Britain's fleet fallen so low in size. Strategists became seriously alarmed at our naval weakness, particularly when the Navy League published a statement showing that Britain had fewer than 100 warships of all types in active commission.

The Home Fleet had almost ceased to exist; the Mediterranean Fleet included two aircraft carriers, four cruisers, two flotillas of destroyers, seven frigates and sloops and eight submarines. In the West Indies were one cruiser and two frigates, and in the East Indies two cruisers and four frigates. The South Atlantic station comprised one cruiser and two sloops; while the British Pacific Fleet had shrunk to two cruisers, two destroyer flotillas and a handful of submarines. Commented a senior American admiral, 'The United States now has more absolute control of the sea than was possessed by Britain.'

Even so, the Navy managed to carry out some semblance of its normal peacetime functions, not least important of which is showing the flag. In February 1947 the new battleship *Vanguard* took the King and Queen and the two Princesses on an official visit to South Africa, being escorted for part of the way by the attenuated Home Fleet. The normal summer round of visits to British ports was then carried out, but the Fleet's autumn cruise had to be cancelled to save fuel, being replaced by training exercises conducted in harbour at Portland.

In the Mediterranean British warships visited Greek and other ports in the Levant, and even cruised as far as Sevastopol, the first British naval appearance in a Russian Black Sea port since before the war. Earlier, Admiral Sir Bruce Fraser, Commander-in-Chief, Home Fleet, had paid a visit to Kronstadt in the new aircraft carrier *Triumph* to attend the celebration of Red Navy Day. The small West Indies squadron made a round of all the principal ports of South America, where the ships were received with the utmost cordiality.

But not all was peaceful flag-showing, thus realising the forebodings of some of the gloomier prophets. When, for example, on 30th November 1947 the United Nations approved the partition of Palestine into two independent Jewish and Arab States, the wild rejoicing of the Jews had immediately been countered by riots and violence on the part of the Arabs. In Aden widespread disorders broke out, Jewish homes being looted and burned by Arab mobs. The destroyers *Contest* and *Cockade*, homeward bound from the Far East, were hastily diverted to Aden, where a force of 200 bluejackets from the two destroyers and the survey ship *Challenger* helped to maintain order until military reinforcements could arrive.

At the other side of the globe, when the Governor of the Falkland Islands made the rounds of his dependencies he found British sovereignty being disputed by warships from Argentina and Chile. A show of force was decided upon, but in order to stage this the solitary cruiser flagship remaining on the South Atlantic station had to be rushed across to the area. Before the war three cruisers had formed the South America Division alone of the America and West Indies station.

Farther north in the Western Hemisphere British Honduras* was threatened by the incursion of guerrillas from Guatemala, which country claimed Honduras as 'part of the national territory retained by a powerful Empire'. The Commander-in-Chief in the West Indies, Vice-Admiral Sir William Tennant, flying his flag in the cruiser *Sheffield*, headed at once for Belize where the warship's Marine detachment was landed. But when it became necessary to relieve the Marines by army units, the latter had to be lifted to the trouble spot in the partially demilitarised training cruiser *Devonshire* which was the only warship available.

British naval weakness was further highlighted by an incident which took place in the Far East when, in January 1948 a mob of several thousand Chinese attacked the British Consulate on the island of Shameen, which adjoins the city of Canton. After destroying the building, they proceeded to attack the houses of the British Consul-General and his Press Attaché and the premises of a British shipping firm, all of which were burned down. The British Vice-Consul was injured during these attacks. Shameen was placed under martial law by the Chinese Nationalist authorities, while all British women and children in Canton were evacuated to Hong Kong for safety in British civil aircraft.

The riots arose out of anti-British demonstrations resulting from the eviction of some 2,000 Chinese squatters from Kowloon, on the mainland of Hong Kong, who were living in huts which had been condemned as insanitary and dangerous to public health. The British Ambassador in Nanking made an immediate protest to the Chinese Government after the riots, and General Chang Chun, the Nationalist Premier, expressed deep regret. Local Chinese authorities were ordered to give full protection to British nationals and mete out punishment to the rioters. But when the British Ambassador demanded full compensation, a public inquiry and punishment for those responsible, the Chinese Government promptly presented a counter-Note claiming full compensation for the evicted squatters!

Before the abrogation of our extra-territorial rights in China, at least two British gunboats would have been regularly stationed off

* *Renamed* Belize *in 1973.*

the Shameen, their presence acting as an effective deterrent against physical attacks on the Concession.

As a further contribution towards economy in defence expenditure, it was decided to scrap the Navy's oldest battleships and one remaining battle cruiser. These included the *Queen Elizabeth, Valiant, Malaya, Nelson, Rodney* and the *Renown.* The first three ships had been built between 1913 and 1915, and rendered magnificent service in two world wars. The *Renown,* sister ship of the *Repulse* which, with the *Prince of Wales,* was sunk by Japanese air attack off Malaya in December 1941, had been launched in 1916. The *Nelson* and *Rodney,* the first British battleships to be built after the First World War in conformity with the limitations of the Washington Naval Treaty of 1922, had also performed good service in the second world conflict. All, however, had suffered war damage and were not considered to be worth modernising.

This still left the four modern battleships of the *King George V* class and their recently built sister *Vanguard.* Also scheduled for scrapping were the four remaining battleships of the *Royal Sovereign* class. Launched between 1914 and 1916, they, too, had served in both world wars. In 1944 the *Royal Sovereign* herself had been lent to the Russians who renamed her *Archangelsk,* and returned her in 1949.

Of the war-scarred veterans bound for the scrapyards the *Queen Elizabeth* was given an almost emotional send-off in recognition of a distinguished career. For almost the whole of her thirty-three years' service in the Navy the *Queen Elizabeth* had been a flagship. In 1916 she became fleet flagship of the Grand Fleet and wore the flag of Admiral Sir David Beatty. Afterwards she became principal flagship of the peacetime Atlantic Fleet and subsequently of the Mediterranean Fleet. Her last service as a flagship had been in the Eastern Fleet during the recent war. In all she had worn the flags of sixteen admirals. The most outstanding event of her career took place on 15th November 1918 when Admiral Beatty received on her quarterdeck the German naval representatives and dictated to them terms for the surrender of the High Sea Fleet. When her ensign was hauled down for the last time in Portsmouth harbour in the presence of the Commander-in-Chief and other senior officers, the band of the Royal Marines played a special arrangement of 'Sunset', followed by 'Auld Lang Syne' and the National Anthem.

Other ships towed away to the breakers' yards around this time included 19 ageing cruisers of First World War vintage, 90 destroyers and well over 100 sloops, frigates and corvettes. These mass scrappings occasioned a good deal of public outcry, but much of this was ill-informed since the majority of the ships were old, and those of wartime construction not worth the cost of modernising. Nor in fact did the Navy possess the manpower to keep them in commission.

But not all the accent was on retrenchment. New ships were under construction, albeit slowly since the pattern of the future Navy had not yet begun to emerge. With the advent of atomic power the aim of the designers was directed chiefly towards strengthening and streamlining the hulls of warships and reducing their superstructure as much as possible.

As has been mentioned, work on the two new large aircraft carriers *Eagle* and *Ark Royal* was proceeding slowly in order to incorporate new technical developments, and ten light fleet carriers were still in various stages of construction. The six *Majestic* class of 16,000 tons had all been launched but were incomplete. Eight *Hermes* class of 22,000 tons had originally been projected. Four were cancelled, and of the others only two had actually been launched, with two more on the stocks.

The latest type of cruiser in commission was the *Superb* of 8,800 tons, completed in 1945 and armed with nine 6-inch guns. Of her eleven projected sisters only two were completed. Six were cancelled, and work on the remaining three, *Tiger*, *Blake* and *Defence*, indefinitely suspended. Eight 'super' destroyers were on order, also sixteen new 'A' class submarines of greater tonnage and higher speed than their predecessors; and among the new auxiliaries in the building yard was a deep-diving vessel, the *Reclaim*.

In June 1948 plans to re-establish Singapore as the principal British naval, military and air base in the Far East were announced. The headquarters of the British Pacific Fleet, to be renamed the Far East Fleet, would move there from Hong Kong, which was however to continue to be an important naval station and the fleet's operational and training base. The Singapore naval base had been recovered almost undamaged from the Japanese at the end of the war, and a new airport was being built at Changi, on Singapore Island, which would be able to take the largest civil and military aircraft. The main purpose of the move was to facilitate inter-Service co-operation, since the shore headquarters of the British naval Commander-in-Chief would be in close contact with those of the Army and RAF Commanders-in-Chief.

Early in 1948 important changes were made in the naval cadet entry system. For centuries entry into the Royal Navy as junior officer had been confined to the sons of noblemen and gentlemen. Charles II, with the object of 'giving encouragement to the families of better quality among Our subjects to breed up their younger sons to the art and practice of navigation', introduced the first organised method of junior officer entry by his system of 'Volunteers' or 'King's Letter Boys'. These aspirants for the life of a professional sea officer were appointed into the Navy only by order of the King. Their upper age limit was sixteen, they were to have 'definite places in the ship', and to receive pay at the rate of £24 per annum.

A more unofficial system of entry was that of 'Captain's Servant', whereby captains could take into their ships the young sons of relatives, friends and acquaintances, sometimes at a very early age. It was by this means that Nelson entered the Navy. All these youngsters were in fact the earliest midshipmen, and since they went straight to sea without any preliminary training whatever, they had to learn their profession the hard way.

In 1729 the first instructional establishment for junior officer entries came into being when a Royal Naval Academy was ordered to be built at Portsmouth for forty 'young gentlemen' to be trained for his Majesty's service at sea, this number being later increased to seventy and to include the sons of serving officers. In 1840 these trainees were called 'naval cadets', and in 1857 a training ship for them was established at Portsmouth, the Naval Academy having been taken over for other purposes. Six years later the vessel was moved to the River Dart, and in 1904 the growing number of cadets were transferred on shore to the then newly built Royal Naval College at Dartmouth.

Cadet entry regulations had been varied from time to time by the Admiralty, but these were mostly concerned with alterations to age limits and amendments to the qualifying examinations. By and large, however, up to the outbreak of the Second World War, candidates continued to be drawn chiefly from the ruling classes. Under new regulations introduced by the first post-war Labour Government no candidate was in future to be barred from competing by reason of social status, school or financial standing.

The age limit for entry was raised from $13\frac{1}{2}$ to 16, and the new system was to apply to the Executive, Engineering and Supply & Secretariat Branches. Cadets so entered would spend two years instead of four at Dartmouth, followed by eight months in the training cruiser before joining the Fleet as midshipmen, gradually replacing the earlier entries. Tuition and maintenance would be free, the Admiralty providing uniform and other clothes, pocket money, etc., to be charged up to the parents on a scale decided by their net income. If, however, this was below £300 a year no reimbursement would be required. (Later, all entry fees were abolished.) A written examination for entry would be held three times a year, successful candidates then being required to undergo tests of intelligence, aptitude, character and personality.

At the same time the Special Entry system, under which candidates from public and grant-aided schools, and nautical training establishments such as Pangbourne and HMS *Conway*, would enter as cadets in the Executive, Engineering and Supply & Secretariat Branches between the ages of 17 and 18, was to continue. These entries, who had previously been trained almost entirely afloat, first began to come through Dartmouth in 1939, and it was via this system of entry that Prince Philip himself joined the Navy.

Other sources of officer recruitment would be by special entry into the recently created Electrical Branch—candidates qualifying by possession of the Higher School Certificate and interview—and by commissions from the Lower Deck. These last could be obtained by two methods. The first was called the 'Upper Yardman' scheme whereby outstanding ratings chosen by selection and examination were promoted direct to acting sub-lieutenant on successful completion of educational and professional courses. The other was for Warrant Officers to be promoted by selection to commissioned rank. (The term 'Upper Yardman' derives from the days of the old wooden sailing warships when the most skilled seamen were normally detailed to man the upper yards.) Candidates for 'Upper Yardman' could be accepted up to the age of 23, and Warrant Officer promotees to age 36. The Admiralty announced that in future up to 25 per cent of all officers would be obtained from the Lower Deck.

In addition a small number of selected Boy Artificers could become cadets in the Engineering and Electrical Branches, to undergo one term at Dartmouth before specialising in their branches. For commissions in the Royal Marines a similar entry examination to that for Special Entry cadetships in the Royal Navy would be held three times a year; candidates to be aged between 17 and 19, and those successful becoming probationary second lieutenants

Another fundamental change made at this time was to abolish the title of Warrant Officer. In past centuries these had been the Navy's only 'standing officers', being employed by the Crown and appointed direct by Admiralty Warrant. The oldest and most historic rank in the Navy, Warrant Officers had originally included the Master, Boatswain, Carpenter, Gunner, Cook, Purser, Surgeon, Chaplain and Schoolmaster. But during the eighteenth and nineteenth centuries all except the Boatswain, Carpenter and Cook had become officers of wardroom rank. In 1910 the Cook, who had reverted to rating status, was given the opportunity of promotion to the rank of Warrant Instructor in Cookery, and in 1918 the title of Carpenter was changed to that of Warrant Shipwright. The Gunner and Boatswain alone retained their titles and status unaltered.

Since those early times additional Warrant ranks were created, notably Engineer, Gunner (T) after the introduction of torpedoes, Signal Boatswain, Telegraphist, Master-at-Arms, Wardmaster, Writer, Steward, Mechanician and, with the advance of technology and the creation of the Fleet Air Arm, other technical and air branch grades.

The Warrant List now became the 'Branch List', and Warrant Officers 'Branch Officers' with their rank prefixed by the word 'Commissioned'. Future appointments were to be by commission instead of warrant, the same principle to apply to the Royal Marines. For years Warrant Officers had their own separate messes in large ships and shore establishments, but in small ships lived in the wardroom and took a full share in mess life. All Warrant Officers' messes were accordingly closed down, and the newly titled Branch Officers automatically became full members of wardroom messes ashore and afloat.

Steps were also taken to re-establish the various classes of Reserves, an Air Section of the RNVR being set up and allocated to four air stations. Thus RNVR Air Squadrons were to form up at Abbotsinch for the Glasgow area; at Stretton, in Warwickshire, for the Liverpool/Manchester area; at Culham for the London/Oxford area; and at Bramcote for the Midlands. These new volunteer air squadrons were initially equipped with Seafire, Firefly and Harvard aircraft. In addition to pilots and observers, a limited number of air engineers were attached to each squadron, and it was intended that Reservists should eventually form a considerable proportion of the maintenance complement.

Two new Reserves created at this time were the Royal Marine Forces Volunteer Reserve (RMFVR), and the Women's Royal Naval Reserve (WRNR), the WRNS having been established as a permanent pensionable Service. Established with a strength of 1,500 officers and men, formed originally into Commandos, Sea Service and Amphibious Wings, the RMFVR was to set up headquarters in London, Glasgow, Liverpool, Bristol and Newcastle.

Certain constitutional changes taking place within the Commonwealth and Empire were now to affect the disposition of our armed forces, and relieve some of the strain on the reduced and overstretched Royal Navy.

Thus in 1947 the Government decided to grant full independence to India. Because of the cordial relations he had established with that country's political leaders while holding the post of Supreme Allied Commander, South-East Asia, during the war, Admiral the Earl Mountbatten was appointed last Viceroy of that Dominion to supervise arrangements for the smooth transfer of power. But because of acute political and religious divergencies between Moslems and Hindus, partition was decided upon. Instead of one, two new Dominions, India and Pakistan, came into being, both later becoming independent Republics. The old Royal Indian Navy, which traced its history in unbroken line from the time of the establishment of the East India Company Marine in 1613, became the Indian Navy with its own warships, while the Royal Pakistan Navy was born, to become the seagoing arm of that Republic's defence forces.

In January 1948 Burma also became an independent Republic outside the Commonwealth, and Britain ceased to bear responsibility for that country's defence. Thirty-seven warships were handed over to form the nucleus of the new Burmese Navy. A month later Ceylon (now Sri Lanka) became a self-governing Dominion within the Commonwealth, with Britain continuing to maintain naval and air bases in the island. In due course the Royal Ceylon Navy came into being. Financial and other assistance was given to the newly independent States to form their own defence forces, and facilities afforded for their naval officers to continue to train at Dartmouth and other Royal Naval technical training establishments.

Although the immediate post-war era marked a period of continuing retrenchment for the Navy, it was also one during which scientific and technical advances began to crowd in on a scale even more rapid than that which marked the opening of the twentieth century.

In the forefront of these was the advent of gas turbines for marine propulsion. During the war years a great deal of work bearing on the subject had been carried out in Britain to make possible the jet-propelled aircraft, and some of the components developed for that purpose were now used for an experimental gas turbine which was built under Admiralty contract and installed for trials in a wartime motor gunboat.

Its advantages as a practical prime mover of low maintenance, compactness and light weight, in addition to self-contained operational and quick starting, led the Admiralty to consider the possibility of developing a gas turbo-generator suitable for smaller types of warship. Called the 'Gatric' gas turbine, the unit underwent sea trials in 1947, as a result of which a second small craft was fitted with the new power unit, and further studies put in hand by civilian firms with Admiralty sponsorship with a view to manufacturing larger units for installation in a vessel of the escort type. Later developments in this field were to have a dramatic effect on future warship propulsion machinery.

Experiments were also taking place with some of the new 'A' class submarines using an improved version of the Schnorkel, or 'Snort' tube, a Dutch invention which had been developed by the German Navy during the war. By providing a constant supply of air to a submarine dived to periscope depth, the Snort device enables the vessel to remain under water for long periods and to travel at increased speeds. In 1948 HMS *Alliance* using a new type snort submerged at a point 100 miles south of the Canary Islands and carried out a cruise, first to the latitude of the Equator, then back to Freetown, Sierra Leone, a total distance of more than 3,000 miles, remaining under water the whole time.

These submarines, of which forty-six had been projected as part of the Navy's war programme but only sixteen eventually built, were the most recent to come into service. Completed too late to take part in the war, their design originated from the need for higher surface speed and greater endurance for Pacific operations. Fitted with diesel-electric engines, they were 281 feet long, armed with ten torpedo tubes, one 4-inch gun and one 20mm AA gun, and had a surface speed of $18\frac{1}{2}$ knots, $8\frac{1}{2}$ submerged. A number of these were also undergoing trials with the object of attaining greater diving depths.

Radiological surveys were made by naval scientists to check the penetration of gamma rays into a warship under attack with atomic weapons, and to this end a cruiser due for scrapping was deliberately bombarded with radiation from a specially directed source. Other condemned vessels were used as targets for underwater explosions to test the effects upon hull structure and equipment.

In the field of automatic navigational instruments, technicians of the Admiralty Compass Observatory evolved a transmitting magnetic compass. Primarily intended for small craft such as motor torpedo-boats, where lack of space, limited maintenance facilities, and the shocks and accelerations of high speed manoeuvres rule out the normal gyro compass, the new instrument could operate as many repeaters as were required. Several types of the new compass were produced suitable for larger warships, such as destroyers, and also for commercial vessels.

The increasing growth of London, with attendant impurity of atmosphere and lightness of the sky at night which was interfering with astronomical observations, led to the decision in 1946 to move the Royal Observatory from Greenwich to Hurstmonceux Castle, in Sussex. The position of the prime meridian, from which the world's twenty-four time zones are reckoned, remained unchanged.

The Observatory had been founded in 1675 by Charles II for the advancement of navigation and nautical astronomy, the original building, which was damaged in the Second World War by German bombs, having been designed by Sir Christopher Wren. One of the earliest objects of the Observatory staff had been to determine exact time. Sir Isaac Newton had shown how movements of the moon could be measured, and the idea was to produce an almanac showing the position of the moon among the stars from which a navigator anywhere in the world could determine Greenwich time from his own longitude. The difficulties were great, but eventually the Nautical Almanac was published in 1767 and has appeared annually ever since.

In the nineteenth century the work of the Observatory, which came under the jurisdiction of the Hydrographer of the Navy, was greatly expanded with new and larger instruments, and, later, by photographic aids. The first Greenwich time signal was instituted in 1833, when a time ball was installed on the tower which dropped at 1 p.m., enabling ships in the Thames to set their chronometers. This practice ceased when the Observatory was evacuated during the bombing of London in the Second World War, but was later revived to continue indefinitely, with the difference that the ball is now dropped at noon instead of 1 p.m. The special importance of Greenwich in the measurement of time and longitude received international recognition in 1884 when the meridian of Greenwich was accepted as prime meridian for the whole world.

In April 1965 responsibility of the general administration and financial control of the Observatory was transferred to the then newly formed Science Research Council.

The year 1946 also saw the setting up of a Naval Meteorological Committee to consider the future of meteorology in the Navy. The first Naval Meteorological Service had been formed during the First World War with the development of the Royal Naval Air Service. In 1919 the Meteorological Office itself was placed under the newly constituted Air Ministry, and the Naval Meteorological Service followed it a year later, becoming the Naval Division of the Meteorological Office. After seventeen years, during which the Fleet Air Arm was developing with the consequent increase in meteorological requirements, the Naval Division returned from the Meteorological Office to the Admiralty where it became a branch of the Hydrographical Department.

The Committee now decided that a specialised weather service was necessary to meet naval requirements, and the Naval Weather Service was duly established, to come into official existence on 1st April 1950. Relying on British and Commonwealth meteorological services for basic information and research, the Naval Weather Service confines its activities to satisfying the specialised operational requirements of the Navy. Its personnel are provided mainly from the Instructor Branch who fill all seagoing appointments, but WRNS officers with scientific qualifications are also entered for service as forecasters in naval shore establishments.

Another development arising directly out of the war was the institution in 1948 of a Naval Lifesaving Committee to study the design and development of suitable equipment to improve the chances of survival of warship crews when abandoning ship. Exhaustive tests were carried out on known types of lifesaving equipment, not only those in use in Britain, but other countries such as the United States and Germany. New types of life jacket were experimented with and tested by human guinea-pigs from warships sent to cruise in Arctic waters.

The Committee's efforts were chiefly directed to three essential items of lifesaving equipment: an effective life jacket for individual issue; a life float to accommodate and protect survivors; and an exposure suit to improve the chances of survival of the occupants of a life float in Arctic waters. The result was the introduction of an inflatable life-raft capable of carrying up to twenty-seven men yet of being stowed when not in use in a small canvas valise. Inflated by gas bottles, the raft had a double skin tent cover for protection against cold winds in northern waters and for use as an awning in tropical seas, air cushion seats, and its equipment included special survival rations, water, signal lights, fishing line, sea anchor, first-aid kit and a radar reflector.

For individual wear a rubberised cotton fabric inflatable life-jacket, shaped to fit round the neck of the wearer and rest on his chest, was substituted for the old wartime stockinette-covered rubber tube. The jacket is fitted with a light, whistle, toggle and line, and is inflated orally through a mouthpiece and non-return valve. While finality was not achieved in design, since the problem of protection against exposure is one which affects the other Services, an exposure suit capable of giving considerable protection to survivors from cold and wet when adrift on a float was also developed.

Mention must also be made of the work of the Navy's Wreck Dispersal Organisation. This was begun on a limited scale during the war, the scratch dispersal fleet consisting only of a converted railway cargo vessel, a captured German fishing trawler and a German coastal vessel, two former minesweepers and a Dutch *schuyt*. With these few ships well over 100 wrecks were disposed of. But when the war ended eighteen trawlers were specially converted for the work. At first the vessels were manned by Reservists, but as demobilisation proceeded Royal Navy personnel took over, working under the orders of the Commander-in-Chief, The Nore.

At the end of the war there were around the coasts of the British Isles at least 500 wrecks, most of which were of vessels sunk by enemy action, obstructing the approaches to ports and harbours and dangerous to navigation. Ninety per cent were on the south-east and east coasts of England between Dungeness and Flamborough Head, while the Thames Estuary was particularly congested. Each wreck had to be searched for and found with the help of the latest navigational radio aids and by means of echo-sounding and asdic equipment. They were then broken up and dispersed by means of electrically fired depth charges, sometimes as many as 200 or more charges being required for the more obstinate.

The work was difficult and dangerous, the charges having to be placed in position by divers, and was not accomplished without a number of fatal accidents. The aim was to disperse wrecks to a depth of 45 feet at low water to enable the largest ships to pass over them in safety. Where tidal streams running past a sunken ship had scoured depressions into the sea bed, it was possible to bury the blown-up wreckage in the hole with comparatively little trouble. But where the sea-bed was hard the task was much more difficult. By 1950 most of the work was thought to have been completed, but in fact the Wreck Dispersal Organisation was not wound up until eight years later, by which time nearly 800 wartime casualties had been pinpointed and finally dealt with.

Working parallel to the Wreck Dispersal Organisation was the Admiralty Salvage Department. Prior to the outbreak of the Second World War no salvage organisation as such existed within the Admiralty. Soon after the outbreak of hostilities, however, the need for such an organisation capable of assisting casualties and raising sunken ships became apparent, and the Salvage Department came into being. Comprising the principal commercial salvage firms in the United Kingdom, who acted as agents and managers of civilian-manned vessels, and a number of ships manned by naval personnel with a shore-based staff of officers and ratings, it was gradually built up into an efficient organisation. When hostilities ended, the Salvage Department took over the work of clearing the fairways and the removal of wrecks left as the aftermath of war.

By the end of 1946 considerable progress had been made with harbour clearance work, when charge of the organisation was assumed by the Director of Boom Defences and became an integral part of his department. The arrangements with commercial firms were terminated, but a nucleus of trained personnel, both naval and civilian, was retained, since salvage is a defence measure necessary to a maritime nation and port clearance an important factor in modern amphibious operations.

By 1950 well over 200 cases of salvage and wreck clearance at home and abroad had been successfully dealt with, ranging from small craft of 50 tons to major vessels of 12,000 tons.

Resulting from the employment by this department of frogmen divers, a new technique in underwater cinephotography was developed by Admiralty scientists. Using a specially designed cine-camera, electrically driven and powered by portable batteries enclosed in watertight cases of slight positive buoyancy, the frogman diver was able to swim freely while holding the camera at depths of up to 100 feet, adjusting aperture and focusing controls while swimming. The equipment included artificial light projectors for siting on the sea bed, by means of which objects up to 30 feet away could be sharply recorded.

The new technique enabled graphic pictures to be obtained of submerged wrecks, submerged parts of ships, underwater defences, propeller performance, and sea bed topography. Slow-motion films were taken of the discharge of torpedoes from a submerged submarine, opening up exciting possibilities for the use of underwater cinephotography. Subsequently underwater television was to make its appearance.

Another field of scientific endeavour in which considerable technical advances were made was in the work of the Surveying Service. Following the appointment of the first Hydrographer of the Navy in 1795, British naval surveying rapidly earned a high international reputation, and British Admiralty charts were considered to be the best in the world. During the war the knowledge and skill of the hydrographic surveyor were fully utilised. But in 1939 the shortage of small craft for convoy escorts and other duties was so acute that the number of surveying ships in commission was drastically reduced, and makeshift craft had to be employed for surveys required for fleet purposes in connection with the siting of minefields, amphibious landings, and the surveying of re-occupied ports.

Maps, charts and associated diagrams produced by the Hydrographic Department for use by the three Services ran into astronomical figures. The naval requirements for the British sector alone of the Normandy landings in 1944 demanded the printing of nearly 1 million charts. Naval surveyors penetrated enemy defences to obtain last-minute information of vital importance to the success of each Allied landing. Gridded charts of hundreds of miles of enemy-held coastline prepared by the Hydrographer's department enabled warships to back up the land forces by blasting important inland strongpoints with their big guns.

When the war ended only three surveying vessels remained with which to tackle the immense backlog of work which had piled up because of the suspension of normal surveying during hostilities, and to meet the many commitments at home and overseas. Two converted minesweepers and a number of motor launches were added to the surveying fleet, and by 1948 the first of four frigates converted for surveying duties was about to come into service. Surveys were at once put in hand round the British Isles—wartime wrecks being swept both before and after being blown up by the Wreck Dispersal

Organisation—in the coastal waters around Malta, Libya, in the Persian Gulf, around Borneo, Malaya, and off the coast of China.

In September 1949 the Damage Control and Ship Fire-Fighting Schools at Portsmouth, both wartime products, combined with the Chemical Warfare Training Establishment to become the Royal Naval Atomic Defence and Damage Control School under the appropriate ship name HMS *Phoenix*. Damage control in the Navy dates back more than 300 years, the earliest record of such an organisation in the Fleet being contained in an order dated 29th May 1617, 'to be observed by the Commanders of the Fleet and Land Companies under the charge and conduct of Sir Walter Raleigh, Knight, bound for the South Parts of America and elsewhere'.

This order instructed that 'an officer or two shall be appointed to take care that no loose powder be carried between decks, or near flint, stock or match in hand. You shall saw divers hogsheads in two parts and filling them with water set them aloft the decks. You shall divide your carpenters, some in hold if any shot come between wind and water, and the rest between decks, with plates of lead, plugs and all things necessary by them. You shall also lay by your tubs of water certain wet blankets to cast upon and choke any fire.' More than three centuries later the principles of damage control and fire-fighting remain unaltered: precautions taken beforehand, provision of material for counter-measures, and dispersal of key personnel.

Experience arising from the loss of ships early in the Second World War emphasised the need for the thorough training of officers and men in the use of the equipment provided for the control of all types of damage in the modern complex warship. The possibilities of nuclear warfare added further complications to the problem of the defence of ships in order that they continue to float, move and fight. A Damage Control school for officers was opened in London in 1942 in order to spread knowledge of the principles of ship stability, damage control organisation and methods which reports of Boards of Inquiry held after ship sinkings had shown to be lacking. Schools for teaching fire-fighting methods had already been started in the three home ports, also short courses in damage control for ratings. After the war the two separate schools teaching damage control and fire-fighting were merged.

The discovery of the existence of 'nerve' gases in 1945 gave impetus to the study of chemical defence in ships, and it was soon realised that the problem of defence against biological attack and also against radiation following nuclear attack were basically similar, and could be directly linked with the other forms of warship defence—damage control and fire-fighting. Thus Atomic, Biological and Chemical protection, Damage Control and Fire-Fighting (A,B,C,D) were combined in HMS *Phoenix*, and 'ABCD' courses became standard for officers and senior ratings of all branches in similar smaller schools set up in Chatham and Devonport. Special courses were also instituted for senior officers and for officers of the Royal Fleet Auxiliary Service and the Merchant Navy.

The scientific manpower of the Navy grew to a considerable extent during the war, the only conflict in history whose outcome was decisively influenced by weapons unknown at its commencement. Thus in 1939 the total number of scientists in naval research establishments was only thirty-seven. By 1944 this number had increased to 130, not counting those employed in technical departments which came into being during the war, such as Anti-Submarine Material, Radio Equipment, Miscellaneous Weapons Development, Combined Operations Material and Naval Operational Research.

In 1945 it was decided to create a Royal Naval Scientific Service which would be a self-contained branch of the Scientific Civil Service, working entirely for the Admiralty, to co-ordinate all research policy and maintain the Navy in a high state of technical preparedness to counter whatever weapons and techniques that might be brought to bear against British sea power. The new Service would include existing Admiralty scientific, technical and chemical establishments and their staffs of theoretical and practical experts in the fields of engineering, chemistry, oceanography and mathematics, and designers and draughtsmen.

Chief among the latter was the long-established Admiralty Research Laboratory, which was mainly concerned with investigations into such subjects as propeller cavitation, the behaviour of torpedoes, air flow over ships, noise suppression, night vision and oceanography. Other establishments included the Admiralty Materials Laboratory, whose work involved investigating problems of corrosion, fungal deterioration, energy conversion, rubber and plastics; the Services Electronics Research Laboratory, which was set up in 1945 to conduct advanced research for all three Services into valves for radio and radar, electronic equipment and lasers; and the Royal Naval Physiological Laboratory, which had come into being during the war to investigate naval physiological problems such as living conditions in submarines and the underwater endurance limits of divers.

It is now necessary to glance briefly at certain political events which were taking place in Europe and elsewhere and were to influence the future role of the Royal Navy.

At the end of the war against Nazi Germany the Western Powers began to withdraw the bulk of their armed forces, speeding up this process as soon as Japan surrendered. Thus in May 1945 America was deploying more than 3 million men in Europe, but a year later this total had been reduced to fewer than 400,000. In the same period British forces in Europe dwindled from more than 1 million to less than half that number. The Russians, however, continued to maintain over 4 million men under arms and, in defiance of the peace treaties signed in 1947, were setting up satellite armies in the countries which had come under their influence.

In his famous 'Iron Curtain' speech at Fulton in 1946, Sir Winston Churchill had proposed a union of the Western nations for defence against Russia. But the time was not then ripe. The first step in this direction, although principally aimed at Germany as a possible future aggressor, was taken in March 1947 when Britain and France signed the Dunkirk Treaty of alliance and mutual assistance. In February 1948 Communists in Czechoslovakia, with Soviet backing, secured control of that country's government and abolished civil liberties, an attempt by the United Nations to inquire into the coup being vetoed by the Russians.

This led to a more positive move being made towards countering the gradual westward infiltration of Soviet Communist influence when Belgium, France, Luxembourg, the Netherlands and the United Kingdom signed the Brussels Treaty in March 1948. For this treaty provided not only for economic, social and cultural collaboration between the countries concerned, but also collective defence, assuring automatic assistance to any of the signatories who might become the object of armed attack not only in Europe but outside that continent.

Permanent consultative and military committees were set up to deal with problems and threats to this newly formed 'Western Union'. To provide a framework upon which a unified command organisation could be built, nucleus land, air and naval commands were created, under the presidency of Britain's Field Marshal Montgomery, with a French general in charge of the land forces and a senior RAF officer to command the air forces. There was no overall naval command, but a French admiral was appointed as naval representative with the title of Flag Officer Commanding Western Europe.

Known as the 'Western Union Defence Committee', this body was, however, only a planning organisation and lacked executive powers. The germ of the idea of a European Western Union had in fact been propagated when, in September 1947, all American countries signed the Rio de Janeiro Treaty of Mutual Self-Defence, the first regional grouping to take place outside the United Nations. Three months after the signing of the Brussels Treaty the United States Senate recommended the association of that country with 'such other regional and collective arrangements as are based on continuous and effective self-help and mutual aid'. This statement of American policy directly paved the way for the North Atlantic Treaty and for the organisation (NATO) which it subsequently set up; also for the supply of arms to the countries concerned.

The treaty itself was signed in Washington on 4th April 1949, by Belgium, Canada, Denmark, France, Iceland, Italy, Luxembourg, the Netherlands, Norway, Portugal, the United Kingdom and the United States, to be joined by Greece and Turkey in 1951 and the Federal German Republic in 1954. Under this treaty the responsibilities of the Royal Navy were linked with those of the navies of the other signatories. Europe's military resources and America's monopoly of strategic weapons were pooled, and the signatories agreed that an armed attack against one or more of them in Europe or North America would be considered an attack upon them all. It remained for a military command structure to be set up and for appropriate forces to be allocated for use in an emergency, and to maintain the security of the North Atlantic area.

Before this came about, however, warships of the Western Union nations began to carry out a series of combined exercises. The first of these historic 'get togethers' took place in June 1949 when more than 100 vessels, British, French, Dutch and Belgian, assembled at Penzance for 'Exercise Verity'. Admiral Sir Rhoderick McGrigor, Commander-in-Chief, Home Fleet, was in overall command, flying his flag in the aircraft carrier *Implacable*. With him in the flagship was Field Marshal Montgomery, President of the Western Union Defence Committee.

The allied force, in which British ships predominated, included the battleship HMS *Anson*; four aircraft carriers, three British and one French; nine cruisers; thirty-four destroyers and escort vessels; seventeen submarines; and radar training ships, minelayers and minesweepers, motor torpedo-boats and support craft. The principal object of the exercise was to test communications and, after carrying out harbour drills, the whole fleet put to sea for combined manoeuvres in the Bay of Biscay area, subsequently returning to Weymouth for a conference of senior naval officers of the four Powers.

The Naval Estimates for 1948–9, which totalled £153 million, showed a further decrease of some £44 million in expenditure on Britain's first line of defence. In the accompanying statement the First Lord explained that the Admiralty policy of deliberating accelerating reductions in the Navy to approximately the manpower level contemplated for succeeding years necessarily involved some temporary dislocation and lack of balance, and for a time the immobilisation of certain units of the fleets. Once these reductions had been effected the Navy could regain stability and normal peacetime efficiency. The total manpower strength of the Royal Navy, Royal Marines and ancillary forces was to be 167,000.

Naval shore establishments and installations in Germany were still being demilitarised, but all Naval Officers in Charge of the various enemy ports had been withdrawn, and the strength of the British Naval Occupation Forces reduced to some 200 by 1948. In Japan Royal Naval and Royal Australian Naval Forces had been withdrawn and the base at Kure closed down. All Royal Naval forces had left Italy.

All practicable sweeping of moored minefields in north-west European waters had been completed and a number of important fishing areas re-opened to fishermen. The sweeping of ground mines in the Thames estuary would continue throughout the year. In the Mediterranean the British area of responsibility had been completed, and three remaining areas in the Red Sea would soon be cleared. British minesweepers had swept 246 mines during 1947, making a total of nearly 35,000 swept since the outbreak of war. The number of minesweepers in commission had been reduced from 65 in 1947 to 21. In 1946 some 5,400 officers and men were employed on this important work, but by the end of 1947 the number had dropped to approximately 1,400.

Restrictions on labour, finance and material resources had delayed the rehabilitation and modernisation of the Royal dockyards, which had been extensively damaged by enemy action during the war, and similar considerations were holding up the promised provision of married quarters for the Navy.

Details relating to the strength of the Fleet showed that of our five remaining battleships only the *Vanguard* and *Duke of York* were operational. The *Anson* and *Howe* had become training ships with special complements, and the *King George V* was in reserve. No fleet carriers were operational, the four remaining in service being either temporarily immobilised or in reserve. Two were still in the building stage. Three light fleet carriers were shown as being operational, and ten under construction. One escort carrier was in reserve. Fifteen cruisers were in service, two being used for training and thirteen in reserve. Three more were building. Thirty-four destroyers were in full commission, eighteen others were undergoing refit and sixty-five in reserve. Ten new ones were building. Twenty-five frigates were operational, eighteen were in dockyard hands, and 136 in the Reserve Fleet, with two building. Twenty-six submarines were in commission, eight refitting or on special duties, and thirty-one in reserve. Some 300 vessels had been disposed of by loan, sale or scrapping, among them thirty-three destroyers and escort vessels which had been received as reparations from Japan.

Despite this drastic run-down in ships and men, the Home Fleet was yet able in May to stage the largest sea and air exercises held since the war, with nineteen surface ships and eight submarines taking part. Later in the year the fleet was able to set out again on its regular autumn cruise, having been brought up to a strength of one battleship, three aircraft carriers, three cruisers and a number of destroyers, frigates and auxiliary vessels.

The Mediterranean Fleet, which comprised two aircraft carriers, seven destroyers, three frigates, two sloops and three submarines, and was still only a shadow of its former self, nevertheless paid visits to Turkey, Greece, Cyprus, the Dodecanese, Egypt, Sicily, Corfu, Italy, Tunisia, and ports in France, Sardinia and Corsica.

The small America and West Indies squadron carried out exercises with the Royal Canadian Navy, and visited Esquimalt, Vancouver, Seattle, San Francisco and Acapulco, and even found time to call for the first time at the tiny West Indian islet of Dead Man's Chest, where fifteen sailors carrying a bottle of rum were solemnly landed!

The Far East Fleet visited ports in Japan and, during one cruise of this attenuated squadron, HMS *Cossack*, successor to the famous wartime destroyer of that name which, in 1940 under Captain (later Admiral of the Fleet Sir) Philip Vian, had rescued British sailors held captive in the German prison ship *Altmark* in a Norwegian fjord, performed a rescue of a different kind. The Chinese transport *Yinghung* with nearly 1,300 Chinese Nationalist troops on board had gone aground on rocky shore in the island of Formosa. Two officers from the *Cossack* swam through rough seas to take lifelines to the stranded ship, and led rescue parties which brought the Chinese soldiers to safety.

Early in 1949 the aircraft carrier *Vengeance*, two destroyers, a frigate, a submarine and a tanker voyaged deep into the Arctic Ocean to test armament and equipment, and to study the effects of Arctic weather upon officers and men. Despite the intense cold, all types of naval aircraft, including the new jet-propelled Sea Vampire and a Westland Sikorsky helicopter, were successfully operated from the carrier. Officers and men tried out special Arctic clothing of different patterns and materials, and were fed on a special diet containing one-third more calories than in normal naval rations.

At the other end of the world the frigate HMS *Sparrow* belonging to the America and West Indies squadron was trapped by pack ice in Admiralty Bay, in the South Shetland Islands. Fortunately after ten days the exceptionally severe weather conditions which threatened to imprison her for the whole of the winter moderated, and the warship was able to free herself. Since both Chile and Argentina continued to lay claims to the Falkland Islands Dependencies, it had become the practice to despatch a frigate of the America and West Indies squadron to that area at regular intervals. Subsequently a permanent patrol vessel of the Royal Navy, specially strengthened against ice, was sent to assist the Governor of the Falkland Islands and Dependencies in maintaining the security of the territories under his jurisdiction. Carrying helicopters and a Royal Marine platoon, she would spend some six months each year operating in Antarctic waters for the purpose of ice spotting, supporting civilian bases and carrying out scientific work on behalf of the Hydrographer of the Navy.

In April 1949 it was announced that the Air Branch of the Navy was to be absorbed into other existing branches, and that the distinguishing letter 'A' worn inside the curl of officers' sleeve lace was to disappear. All Air Branch officers, other than Air Engineers, would be transferred to the Executive Branch, and Air Engineers to the Engineering Branch. Ratings were no longer to be entered for flying duties, all air crews being provided from officer pilots and observers. Pilots and Observers would be drawn from permanent RN officers who volunteered for specialisation in flying duties. Short Service commission officers entered for flying duties for eight years' full time service followed by seven years on the Emergency List would in future be entered in the Executive Branch, and given the option of a permanent commission at the end of the eight-year period.

More money was to be spent on naval aviation, chiefly on carriers. Helicopter trials were started, and, to stimulate national interest in naval aviation, public displays were staged at various naval air stations. Unwittingly focusing the spotlight on the aerial future of the Navy, four Sea Furies joining the Mediterranean Fleet as part of the normal replenishment programme created a record by flying the 1,300 miles to Malta non-stop in just over three hours.

Three months later it was announced by the Admiralty that of the Navy's five remaining battleships, the four vessels belonging to the *King George V* class were to be placed in reserve. The fifth, the *Vanguard*, which had been acting as flagship of the Mediterranean Fleet, was to become flagship of the Training Squadron. This move had been decided upon so that a larger number of smaller ships could be kept in full commission to meet peacetime commitments, and to ensure that maximum provision for convoy protection could be made in the event of an emergency.

In response to shocked criticism the Admiralty emphasised that the decision to reduce the number of battleships in full seagoing commission did not imply that there was no further use for these vessels. In the foreseeable future the battleship had a positive role to play, and in war would have important tasks. It remained the best form of distant or close cover for ocean convoys and the best deterrent to surface attack on shipping lanes. The battleship was still the most effective seagoing anti-aircraft platform, possessing the most comprehensive forms of radar and gunnery control. Its hitting power was enormous and, above all, was still the most difficult ship to sink.

Nevertheless, despite these encomiums, there was little doubt in the minds of the informed that the era of the battleship was coming to an end. The Americans thought as we did, for of the fifteen still retained in the US Navy only one was in active commission and she, too, was a training ship. Within a few years in fact they would all be gone.

The Naval Estimates for 1949–50 showed an increase of slightly over £30 million on those of the previous financial year. But as affecting future naval strength the increase was more apparent than real, for more than half the extra sum was needed to meet higher costs of building and equipment and spiralling wages in industry.

Total manpower of the Royal Navy and Royal Marines had fallen to 153,000, some 14,000 fewer than anticipated in 1948. Recruiting was reasonably good but wastage was high and re-engagements had fallen below the pre-war level, due to full employment ashore and higher wages. The RNVR was expected to reach its full establishment of 5,000 ratings during the year, and the RMFVR half its interim establishment of 200 officers and 1,300 other ranks.

The First Lord announced that the Government had set on foot a comprehensive review of the future structure of the armed forces for years to come. This took the form of an inter-Service inquiry conducted under the direction of the Chiefs of Staff with the object of establishing the relative roles of the three Services under modern conditions, so that the nation would receive full value for money and properly balanced forces able to make a worthy contribution to the Western Union and Atlantic Pact. In the course of the review recommendations for certain economies had been made and accepted.

From a naval point of view this had an ominous ring, for, despite the Government's reiteration of its determination to improve by all possible means the state of readiness of the Fleet, the reductions in ships and manpower were alarming. Officers and men were getting too little sea experience, and there was a shortage of skilled senior ratings. The customary explanatory statement showing the strength of the Fleet revealed that the battleship situation remained unchanged. Of 6 fleet carriers, 3 were operational and 3 in reserve. Seventeen cruisers were in commission, with 12 in reserve. 118 destroyers were on the active list, but more than half of them were in reserve. There were 173 frigates and sloops, but only 44 were in full commission. Sixty-five submarines were listed, some 50 per cent of which were operational; and 76 minesweepers, the bulk of them in reserve.

Highlighting our continuing naval weakness, Communist-inspired elements were busily stirring up trouble in various parts of the world. Outside Europe, they were to meet with their greatest success in the Far East.

During the war with Japan, the Chinese Nationalist Government under Generalissimo Chiang Kai-shek, sharing an uneasy alliance with Mao Tse-tung against the common enemy, had been forced to retreat to Chungking. In 1946 the Nationalist Government returned to Nanking, but the Communists, using arms and equipment captured from the Japanese, resumed their pre-war struggle against Chiang. By 1947 Mao Tse-tung's forces, calling themselves the 'People's

Liberation Army', had captured Manchuria, Peking and Tientsin, and were rapidly pressing southwards.

Early in 1949 Chiang Kai-shek was compelled to resign as President, and General Li Tsung Jen took over. The latter tried to make terms with the Communists, but his peace delegation defected to the enemy. In April the Nationalist Government fled to Canton and their army retreated behind the Yangtse. Upon reaching the opposite bank, the Communists began to build up their forces preparatory to launching a final assault on Nanking. This was the situation when, on 20th April 1949, the British frigate *Amethyst* of the Third Frigate Flotilla, Far East Fleet, was making ready to proceed up river with supplies for the British Embassy at Nanking and to relieve the destroyer *Consort* which was acting as guardship at that port.

Launched in 1943, the *Amethyst* had distinguished herself by sinking a U-boat off Ireland in February 1945, and after transfer to the Far East had been present at the Japanese surrender in New Guinea. She displaced 1,495 tons, was armed with six 4-inch guns in twin turrets and six smaller weapons, could steam at 18 knots, and carried a crew of 170 officers and men. Prior to her present assignment she had been employed on anti-bandit patrols off the Malayan coast, of which mention will be made later. In command of the *Amethyst* was Lieutenant-Commander Bernard Skinner.

After the end of the war it had been agreed with the Chinese Nationalist Government that in view of the considerable British interests in China and the presence of large British communities, our Ambassador and other consular officers should remain at their posts, and permission was obtained for a British warship to be stationed at Nanking so that in the event of a breakdown of law and order resulting from the civil war, she would be able to assist in the protection and, if necessary, evacuation of British nationals.

Britain's policy in this respect was governed by the Moscow Declaration of December 1945 by which the United Kingdom, the United States and the Soviet Union had affirmed that they would not intervene in China's internal affairs. Accordingly, other foreign Powers retained their diplomatic representatives in China, and some also stationed warships at Shanghai and Nanking.

In view of the situation prevailing on the Yangtse in April 1949, efforts were made through diplomatic channels to come to an arrangement with the Communists regarding the proposed passage of the *Amethyst*, but these approaches were rejected. The People's Liberation Army had delivered an ultimatum to the Nationalists before

Helicopters over the Malayan jungle

Daring class destroyer

The destroyer *Relentless*, converted to anti-submarine duties

HMS *Belfast* during her last commission

Whirlwind helicopter over Borneo

Vaporised in the Montebello test—HMS *Plym*

Old storehouses in the Royal Victoria Victualling Yard

Filling rum casks

Coronation Review, 1953

launching their attack across the Yangtse, but this was not due to expire for several days. As the *Consort* was overdue for relief and running short of supplies, it was decided that the *Amethyst* should make the passage up river before the time limit for the ultimatum expired. She therefore sailed from Shangai on 19th April flying large White Ensigns and with Union Jacks painted on her sides, so that there could be no doubt as to her identity.

When, however, soon after nine o'clock next morning, she had reached a point some sixty miles from Nanking, Communist batteries on the north bank opened fire on her, causing considerable damage and casualties. The captain received wounds from which he subsequently died, and an enemy shell wrecked the low power room on board, putting the vessel's gyro compass, wireless, lighting and gunnery control out of action, and also killed the ship's doctor. The frigate went aground on a sandbank known as Rose Island. The First Lieutenant, himself severely injured, decided to land some of the crew, including the wounded. These managed to get ashore either by swimming or in sampans manned by friendly Chinese fisherfolk, being shelled and machine-gunned as they went. Most of them eventually reached Shanghai.

As soon as he received the *Amethyst*'s signal reporting that she was being fired on, Vice-Admiral Madden, Flag Officer and Second in Command of the Far East Fleet, the Commander-in-Chief being away in the United Kingdom at the time, ordered the *Consort* to leave Nanking and go to the frigate's assistance. The destroyer arrived early that afternoon and was at once heavily engaged by Communist batteries. As the firing was too hot to allow her to approach the stricken frigate, she continued down river at high speed; then turned back and, although being fired on the whole time, twice endeavoured take the *Amethyst* in tow. During these efforts she sustained further damage and casualties and her steering was affected. She therefore resumed her passage down river, while the *Amethyst*, whose survivors had lightened the ship by jettisoning various items of gear and equipment, managed to refloat her. But after warning shots had been fired she was compelled to re-anchor.

Meanwhile the cruiser *London* wearing the flag of Admiral Madden and accompanied by the frigate *Black Swan*, was heading up river at top speed. The damaged *Consort* was met *en route* and ordered to carry on down to Shanghai. But before the new arrivals could reach Rose Island they, too, came under heavy fire which inflicted damage and casualties. The fire was returned, but Admiral Madden decided that it would be impossible to extricate the *Amethyst* from her predicament without further serious loss of life in all three ships. Accordingly the *London* and *Black Swan* returned to Shanghai to land their dead and wounded and effect repairs.

Later the same day an RAF Sunderland aircraft with a naval and an RAF doctor on board and medical supplies was flown to the *Amethyst* from Hong Kong. Both the aircraft and the frigate were fired on, but the Sunderland managed to transfer the RAF doctor and some of the medical supplies to the warship before being forced to take off again. That night more wounded were put ashore from the *Amethyst* and she managed to creep a little farther up river.

There now remained on board three of her own officers and the RAF doctor, and sixty naval and Chinese ratings. Soon afterwards Lieutenant-Commander J. S. Kerans, Assistant Naval Attaché at Nanking, reached the ship, having been ordered to travel overland from that city and take command. Wireless communication had been re-established with Admiral Madden and, after various alternative courses of action had been considered, it was decided that the *Amethyst* should remain where she was to avoid further casualties. Meanwhile the Communists had crossed the river lower down, and on 23rd April they entered Nanking.

All attempts by diplomatic means to obtain the release of the *Amethyst* failed, and the damaged ship, kept ready to be scuttled in the event of an all-out attack by the Communists, remained marooned in the Yangtse under constant threat. As the weeks dragged by Kerans attended meeting after meeting with local Communist leaders in endeavours to obtain a safe conduct for the ship's departure, steadfastly refusing to accede to their reiterated demands that he should admit that the *Amethyst* had infringed Chinese sovereignty, accept blame for the incident and agree to compensation for the Communist troops killed by the warship's return fire. In this stand he had the full backing of the Commander-in-Chief, Far East Fleet, Admiral Sir Patrick Brind, now back on the station. To augment his forces a cruiser and two frigates had been ordered to China, and an aircraft carrier was standing by to proceed to the Far East if required. Two American cruisers also arrived at Shanghai.

Finally, after three months of fruitless negotiation, Kerans determined to make an attempt to break out. Supplies on board the warship were rapidly dwindling, fuel was low, and the ship's only serviceable armament now consisted of one 4-inch gun and one Oerlikon. The distance to Woosung was 150 miles, and the passage would have to be made under the cover of darkness, during which the damaged vessel would be compelled to pass through a boom across the river and run the gauntlet of enemy batteries on either bank. Nevertheless, when Kerans consulted them, all hands were unanimous that the attempt should be made.

Thus, as midnight approached on 30th July, the *Amethyst* quietly slipped her previously greased cable, and with steam up for maximum speed, moved off down river. She followed closely in the wake of a Chinese merchant ship as far as the boom, then during the confusion caused when a shore battery mistakenly opened fire on the merchantman, made smoke and increased to full speed, returning the enemy fire as she went. By 2.45 a.m., she was 100 miles down river. speeding at 22 knots, and an hour and a half later sighted the British destroyer *Concord* off Woosung. It was then that the jubilant Kerans made a signal to the Commander-in-Chief that was to be headlined throughout the Press of the free world :

Have rejoined the Fleet south of Woosung. No damage or casualties. God Save the King !

CHAPTER THREE

Making Haste Slowly

The nineteen-fifties opened on a sombre note with two naval disasters. The first of these occurred on 12th January 1950. In the evening of that day the submarine *Truculent* was returning to the dockyard at Sheerness from the submarine exercise area in the Thames Estuary on completion of diving trials after a refit when she collided with a Swedish motor tanker.

The submarine, which was travelling on the surface at the time, was badly holed on the starboard bow and sank almost immediately. On board were sixty-one officers and ratings and eighteen dockyard technicians. The *Truculent*'s captain, three other officers and a look-out who were on the bridge at the time of the collision were thrown into the water, and subsequently picked up by a Dutch steamer. Most of the submarine's crew managed to reach the engine room and after part of the boat and eventually got away through the after escape hatch, using the Davis Submarine Escape Apparatus (DSEA).

Unfortunately more than an hour passed before the first news of the sinking was received by the naval authorities. By the time that rescue vessels reached the scene of the disaster the majority of the men who had managed to make their escape had been swept out to sea on the strong ebb tide and drowned. Only ten of them, including two dockyard workers, were saved.

The *Truculent* was one of a class of submarines built between 1942 and 1944 and, except for the newest 'A' class, were the Navy's largest patrol submarines. They were 265 feet long, displaced 1,575 tons, were armed with eleven torpedo tubes, and had a speed of $15\frac{1}{2}$ knots. Their normal complement was sixty-five officers and men. The last peacetime submarine disaster had occurred on 1st June 1939 when the *Thetis*, an earlier version of the *Truculent* class, sank in Liverpool Bay while on acceptance trials with a loss of ninety-nine officers and men, including some of the employees of the shipbuilders. Subsequently she was raised and, renamed *Thunderbolt*, performed distinguished war service before being sunk by enemy action in the Mediterranean in March 1943.

As was normal at the time, the *Truculent*'s escape apparatus included two indicator buoys, three escape trunks and associated equipment, DSEA sets for all on board with a margin of spares distributed throughout the vessel, and other ancillary equipment such as flooding valves, pressure torches and submerged signal ejectors. But she had foundered very quickly with a loss of all electrical power and before the watertight doors could be closed. As a result the whole forward part of the submarine and control room were flooded. Eventually she was raised by the Salvage Department, taken to Sheerness dockyard for examination, and afterwards scrapped.

The disaster, however, drew attention to the need to provide measures to keep men alive in the water after they had escaped from a sunken submarine, and a careful review of existing arrangements was made by the Admiralty and the Flag Officer, Submarines.

In the nineteen-twenties salvage had been considered the best method of rescuing survivors from a submarine accident. But when this proved ineffective, attention was given to methods of individual escape. In 1930 after trials had been carried out with various types of breathing apparatus, the Davis Submarine Escape Apparatus was adopted for individual issue in the Royal Navy. This consists of a mouthpiece connected by a flexible tube to a rubber bag, attached to which is a metal container charged with oxygen under pressure. By this means the wearer is able to breathe under water during ascent. The bag has to be charged with oxygen at a pressure equal to that of the water at whatever depth from which the escape is to be made. On the way up the apparatus automatically releases some air from the breathing bag as the pressure of the water decreases. Goggles are worn to protect the eyes, and the nostrils are pinched by a clip so that breathing is only possible through the mouthpiece.

Special flood valves were fitted in submarines, the idea being that escapes should be made through the conning tower hatch after pressure inside the vessel had been equalised by partial flooding to enable the hatch to be opened. Then, in order to shorten the time that men would be under pressure while waiting to quit the vessel, special escape hatches were fitted together with twill trunks—canvas cylinders which could be pulled down into position under the escape hatch. The twill trunk made it possible to equalise the pressure and open the hatch without a large bubble going out and letting it slam down again. Men waiting to escape could stand with their heads in the air.

Before the *Thetis* disaster the rule had been that no escapes should be commenced from a sunken submarine until it was known that surface ships would be available above to pick up survivors. The *Thetis* was not, however, found for seventeen hours, during which time the survivors did their best to bring their vessel to the surface. Eventually the air in the submarine became practically exhausted, by which time the men were so drained of energy that they were unable to don their DSEA sets and thus perished.

At the end of the Second World War a committee was appointed to inquire afresh into the whole question of submarine escape and rescue. Every known escape from submarines of all nations in peace and war was studied from the material and physiological aspects. Among the committee's recommendations was the provision of a 'mixture' breathing set to replace the DSEA gear in existing submarines for use with the twill trunks to protect survivors against CO_2 poisoning during the period of flooding-up. This was not found practical, however, and a device known as the 'Built-in Breathing System' (BIBS) was designed, successfully tested in the specially built escape training tank at Submarine Headquarters, and fitted for trials in a seagoing submarine.

The system consisted of a number of large bottles of a mixture comprising 40 per cent oxygen and 60 per cent nitrogen built into the submarine, with a tube and mouthpiece for each man to breathe through while awaiting his turn to use the escape chamber. It was also recommended that existing submarines should be fitted with radio indicator buoys equipped with a flashing light, reflecting studs and a flagpole with red nylon flag; and underwater telephones and underwater signal ejectors for firing smoke candles from each end of the vessel.

The earlier committee had recommended that a special escape suit should be provided for every man in a submarine's crew, and at the time of the *Truculent* tragedy just such a suit was coming into production. Made of double-skinned waterproof nylon, it could be stepped into and pulled up over ordinary clothes, then inflated by means of a non-return valve. Neck and wrists were self-sealing, and gloves protected the hands against frostbite. A pressure-tight lamp on the shoulder was automatically lit by a seawater battery. This immersion suit could keep a man afloat, insulated from cold, for many hours. Later, as new submarine escape techniques were developed, the immersion suit, which eventually became standard equipment in British submarines, underwent further changes in design and material.

In the spring of 1951 came an even more tragic submarine disaster which was to have a far-reaching effect on underwater search techniques.

On Monday, 16th April HMS *Affray*, one of the sixteen all-welded 'A' class submarines of 1620 tons, sailed unescorted from Portsmouth to carry out a practice war patrol. On board she carried in addition to her crew of four officers and forty-six ratings, twenty young officers on a training course, who included Sub-Lieutenant Anthony Trew, a survivor from the *Truculent*, and four Royal Marines undergoing training. In command was Lieutenant John Blackburn, DSC, an experienced submarine officer.

The *Affray* had recently completed a 51,000-mile voyage, during which she visited India, Ceylon, Singapore, Hong Kong, Australia and South Africa. Her orders were to dive off the Isle of Wight and proceed submerged to Falmouth, where she was due to arrive on Thursday, 19th April. Each morning she was to surface to snort depth and report her position by wireless. When she failed to report on Tuesday, however, the 'Submiss' routine for an overdue submarine was put into operation by the naval authorities at Portsmouth, and a search was organised using aircraft, helicopters, surface vessels, submarines and the new experimental diving and salvage vessel *Reclaim*. Every effort was made to contact the *Affray* by wireless.

After seventy-two hours had elapsed without discovering a trace of the submarine, by which time it was considered that her oxygen supply would have been exhausted, hopes that the crew might still be alive were abandoned, but the search went on. More than 1,000 square miles of the sea bed between the Isle of Wight and Start Point were scoured by a force of vessels using asdic equipment, the operation being complicated because of the large number of wartime wrecks littering the area. Divers who went down to examine contacts in doubtful cases were hampered by tides and weather. Eventually the main force was called off, but the *Reclaim* continued the search. She had now been equipped with a new aid in the hunt for the missing submarine.

As soon as the *Affray* had been reported lost, four members of the Royal Naval Scientific Service set to work to produce a portable underwater television camera such as those used in outside broadcasts. They mounted the camera in a welded watertight container, and designed remote controls so that the set could be operated from a surface ship, together with underwater lighting apparatus. Within three weeks the equipment was ready, and successful tests on various wrecks were carried out by the *Reclaim*.

Then, two months after the *Affray* had disappeared, she was finally located by the *Reclaim*, which had first pinpointed the position of a sunken ship with her asdic, then identified and examined her with the aid of the underwater television camera. The submarine was lying on even keel in 288 feet of water on the edge of the Hurd Deep, an undersea canyon north-west of the Channel island of Alderney, and thirty-seven miles off her scheduled course. It was evident that no attempt to escape had been made, which pointed to rapid flooding and a swift death for all on board. The submarine's snort tube, which was in the operating position, had been badly damaged, which appeared to indicate that she had been in collision with a surface ship while snorting. No proof of such an accident could be obtained, however, and because of the difficulty of the operation, it was decided not to attempt salvage.

But the new addition to the Navy's underwater search equipment, subsequently developed and improved, which can be used in tidal conditions too risky for a manned observation chamber, and might well prove to be of vital importance in future lifesaving operations, can perhaps be considered as compensating in some small degree for the tragic loss of the *Affray* and her seventy-five officers and men.

Submarines and measures to counter their potential menace constituted the chief preoccupation of the navies of the Western Union Powers at this time, particularly in view of the rapid growth of the Russian Navy. Reliable intelligence indicated that the Soviets were concentrating on building up a powerful underwater fleet. More than 300 submarines were in service in the Russian Navy, with another 120 building. These included oceangoing boats, German vessels of advanced design captured at the end of the war, and minelaying boats with a submerged speed of 20 knots or more. Many were snort-fitted, enabling them to cruise submerged for long periods. Russia had also obtained the services of some first-rate German scientists who were carrying on research into methods of high-speed underwater propulsion. The Russian programme of warship construction also included a new class of heavy cruiser. Designed as commerce raiders, they were of 10,000 tons, armed with 12-inch guns and had a top speed of 35 knots.

Thus the statement which accompanied the Naval Estimates for 1950/51 emphasised that attention was to be concentrated on building new anti-submarine frigates, and converting existing vessels to enable them to hunt the new fast battery-drive type of submarine.

The possibility of introducing anti-submarine frigates of simpler design, cheaper and easier to build in large numbers was under consideration. In research work the highest priority was being given to the development of anti-submarine weapons for ships and aircraft. New types of homing torpedoes were being developed which could be launched on the surface or from aircraft, or from under the surface.

Naval aviation resources were also being largely devoted to the submarine threat. A new aircraft able to combine the powers of detection and destruction was being developed, and a prototype had been deck-launched successfully. A new attacker jet aircraft with a maximum speed approaching 600 mph was also in the production stage. An experimental minesweeping flotilla was to be commissioned principally for investigating methods of sweeping mines which did not respond to orthodox methods. Scientific effort was being chiefly directed to counter-measures against high-speed aircraft, high-speed missiles and high-speed submarines. These demanded guided weapons, longer range and more rapid radar, better anti-aircraft guns and proximity fuses, and other new and improved weapons. All these devices, however, called for more weight and space in warships, and to provide it the Admiralty was developing more efficient propulsive machinery which would occupy less weight and space, a reference to the gas turbine experiments.

The Estimates for the year totalled £193 million, some £4 million more than the year before. The post-war process of living on the Navy's own fat had now almost come to an end, but before building up anew a review of the basis of the provision and maintenance of the Fleet was being undertaken.

On the subject of manning it was predicted that wastage during the coming year would be greater than in previous years because of the large numbers of men reaching the end of their current terms of service, and the reluctance of long-serving men reaching the end of their twelve-year engagements to re-engage for further service. Thus there was a shortage of experienced ratings—a cry to be constantly repeated. Special measures calculated to attract a higher proportion of men to re-engage were being examined. Manpower, which had been reduced to a total of 145,000, was expected to fall still further to about 127,000. There was a growing shortage of air crews, and to deal with this problem improvements were being considered in conditions of service. As part of the measures to compensate for the reduced intake of National Servicemen, recruitment for the Royal

Naval Reserve, which had ceased at the beginning of the war, was re-opened.

The RNR first came into existence in 1859 to provide a reserve for the Royal Navy from Merchant Service personnel, the primary qualification for entry being that candidates should be following the sea as a profession. Entries were open for the Executive, Engineering, and Supply & Secretariat Branches for officers, and for seamen and engineering ratings. Similarly, ratings who had served in the Navy during the war and had subsequently entered the Merchant Navy or fishing fleet were encouraged to join the RNR. Increased training fees were introduced for officers and larger retainers for ratings than had been paid in the pre-war Reserve.

To provide an additional source of potential naval manpower in emergency, 80 per cent of the Navy's intake of 2,000 National Servicemen for the year were required to have enrolled in the RNVR, RNVR Air Squadrons, RNV(W)R or the RMFVR, provided that they could perform one year's training commitment prior to being called up. It could then be guaranteed that they would spend their National Service in the Navy, and also stand a chance of being selected for a commission either in the RNVR or RMFVR. RNVR training was stepped up, with cruises to Continental ports in mine-sweepers and motor launches being arranged, while RNVR Air Squadrons were given flying training in carriers of the Home Fleet and Training Squadron. In October 1950 routine training for the Royal Fleet Reserve was recommenced, the men being required to serve afloat for one week in every alternate year.

Despite the small increase in its estimates the Navy was still working to a limited budget, and substantial administrative economies, particularly in training establishments and other shore bases, were being made. Among these were the abolition of the Chatham Group, Royal Marines and the closure of Bermuda dockyard, one of the oldest of the Navy's overseas yards but the most expensive to run in relation to its usefulness.

Bermuda had been taken over by the Crown in 1684, and a century later when the French Revolutionary Wars began the construction of a dockyard there was recommended to the Admiralty. Ireland Island was selected for the site, but work did not begin until 1810. To carry it out convicts were imported from England, and some 9,000 English criminals were eventually sent out. The first Commissioner was appointed at about the same time, and during the

American War of 1812–15 Bermuda grew in strategical importance, and the establishment of the base was considerably increased.

After the end of hostilities with America it was found necessary to make certain additions at Bermuda and the significance of the dockyard increased. It became an important naval and coaling station, and in 1889 a large iron floating dock was towed across the Atlantic and placed in position at St. George Island, subsequently being replaced by a larger one in 1902. During the Second World War Bermuda formed an important base link in the anti-U-boat campaign in the Atlantic from which sea and air patrols provided cover for convoys. In 1940 facilities for setting up naval and air bases in the islands were granted to the United States as part of a larger agreement involving the transfer of American destroyers to the Royal Navy.

Now it was decided that, although Bermuda would continue to be the headquarters of the America and West Indies squadron, in future that squadron would be maintained by ships of the Home Fleet, and refits and repairs carried out in the United Kingdom. Accordingly after the stores and equipment had been transferred or sold, and the floating dock towed away, the White Ensign flying above HMS *Malabar*, the shore base, was hauled down on 1st April 1951.

One result of continuing post-war austerity was the disappearance of naval officers' ceremonial uniforms which had been worn up to the commencement of the Second World War. In April 1950 the Admiralty announced that as there was little possibility in the foreseeable future of the reintroduction, even in modified form, of such rigs as full dress, epaulettes, cocked hat, frock coat, ceremonial sword belt and other accessories these were no longer to be worn, even if held by individual officers. Normally in peacetime the naval officer's Number One, or full dress, was so costly that junior officers had been excused its upkeep until they attained a certain rate of pay. In addition he was required to maintain thirteen other dresses, or 'rigs'. Each was referred to by a number in the Dress Regulations and carefully described down to the smallest button, together with the occasions when to be worn.

First introduced in the reign of George II, the British naval officer's full dress, 1939 style, consisted of a double-breasted frock coat of fine blue cloth lined with white kerseymere. The skirts were edged with inch-deep gold lace, the collar piped with gold oak leaves, and the cuffs slashed with white cloth and embroidered with the appropriate distinction lace of rank. The trousers were decorated with a wide gold stripe running down each outside seam, dubbed irreverently by the wearers 'lightning conductors', and the epaulettes of pearl and gold lace embroidered with gold oak leaves and acorns, with gold bullions, or tassels, pendant from each. Known as 'swabs', epaulettes were originally added to British uniforms in the eighteenth century because foreign sentries thought that officers without them could not be officers and thus failed to pay them proper respects.

The sword belt was of black silk embroidered with gold oak leaves, and the cocked hat of black beaver with golden tassels and a cockade of bullion. This headgear, worn fore and aft, was known in the Fleet as a 'scraper' from the days before the hand salute was introduced, and officers lifted their hats and bowed to their superiors—hence the phrase 'bowing and scraping'.

The naval officer's Number Two rig was almost as gorgeous as the full dress. It was a super evening dress consisting of mess jacket with epaulettes, gold-laced trousers, white waistcoat, sword and full dress belt. Discreetly covered by a boat cloak made of blue cloth lined with white silk while *en route* to the wearer's destination by boat or other conveyance, the dress was for wear at official balls, dinners and other public junketings of importance.

Now all this glory was to depart—for ever as it transpired—in favour of the old Number Five dress of blue monkey jacket and trousers. With this everyday mundane rig, however, the King approved the wearing on appropriate occasions of orders, decorations and medals, and a wing collar and bow tie for ceremonial occasions.

Despite the abolition of this naval sartorial magnificence there were comparatively few complaints afloat, for even before the war the cost was astronomical, and not all of the most senior officers could afford to provide themselves with the full range of rigs officially laid down in the Dress Regulations. In 1959, however, some semblance at least of the old splendour was restored when a ceremonial frock coat was again introduced for flag officers. The new garment had only six buttons on each side in place of the former eight, no flash on the sleeves, a stand collar with gold-laced edgings and, instead of epaulettes, a shoulder strap. An ordinary flat cap replaced the prewar cocked hat. Still later, the number of buttons on the ceremonial coat was increased to eight for Admirals of the Fleet, and the old oak leaf-decorated sword belt restored.

Soon afterwards a complete list of revised dresses for officers was issued by the Admiralty. They numbered nineteen, five more than in pre-war days, but including simpler informal rigs previously unheard of, such as blue battledress, blue shirts and shorts for tropical, working and action dresses, and even sandals.

Another uniform change for officers came about in April 1951 when all RNR and RNVR officers were directed to wear the same straight stripes and curl on the sleeve according to rank as those worn by RN officers, but with an 'R' in the curl, the latter being omitted when mobilised. In the same way RNVR officers of the Air Branch were to wear an 'A' inside the curl. Temporary officers were also allowed to wear straight stripes, but with a wavy curl instead of the normal RN curl; Air officers wore an 'A' in the curl. All newly entered chaplains were for the first time to wear uniform but with no rank badges.

For ratings, too, there were various alterations to uniform. These included the substitution for the old unsightly overalls worn in pre-war days of a new working dress consisting of a light blue shirt and trousers of darker blue denim. Other innovations were plastic-topped white caps for both officers and men, to be worn all the year round at home and abroad. Previously blue caps had been worn during the winter months in home waters. The traditional 'square rig' of collar, jumper and bell-bottomed trousers was given a new look by the introduction of a coat-style, zip-fronted jumper made of diagonal serge cloth. The trousers were also zip-fastened and fitted with side and hip pockets. The new uniform was also issued in white drill for wear in tropical climates.

In 1956 junior ratings of the Supply & Secretariat, Sick Berth and Coder Branches who had previously worn the Class III rig of 'fore and aft' jackets with black buttons, straight trousers and a peaked cap with a red badge, changed to the square rig of bell-bottomed trousers, jumper with collar, and round flat white-topped caps along with seamen and junior engineering ratings.

Raincoats with warm detachable linings were supplied for officers and ratings, and the old oilskin clothing for use in foul weather was replaced by waterproof garments made from PVC-impregnated fabric. For wear in cold climates kapok-lined cotton garments to be worn under the waterproofed clothing superseded the wartime duffel coat. Sailors were issued with sheets and pyjamas in seagoing ships as well as shore establishments, also pillows and pillow cases for use in the camp-bed hammocks being supplied. As new ships with improved habitability came into service, the sailor's traditional hammock was soon to make its final bow in favour of tubular steel and canvas bunks.

Following the success of the Western Union's 'Exercise Verity', the nineteen-fifties saw the establishment of international naval co-operation on a scale never previously attempted or achieved in time of peace.

During the spring cruise of the Home Fleet in January 1950 to Gibraltar and the Western Mediterranean, its ships joined those of the Mediterranean Fleet and a French squadron in full scale combined exercises. At the same time warships of the America and West Indies squadron joined those of the Royal Canadian Navy and the United States Navy for anti-submarine and air defence exercises in the Caribbean under the overall command of an American admiral. In the waters between India and Ceylon the British East Indies squadron exercised with warships of the Royal Indian Navy.

Later in the year there was fuller and more effective co-operation among the Western Union navies when warships from Scandinavian countries for the first time joined Great Britain, the Netherlands, France and Belgium in a series of smaller exercises. In the Channel and North Sea a flag officer of the Royal Netherlands Navy was in overall command of an exercise in which British, French and Dutch warships and aircraft of the RAF took part. In the Mediterranean British warships exercised with Greek, Italian and American naval squadrons.

These extensive programmes of combined exercises, some within the framework of the Western Union alliance, some the North Atlantic Treaty, and others organised purely on a basis of common defence, having as their aim the development of common tactical doctrines and practical understanding, were to prove valuable training for the later formation of a common NATO defence force.

Later in the year a top level committee of naval representatives of Britain, the United States and Canada met in Washington to work out standardised procedures to be adopted for the North Atlantic area similar to those made by the Brussels Treaty Powers. These covered command of the sea and tactical requirements, communications, the control of shipping, air operations and the air defence of forces at sea, submarine and anti-submarine operations, minelaying and mine countermeasures, operations by coastal forces, amphibious operations, the defence of ports and bases, sea exercises and training, and logistic doctrines.

While these mutually protective measures were taking shape, world attention became focused on the Far East where the threat of a new global conflict had abruptly arisen. For on 25th June 1950, without any prior ultimatum or formal declaration of war, the North Koreans launched a full-scale attack on South Korea. This was to be the first test of the efficacy of the United Nations.

At the Postdam conference in 1945 after Germany's surrender, the Western Allies and Russia had agreed that when Japan was defeated Korea should be given back the independence she had lost in 1910 when the country had been absorbed into the Japanese empire. It had also been arranged that Russia should take the surrender of Japanese troops north of the 38th parallel of latitude and America those south of that line. It was never intended, however, that the 38th parallel should divide Korea into two states.

All efforts to establish a united Korea failed, due to Russian intransigence, and in 1948 the democratic Republic of South Korea came into existence under United Nations auspices, while in the north a Korean Communist People's Republic had been formed and equipped with a large army, the growth of which was supervised by the Russians. Soon afterwards American forces were withdrawn from South Korea leaving behind a handful of military advisers, and in the north the Russians withdrew their troops except for a number of technicians. North and South Korean soldiers now faced each other across the demarcation line of the 38th parallel, and border incidents became numerous.

A United Nations Commission had visited Korea to discuss unification of the country only a short time before the North Koreans launched their unprovoked attack. Some 60,000 of their troops poured over the border, supported by Russian-built tanks and jet aircraft. Against them the South Koreans, virtually lacking artillery, armour and aircraft, could oppose only small forces which were compelled to fall back rapidly.

The Security Council of the United Nations met at once and ordered the North Koreans to cease hostilities and to withdraw to the 38th parallel. The Soviet Bloc dissented from this action, but as Russia was boycotting the Security Council at the time there was no veto. Since Russia was always ready to extend further her sphere of influence, it was impossible to believe that she had not given the North Koreans prior approval for their act of aggression.

Its demands ignored, the Council then formally imposed economic and military sanctions and called on all members to rally to the support of South Korea. It was agreed that direction of military operations should be undertaken by the United States, General Douglas MacArthur being appointed supreme commander, and President Truman ordered American naval and air forces into action. But before anything more than advanced elements of troops transported by air from American occupation forces in Japan could arrive, the North Koreans had overrun the south, capturing Seoul, the capital, and advanced to within fifty miles of the south coast port of Pusan.

The British Government promised all available help, but it was difficult to give immediate military assistance to the hard-pressed South Koreans. Naval aid was, however, easier to provide. When hostilities began, Britain's Far Eastern Fleet comprised twenty-two warships, which included the aircraft carrier *Triumph*, the cruisers *Belfast*, *Kenya* and *Jamaica*, seven destroyers, seven frigates and smaller vessels, together with Royal Fleet Auxiliary ships and the hospital Ship *Maine*. A squadron consisting of just over half of these vessels was cruising in Japanese waters under the command of Rear-Admiral W. G. Andrewes, Flag Officer, Second-in-Command, when the Government decided to support the United Nations action in Korea.

From his headquarters in Singapore the Commander-in-Chief, Admiral Sir Patrick Brind, ordered them to co-operate in conjunction with the American Seventh Fleet. Within five days of the outbreak of hostilities the *Triumph*, *Belfast* and *Jamaica*, together with the destroyers *Cossack* and *Consort,* the frigates *Black Swan*, *Alacrity,* *Hart,* and a number of auxiliaries had begun operations with the Seventh Fleet under the orders of the American Vice-Admiral Commanding.

The *Jamaica* and *Black Swan* were despatched up the east coast of Korea to join with US warships harassing the enemy's left flank. *En route* they were attacked by a force of six North Korean E-boats, all but one of which was sunk. Meanwhile the west coast was blockaded to prevent supplies reaching the enemy by sea. Together with planes from an American carrier, aircraft from the *Triumph* were employed in seeking out and destroying enemy vessels in creeks and harbours and in strikes against shore targets.

By 5th July the British ships had been reinforced by warships of the Royal Australian, Royal Canadian and Royal New Zealand navies, so that within about ten days of the North Korean attack seventeen British and Commonwealth warships and some 7,000 officers and men were operating in Korean waters. The Americans were deploying about the same number. Admiral Andrewes assumed responsibility for the west coast blockade, and an American admiral was in command on the east coast. An escort force under British command convoyed troop and supply ships to and from the American Naval Base at Sasebo, in Japan.

Until adequate reinforcements could arrive the British ships had to remain on patrol to the limit of their endurance in order that the blockade should be completely effective. Thus there was little time to return to port, store and refuel and rejoin the patrol. The ships were also operating under exceptional navigational difficulties, since the coastal waters round Korea had not been charted for many years. During the course of their blockade duties the ships steamed thousands of miles in a climate which ranged from the tropical to the arctic.

On 29th August the aircraft maintenance carrier *Unicorn* and the cruiser *Ceylon* arrived with 1,500 troops of the 1st Battalion Argyll and Sutherland Highlanders and the 1st Battalion Middlesex Regiment with 800 tons of stores. By now the United Nations forces had been pushed back until they were confined in what was little more than a bridgehead around Pusan. At the beginning of September the North Koreans launched a violent onslaught against the bridgehead. But, aided by the fire of the warships and naval air strikes, the perimeter was held. As the strain of their swift advance and stretched communications began to tell, the enemy attack lost impetus and eventually petered out.

Meanwhile logistic support for the Commonwealth Fleet, operating more than a thousand miles from its base, had been instituted. The *Unicorn* brought replenishment aircraft for the *Triumph* and crammed the rest of the available space on board with stores. Later the carriers *Ocean* and *Warrior* were used to ferry aircraft, men and materials direct from the United Kingdom. The newly activated Fleet Train grew steadily in size and eventually included, besides nine supply ships and oil tankers, the hospital ship *Maine*, incidentally the only one in the area since the American hospital ship *Providence* intended for Korea had been sunk in a collision off San Francisco. From mid-July until almost the end of August the *Maine* was employed in evacuating wounded from the fighting zone. During this period she steamed 4,654 miles in the process of evacuating 1,315 casualties, earning thereby the special gratitude of the Americans whose wounded formed the bulk of the evacuees.

By the middle of September MacArthur was ready to mount a counter-offensive. This began with the landing at Inchon, on the west coast of Korea and well inside enemy-held territory, of the American Tenth Corps. Their aim was to cut the North Korean lines of communication and recapture Seoul. Thus the enemy force besieging Pusan would be virtually cut off. Commonwealth naval forces played an important part in this amphibious operation.

The cruisers *Jamaica*, *Ceylon* and *Kenya*, with the *Triumph* providing air spotting, formed part of the bombarding force. Destroyers and frigates acted as escorts and screened the bombarding ships. The landing was a success, and within a fortnight Seoul was recaptured. Following the Inchon landings United Nations forces at Pusan broke out of their bridgehead, and their offensive was so successful that by 1st October the North Koreans had been driven back beyond the 38th parallel. A week later, having received the approval to do so of the UN General Assembly, MacArthur crossed the parallel and pursued the beaten enemy as far as the Yalu River, where he called upon North Korea to surrender and end the war. Throughout these operations the naval forces provided valuable support on the flanks of the advancing army, ships of the Commonwealth navies steaming a total of nearly 60,000 miles.

As a result of the precipitate retreat of the North Koreans many islands on the west and south-west coasts had to be liberated, the majority of these missions being carried out by Commonwealth destroyers and frigates. Large quantities of rice were landed to feed the starving islanders and the lighthouse keepers who had remained at their posts although marooned by the tide of war. Safe areas for fishing were established, the sick tended, and supplies of clothing handed out to the liberated and ragged villagers. On 9th October the aircraft carrier *Theseus* arrived in Korean waters and replaced the *Triumph*.

Mention must here be made of a unit of the Royal Marines, which was subsequently to cover itself with glory and earn an American Presidential citation. After the United States Tenth Corps had carried out the Inchon landing and linked up with the Seventh Army coming from the south, MacArthur switched them by sea to the right flank of his forces to continue pursuit of the North Koreans. Their objective was the Chosin Reservoir, principal source of power supply to the industrial areas of the north. The British military contribution to the United Nations force in Korea was a Commonwealth Division, which eventually comprised in addition to a United Kingdom

Brigade, Canadian, Australian and New Zealand troops. Although Royal Marine detachments were carried on board the Navy's larger ships in Korea and had taken a small part in the Inchon landings, it was decided that Royal Marines should also be represented in the Commonwealth Division.

Accordingly No. 41 Independent Commando was formed at Plymouth in August 1950, and in plain clothes flown out to Japan where it was fully equipped by the Americans. On arrival the Commando was augmented by volunteers from the Far Eastern Fleet who were already in training. Working under the direction of the US Army Special Raiding Forces, the Commando carried out a number of successful amphibious coastal raids to destroy enemy communications and tie up Communist forces in coastal defence. In November, after hard fighting, they joined the First US Marine Corps Division in the Chosin area, within two miles of the Yalu River.

Now a new enemy appeared. In October before the UN forces crossed the 38th parallel, the Chinese had declared that they would not stand idle if North Korea was invaded. MacArthur, however, ignored this threat despite reports of large Chinese troop movements near the Korean border and had left his forces thinly deployed along a lengthy battle line.

At first United Nations air superiority began to be challenged by Russian-built MiG aircraft operating from bases inside Manchuria. Then, towards the end of November, fourteen Chinese divisions were suddenly hurled against the UN line. Bad weather had by now set in, bringing biting arctic winds, blinding snowstorms and temperatures well below zero, preventing UN aircraft from giving their usual support to the ground forces. The UN line was pierced and the whole army threatened. A spearhead of eight Chinese divisions was aimed at Tenth Corps, which was soon surrounded and heavily outnumbered.

While the main United Nations forces hastily fell back to the 38th parallel, the Tenth Corps was compelled to fight its way back to the sea. Attacked from all sides, ambushed and sniped at from ditches alongside the track, the Marines, with 41 Commando acting as rearguard, doggedly struggled back to the coastal bridgehead at Hungnam, on the east coast. From thence, with naval support, they were evacuated to Pusan.

After fruitless attempts by the United Nations to end the fighting, the Chinese launched a fresh offensive all along the line in January 1951, and again Seoul was captured. The evacuation of UN forces was once more covered by Allied naval units, whose supporting fire helped to blunt the impetus of the Communist attack. A counter-offensive retook Seoul and drove the enemy back to the 38th parallel, where a strong defensive line was formed. After hard and bitter fighting another ferocious Chinese thrust was checked, not least by the gallant stand of the 1st Battalion the Gloster Regiment on the Imjin River, and a fresh drive by UN forces, now under command of the American General Ridgeway who had been appointed to supersede MacArthur as Supreme Commander, finally forced them back behind the 38th parallel.

In July 1951, at the suggestion of the Russians, truce talks began, but while these were going on sporadic fighting continued, with Allied warships bombarding enemy lines of communication, so re-ducing their supplies, and defending UN-held offshore islands. Allied carrier-borne aircraft continued to range over enemy territory, des-troying road and rail bridges, bombing enemy positions, supply bases, industrial centres and other strategic targets. An armistice was finally signed two years later.

Apart from the devastation and suffering, this undeclared war had caused more than three million casualties on both sides. One sig-nificant result was that Red China had emerged as an aggressive force in the Far East with aims beyond her own borders.

A total of seventy-five warships of the Commonwealth navies and of the Royal Fleet Auxiliary Service had been engaged in the fight-ing for varying periods. They comprised thirty-four ships of the Royal Navy (including four light fleet carriers and six cruisers), eighteen ships of the Royal Fleet Auxiliary Service and one hospital ship; nine ships of the Royal Australian Navy (including one carrier); eight destroyers of the Royal Canadian Navy, and six frigates of the Royal New Zealand Navy. The British ships alone steamed a total of 2,100,500 miles and used up over 633,000 tons of fuel.

During hostilities, which lasted 1,128 days, 23,000 rounds of 6-inch and 148,000 rounds of 4.7-inch shells were fired by HM ships in bombardments; 15,200 bombs of various weights were dropped, and 57,600 3-inch rocket shells were fired from aircraft. In addition, nearly 3.5 million rounds of 20 mm gun ammunition were fired. Other nations who contributed naval units included the Republic of Korea, the United States, France, the Netherlands and Thailand. These combined forces were mainly responsible for the control of sea communications and seaborne air and gun support on the flanks of the ground troops. Tactical co-operation when warships of the various nations were employed together proved excellent and effective throughout.

The spearhead of the Commonwealth naval forces was the striking power of their air squadrons. The tours of duty in the war zone of the five carriers employed lasted approximately six months. They were HM ships *Triumph, Theseus, Glory, Ocean* and HMAS *Sydney*, supported by the repair and maintenance carrier *Unicorn*. HMS *Glory* did three tours of duty, HMS *Ocean* two, and the other ships one tour each. Fourteen British and two Australian squadrons operated from these ships, totalling some 480 aircrews. The squadrons flew 25,000 operational sorties for the comparatively low casualty record of twenty-one aircrew killed in action, mostly shot down by anti-aircraft fire, and fourteen killed in accidents.

A noteworthy feature of the air operations in the war zone was the value of helicopters, which were much used by the Americans for difficult tasks in the mountainous regions of Korea. Thus they were utilised for spotting, reconnaissance, evacuating casualties and air-lifting small parties of troops and local force commanders. A number of them were lent to the British carriers, and helicopters subsequently became standard additions to our own carriers. Westland Sikorsky S.51s had already been used experimentally by British ships in home waters for mail carrying and the transport of senior officers to and from ships at sea.

The outbreak of the Korean war had found the British Army widely dispersed, heavily committed and unprepared for what seemed a renewal of global warfare. Thus there was difficulty in assembling one brigade for service in the Far East. But these were soon joined by contingents from Australia and Canada until, by the end of the war, the Eighth US Army, which formed the bulk of the United Nations force, was supported by military units from twenty-one different countries.

Proportionately, however, the strength of the Commonwealth naval force was much larger than its contribution to the ground forces. While ships of each category were relieved at regular intervals, its total strength at any one time was never less than one aircraft carrier, several cruisers, a score or more of destroyers and frigates, and a fleet train of tankers and supply ships.

When hostilities began the Western Union nations pledged themselves to hurried programmes of re-armament. Thus the British

Labour Government, which had been preoccupied with the country's immediate economic problems, started a crash programme to increase the strength of the Army, strengthen the Navy and RAF and speed up re-equipment. National Service was extended to two years, and a number of Reservists were recalled in order to bring up to wartime strength the complements of ships engaged in the war zone. In addition some 3,600 officers and ratings and Royal Marines who were due for release at the termination of their normal engagements were temporarily retained. The naval building programme was expanded, and eighty-nine ships of the Reserve Fleet brought forward for accelerated refit.

Towards the end of 1951 HMS *Eagle*, the first of the two new fleet carriers which had been under construction when the war ended, commissioned for service. Displacing 36,800 tons, with a length of 803 feet overall and a beam of 112 feet, she was the logical outcome of the trend in aircraft carrier design which started with the *Ark Royal* in 1936, and produced such ships as the *Illustrious* and *Formidable* which were so successful during the war.

She was, however, much larger than her forerunners, due to the increase in the size of naval fighter and strike aircraft and the consequent requirement of larger hangars and longer flight decks; the need for heavy radar gear to be mounted high above the waterline, and the higher minimum standard of crew accommodation. But, side by side with the increase in size, hitting power represented by her strike aircraft, and capacity for defence represented by her fighter aircraft, gun armament and details of her design were also increased.

Her flight deck spanned an area of more than two acres, and in addition to arrester wires and safety barriers, she was fitted with the most modern launching catapults. Her island structure, which housed the radio, radar and plotting rooms, was as large as a frigate; and the twin hangars, big enough to accommodate 263 double-decker buses, could stow 80–100 of the largest naval carrier-borne jet aircraft. At that time these included the Vickers Supermarine Attacker, the Hawker Sea Hawk, and the De Havilland Sea Venom, a two-seater night fighter. The *Eagle*'s four sets of steam turbines could drive her at a top speed of 31 knots, and special damage control headquarters and facilities had been built into the ship so that in case of damage she could speedily be restored to full fighting efficiency. Her gun armament comprised sixteen 4.5-inch and fifty-eight 40 mm guns, and her complement numbered some 2,000 officers and men.

It was in the sphere of crew accommodation, messing and amenities that the new *Eagle* boasted advances that were eventually to become the norm in future British warships. A centralised messing system had been introduced in which the ship's company took their meals in large dining halls. Chief and petty officers were waited on by teams of servers, the junior ratings serving themselves in the second dining hall on the cafeteria system. This had the effect of removing all meals from the mess decks where the old-time sailor had lived, slept and had his being, so that these became solely sleeping and recreation spaces.

On his own air-conditioned mess deck each man had his own kit locker and another smaller locker for personal effects. The ship's company, however, still slept in hammocks. The fully automatic galleys were fitted with the most advanced electric cooking machinery and labour-saving devices, such as sausage-making machines, potato peelers, bread and butter cutting machines, and automatic waste disposal units. Besides a fully equipped laundry, there were two ice cream and soda fountains, a barber shop, library, cinema, and a small air-conditioned chapel. The cost of building this super-carrier, exclusive of her gun armament, was £15.75 million, £6.75 million more than the battleship *Vanguard*.

Also nearing completion at this time were the largest conventional destroyers ever to be built for the Royal Navy. Known as *Daring* class ships after the name vessel of the type, their standard displacement was 2,800 tons, 3,600 at full load. Eight of the class were built and named *Daring, Dainty, Decoy, Defender, Delight, Diamond, Diana* and *Duchess*. They were 390 feet long overall and 43 feet in the beam, carried six fully automatic and radar-controlled 4.5-inch guns in twin turrets; six 40 mm Bofors anti-aircraft guns; ten 21-inch torpedo tubes in two above-water pentad mountings, and a Squid triple-barrelled depth charge mortar.

Of all-welded construction, they were powered by geared steam turbines of advanced design, giving them a speed of 35 knots, and their crew accommodation included electric galleys, a laundry and bathrooms, fluorescent lighting and pastel colours in the living spaces, and labour-saving devices for cleaning ship. Comparable to light cruisers in tonnage and striking power, the *Darings*, which carried a complement of some 300 officers and men, cost between £2 million and £3 million each. Although the wonder of their time, these outsize destroyers were the last to be built as such, and their active life span was comparatively brief.

As a stimulus to recruiting for the regular strengths of the three Services needed by the programme of re-armament, a new pay code was introduced on 1st September 1950. The increases were more generous than those awarded four years earlier and more in line with wages and salaries in the private sector. Thus for the Navy the pay of an Ordinary Seaman after six months' training went up from four shillings (20p) a day to double that amount; able seamen went up from six shillings and sixpence (32½p) to nine shillings and sixpence (47½p); leading rates from eight shillings and sixpence (42½p) to twelve shillings (60p); petty officers from ten shillings and sixpence (52½p) to sixteen shillings and sixpence (82½p); and chief petty officers from twelve shillings (60p) to nineteen shillings (95p).

All seaman branch ratings could specialise in one of a number of technical subjects, such as gunnery, radar, torpedo, and submarine detection, each specialist qualification carrying additional pay of from three shillings and sixpence (17½p) to seven shillings (35p) weekly. Rates of pay for technical and artificer branches went up by comparable amounts. Length of service increments of three shillings and sixpence (17½p) weekly were awarded after four years in any one rating, but good conduct badge pay remained unaltered at two shillings and fourpence (11½p) weekly up to a maximum of three badges after twelve years' service. Kit upkeep allowance was increased from £3 to £3 6s 3d (£3.31), paid quarterly, and marriage allowances,, irrespective of age, ranged from £2 2s 0d (£2.10) to £2 12s 6d (£2.26½) weekly. Royal Marines received similar increases, and National Servicemen serving beyond 18 months received the same rates of pay as those on regular Royal Naval engagements.

Pay for officers, both in the Navy and Marines, was also considerably increased from the rates awarded in 1946. Thus a midshipman would now receive £219 per annum instead of £137; sub-lieutenants £283, an increase of £72; lieutenants from £310 to £392, rising to £584; commanders from £867 to £1,013, rising to £1,195; and captains from £1,186 to £1,551. Flying pay was almost doubled. Members of the WRNS, whose rates of pay were approximately three-quarters of those of corresponding officers and ratings in the Royal Navy, received proportionate increases, and they also became eligible for specialist pay and length of service increments.

Closely following on these pay rises, increased rates of retired pay and pensions also came into force. As an encouragement to ratings already serving to re-engage to complete time for pension, new tax-free financial terminal grants were introduced. Ranging from £100 for able rates to £250 for chief petty officers, these grants were intended to help men leaving the Service in early middle age to settle down in civilian life. Retired pay for officers was increased by amounts ranging from £25 to £200 per annum, dependent on rank, and they could receive a tax-free terminal grant of £1,000.

To assist in overcoming shortages in higher ratings the Admiralty had in the previous year brought in a scheme known as the 'Fifth Five', whereby recommended chief and petty officers of all branches could re-engage for a further term of five years at the expiration of the normal period of 22 years' pensionable service, making a total of 27 years. A further extension of service to 32 years, to be called the 'Sixth Five', was now introduced, which offered not only an enhanced pension but an increased terminal grant of up to £410.

It remained to be seen whether these measures would be sufficient to compete with the lure of full employment and steadily rising wages in civilian life at the dawn of what was to become known as 'the age of affluence'.

But the new defence plan called for the expenditure of millions of pounds, making necessary the reimposition of certain wartime controls and a deflationary squeeze on all other private and public expenditure. A balance of payments crisis was also developing. When a general election, held in the autumn of 1951, returned a new Conservative Government the pace of re-armament was slowed down, and a major review of defence policy undertaken in the light of the development of new weapons and weapon carriers.

In addition to the Korean war other troubles were occupying the attention of our overstretched forces overseas in the early nineteen-fifties, not least of which was an armed insurrection in Malaya which dragged on for several years.

After the Japanese surrender the Federation of Malaya, which comprised all the separate Sultanate States except Singapore, came into being in 1948. But it also brought the beginning of a serious Communist revolt. Communists had hoped to gain control of the country in 1945, but were forestalled by the arrival of British military administration. Between 1946 and 1947 Communist insurgents made determined efforts to paralyse the economic recovery of the country, finally launching a campaign of violence and murder. Their principal targets were British rubber plantations, tin mines, and all who opposed them. The terrorists were armed with captured Japanese weapons and equipment, and operated from jungle hideouts. The police were unable to deal with them, and a state of emergency was declared.

Security forces were accordingly strengthened by Army units and, in June 1950, the headquarters of 3 Commando Brigade with the three Royal Marine Commandos were moved from Hong Kong to Singapore. During its subsequent two years of Malayan service the Brigade, in conjunction with the police, was responsible for the security of the State of Perak, one of the worst bandit black spots. For the Marines there were no spectacular encounters with the elusive enemy, who operated from bases hidden in swamp and primary jungle. But by the time the Brigade moved on to Malta in July 1952 they had accounted for 171 bandits killed and 48 captured for the loss of 4 officers and 15 other ranks killed. In recognition of their successes 18 decorations and 25 Mentions in Despatches were awarded to ranks of the Brigade.

The Navy, too, played an important part in those long drawn out operations. Warship patrols prevented supplies and reinforcements from reaching the insurgents by sea; naval guns bombarded bandit hideouts in the jungle, and assault landing craft fitted out as gunboats operated in the Malayan rivers. Towards the end of 1952 a squadron of naval S.55 helicopters was sent to Malaya to reinforce the smaller RAF S.51 helicopters used for casualty evacuation and air-lifting troops into action in the interior. Nevertheless, in spite of increasingly effective measures taken against them, a hard core of Communists was still in active revolt as late as 1957 when Malaya became an independent State within the Commonwealth. In fact it was not until August 1960 that the Emergency was officially declared to be at an end.

Turmoil in the Middle East also continued to bedevil the international scene and added to the Royal Navy's responsibilities. Much of this stemmed from the establishment of the State of Israel which followed the departure from Palestine of the British High Commissioner in May 1948. Member States of the Arab League, who included Egypt, Iraq, Lebanon, Syria, Saudi Arabia and Jordan, went to the aid of the Palestine Arabs who were fighting the Jews, but only Egypt, Syria and Jordan provided effective forces. The Israelis fought back and inflicted severe defeats on their enemies, the Egyptians particularly coming off badly. Eventually a truce was proclaimed in 1949, but the Arab nations banded together to enforce an economic and political boycott of Israel.

Considering themselves still legally in a state of war, the Egyptians barred Israeli ships from using the Suez Canal, and also tried to prevent shipping using the port of Aquabah, to which the Israelis had restored its Biblical name of Eilat. This action led to interference with British shipping, and warships had to be detached from the Mediterranean Fleet to patrol the area, a strong protest being made to the Egyptian Government. Then, in 1951, the Egyptians abrogated the 1936 Anglo-Egyptian Treaty of Alliance which provided for the establishment of a British garrison for twenty years and recognition of Britain's special interest in the Canal Zone.

Reinforcements were at once sent to the Mediterranean, some by air and others in the aircraft carriers *Illustrious* and *Triumph*. In the interests of international shipping, the Royal Navy took control of key points along the Canal, at Port Said, the Bitter Lakes and at Suez. Since the Egyptian staffs of the vital water services were prevented from working by the threats and intimidation of their own Government, a British cruiser took over the role of shipping office at Port Said, and her sailors, working in half a dozen assault craft, moored and unmoored hundreds of merchantmen of many nations, and thus enabled millions of tons of international shipping to continue to pass through the Canal in orderly convoys. Eight destroyers and frigates were deployed in the Canal area, and fast motor boats provided harbour patrols at night to prevent pilfering.

Rioting and disorders continued throughout Egypt in protest, until finally in January 1952 martial law was proclaimed by King Farouk and troops were called out to quell anti-British demonstrations. Six months later an Army *coup d'état* led by Major-General Neguib overthrew the Government, and shortly afterwards Farouk abdicated in favour of his young son.* For a time comparative calm was restored, and in October 1954 a treaty was signed between Britain and Egypt by which a phased withdrawal of British troops from the Canal Zone would take place on the understanding that our military base would be maintained by British civilian contractors. But this provided only a breathing space for what was to follow.

While the Canal crisis was boiling up, the Anglo-Iranian Oil Company was seeking to re-negotiate its concessionary rights with the Persian Government. But these negotiations failed due to the opposition of the Nationalist Front led by Dr. Mossadeq. When on a

* *In June 1953 the young king was deposed and a Republic proclaimed.*

wave of popular feeling the latter became Prime Minister, the Persian Government nationalised the oil industry and expropriated the Anglo-Iranian Oil Company's wells at Abadan.

The Company and the British Government both petitioned the International Court on the issue, but the Mossadeq regime refused to recognise the Court's jurisdiction. In October 1951 Britain referred the matter to the Security Council of the United Nations, but repeated efforts by the Council, Britain and America to find a solution failed. Anti-British feeling ran high in Persia, all British consulates in the country being closed at Mossadeq's demand early in 1952.

At the outset of the crisis the small Persian Gulf squadron was reinforced by cruisers, destroyers, frigates and tank landing craft, while a paratroop brigade stood by in Cyprus. British warships anchored off the giant oil refinery in the Shatt-el-Arab to keep a watch on the situation. Eventually, however, employees of the Anglo-Iranian Oil Company and their families had to be evacuated by warship to Basra from whence they were flown home, and the refinery ceased to function. The dispute dragged on until 1954 when a settlement was finally achieved, by which time Mossadeq had been toppled from power and sentenced to a term of imprisonment for treason.

CHAPTER FOUR

The New Elizabethan Age

In September 1951 King George VI underwent a serious operation, and by the end of the year appeared to have made a good recovery. But on 6th February 1952 he died suddenly at Sandringham.

Following his operation it had been arranged on the recommendation of his doctors that in the New Year the King should set out on a recuperative cruise in the battleship *Vanguard*, spending a period in South Africa. A Royal tour of Australia and New Zealand which was to have been made early in 1952 would instead be carried out by Princess Elizabeth and her husband, the Duke of Edinburgh, who as a lieutenant-commander had been serving with the Mediterranean Fleet. Accordingly the Royal couple left England by air on the first stage of the tour on 31st January, being seen off from London Airport by the King, and had reached Nairobi when news of his Majesty's death was conveyed to them. The tour was cancelled, and on the Princess's arrival back in this country she was proclaimed Queen Elizabeth II.

On 14th February the funeral of the late King took place following a period of lying in state at Westminster Hall. Strong detachments of the Royal Navy and Royal Marines took part in the funeral processions in London and Windsor, and the gun carriage bearing the King's coffin was drawn from Westminster to Paddington Station, and from Windsor station to St. George's Chapel in the Castle by naval officers and ratings. Thus tradition was continued which had first started half a century earlier at the funeral of Queen Victoria, when the artillery horses which were drawing the gun carriage bearing the coffin broke their traces and were replaced by bluejackets from the naval guard of honour. Both at Westminster Hall and Windsor station naval piping parties piped their Royal admiral 'over the side' for the last time.

In the following January the Queen approved the promotion of her husband to be Admiral of the Fleet, and at the same time appointed him Field Marshal, Marshal of the Royal Air Force, and Captain-General of the Royal Marines. She thus followed historical precedent, for in 1702 Queen Anne made her consort, Prince George of Denmark, Generalissimo of all the Forces, Constable of Windsor Castle, Lord High Admiral, Lord Warden of the Cinque Ports, and Captain-General of the Honourable Artillery Company. Queen Victoria created her bridegroom a Field Marshal, but he never held a commission in the Royal Navy.

The Duke of Edinburgh was, however, a professional sailor, having joined the Royal Navy as a cadet in 1939. He served in a number of ships during the war, and was present at the battle of Matapan while serving as a midshipman in the battleship *Valiant*. In October 1950 as a lieutenant-commander he took command of the frigate *Magpie* in the Mediterranean, and on 30th June 1952 was promoted to commander. On that occasion the Admiralty stated that 'the Duke has been selected for promotion by the Board solely on his merits as a naval officer, and in competition with all the other lieutenant-commanders due for promotion'. Now he took his place at the top of the professional tree with the other twelve Admirals of the Fleet.

The dawn of the new Elizabethan era seemed full of promise. With the abolition of the last of the wartime controls, austerity was ending; there was full employment and production was increasing; average earnings were higher and the general standard of living was beginning to rise. Nevertheless, in order to keep within the limits of the country's economic capacity the big and costly re-armament programme begun in 1951 had to be rephased due to the rising costs of arms and equipment and the rate of technical progress in armament design and production. The chief naval threats were considered to be the mine, the submarine and the air, and the programme was therefore principally directed towards adequate counter-measures. New construction, modernisation and conversion were accelerated, but the bulk of the extra funds available were allocated to naval aviation.

The new aircraft carrier *Eagle* had now joined the Fleet, but the construction of the *Ark Royal* was still further delayed. In fact she did not come into service until 1955. Of the new light fleet carriers under construction, the *Centaur* was completed in 1953, and two of her sister ships, *Albion* and *Bulwark*, in 1954. Two more vessels of the class, *Melbourne* and *Bonaventure*, were being completed for the Royal Australian and Royal Canadian navies respectively.

New naval flying aids coming into use included three revolutionary British inventions: the steam catapult, the angled deck, and the mirror landing device, all of which were subsequently adopted by the navies of other nations.

Ever since the first air-operated catapult for the Navy's aircraft was fitted in HMS *Vindictive* in 1925, there had been steady development to improve the efficiency of aircraft launching by this means. The air-operated catapult gave way to one operated by cordite, and this in turn was replaced by a hydro-pneumatic type. In this type of catapult the accelerating force was transmitted to the aircraft by means of steel wires passing round pulleys, to the ends of which were attached a small trolley running along a track sunk flush in the flight deck. Hooked to this trolley was the towing bridle which hauled the plane along the deck. But the increasing weight and higher speeds of naval aircraft called for larger and heavier power units, and correspondingly heavier ropes and pulleys. These eventually reached a size and weight which made further improvement impossible, since the mechanism would be too heavy to install in an ordinary ship, and a new launching method was sought.

The invention of Commander Colin Mitchell, an RVNR Engineer officer, the steam catapult works on the principle of the slotted cylinder, and has no rams or hydraulic purchases. The hook to which the aircraft is connected is directly attached by a shuttle to a pair of pistons driven along sealed twin cylinders by high pressure steam from the ship's main boilers, fed off into storage tanks housed below the flight deck. When about to be launched, the aircraft is connected to the shuttle by a towing bridle at the fore end and secured to a 'holdback' hooked into a deck fitting aft. The aircraft's engines are then run up to full power, the launching valves of the catapult opened and steam admitted from the storage tanks to the after ends of the pistons in the power cylinders. This generated force snaps a calibrated link in the 'holdback' and thrusts pistons, shuttle and aircraft forward at the required velocity.

First tested in the British aircraft carrier *Perseus* in 1950, the new catapult proved so powerful that it could hurl into the sky the heaviest jet aircraft, even with the carrier steaming downwind or alongside in harbour.

The angled deck, second of the new devices, which had been evolved by Captain Denis Campbell, DSC, RN, in collaboration with a technician of the Supply Ministry, involved a modification of the conventional shape and layout of a carrier's flight deck to enable aircraft to land on at an angle instead of from directly astern as formerly. Thus a pilot making a faulty landing can fly straight off and circle for another attempt with no danger of colliding with personnel and parked aircraft through overshooting the arrester wires and crash barriers. With the angled deck not only are crashes extremely rare, but as the arresting area can overlap the midships parking place, the layout has the effect of increasing the size of the deck park forward and enables aircraft to be catapulted off without interfering with the landing area.

The mirror landing aid, invention of Commander Hilary Goodhart, a naval engineer and test pilot, is a robot signalling light system, effective by day or night, which visually beams the pilot of an aircraft on to the flight deck, replacing the old batsman whose inherent human errors could not be accepted at the higher approach speeds of new aircraft.

The device comprises a large curved mirror flanked at either side by a row of coloured lights, a gyro-operated mounting maintaining the mirror at a constant angle regardless of the ship's motion. A set of white lights placed aft shine into the mirror and produce a blob of light which is watched by the pilot as he approaches. By keeping this blob lined up with the flanking coloured lights the correct vertical angle of approach is maintained. Due to the curvature of the mirror the light blob is visible at all necessary angles in their horizontal plane, thus enabling the pilot to pick it up while circling for landing. The vertical angle of the mirror can be varied according to the type of aircraft being landed, so that as each pilot comes in on the flat beam of light his undercarriage is the right height above the carrier's stern prior to touchdown.

A further contribution to the safe landing of aircraft on to a carrier was the British invention in 1955 of the 'Audio' airspeed indicator. Working on the principle of an electric organ, the device gives assurance of correct speed and warning of incorrect speed in the pilot's earphones, thus enabling him to look round and appreciate the area of approach.

The re-armament programme included no new cruisers, but three existing cruisers, *Birmingham*, *Newcastle* and *Newfoundland* of pre-war and wartime vintage were extensively modernised. Work on the three *Tiger* class vessels was still further suspended pending the completion of trials of a new type of quick-firing, radar-controlled gun. This weapon, along with many other devices and technical equipment was undergoing full scale tests in the trials cruiser *Cumberland*.

Known as the Navy's floating laboratory, the *Cumberland* was a County class cruiser of 10,000 tons completed in 1928. After distinguished war service in most parts of the world from Arctic waters to the Far East, she was converted to become the Navy's first trials

The aircraft carriers,
Hermes, Ark Royal and
Victorious in company

Fairey Gannet, Airborne
Early Warning aircraft

The Mirror landing sight

Whitby class frigate

Transfer of the naval base at Simonstown, 1957

'O' class submarine—conventional patrol type

Naval clearance divers at work

Amphibious warfare group showing the Commando carrier *Bulwark*, HMS *Fearless* with (over-flying) RAF helicopters and Navy Wessex helicopters; and minor landing craft in foreground

A *Tribal* class frigate at speed

ship in 1951. As well as testing guns and associated control systems, radar equipment, fin stabilisers, new type compasses, improved methods of astro-navigation, fibre glass boats, and 'washdown' trials against radio-active fallout, she made important contributions to the habitability of mess decks, testing many new devices aimed at improving the living standards afloat of ratings. In 1958 she was replaced by a trials ship whose principal task was to evaluate weapons and other sophisticated equipment which in the early nineteen-fifties had not progressed beyond the drawing board.

To augment existing cruiser strength, however, the new *Daring* class 'super' destroyers were coming into service, while other fleet destroyers were taken in hand for conversion into fast anti-submarine frigates. Between 1951 and 1955 some forty-six of these vessels were converted, including a number for Commonwealth navies. Armed with 4-inch and 40-mm guns and Squid depth-charge mortars, their speed was in excess of 36 knots, and they were considered capable of dealing with any type of submarine a potential enemy could put into service.

In due course they were succeeded by several new classes of fast frigates, designated either as anti-submarine, anti-aircraft, or aircraft-direction vessels.

Of the smaller warships built under the re-armament programme were a large number of minesweepers. Designed to combat the threat posed by modern mining, these were of two classes, coastal and inshore, and of entirely new type. The coastal minesweeper was 152 feet long with a beam of 29 feet, and displaced some 425 tons. Two Napier Deltic diesel engines developing 3,000 shp gave a top speed of 16 knots. Construction was of wood-planked aluminium alloy, capable of rapid fabrication and largely non-magnetic. Able to operate effectively against contact and influence mines, they were intended for use in shallow coastal waters. Some ninety were built, many being sold to Australia, India, Malaysia and South Africa. The inshore type were 107 feet long with a 22-foot beam, and displaced from 123 to 164 tons. Of wood or composite construction, they were designed to operate in rivers and estuaries.

Another measure taken against the threat of mines in a future conflict was the formation of the Royal Naval Minewatching Service. This organisation was intended to be responsible in wartime for manning posts ashore and afloat around the coasts of the United Kingdom and overlooking the principal navigable waterways. The object of the minewatchers was to spot mines dropped from aircraft, plot and report their positions to local naval headquarters so that shipping could be warned and diverted and steps taken to deal with the mines. It was to be a civilian organisation administered by the Navy. Each Commander-in-Chief would have Minewatching Service officers on his staff, and at each of the large ports there would be a part-time Assistant Minewatching Officer.

Entry into the Service was open to men above the age of 45 and women of 26 and over, volunteers being confined to those who lived in coastal areas or close to the principal navigable waterways. Subsequently these age limits were extended to between 21 and 60 for either sex. In peacetime the volunteer minewatchers would be expected to attend lectures and demonstrations to be arranged in their own localities. In time of war they would be issued with a free uniform consisting of blue battledress, beret and greatcoat with a shoulder flash bearing the initials 'R.N.M.W.S', and a badge specially designed for wear on the beret. A miniature of the same emblem in the form of a lapel badge for men and a brooch for women was supplied for wear in plain clothes. Recruiting for the new Service began in January 1952, and some 5,000 men and women volunteered. Today the title of the organisation has been changed to 'Royal Naval Auxiliary Service', and its scope extended to include many other tasks connected with port protection.

Among the small craft being specially built for anti-submarine work were a number of Seaward Defence boats whose purpose was to detect, locate and destroy submarines, including midget submarines, in the approaches to defended ports. 117 feet long and displacing some 150 tons, they were armed with a 40-mm gun, carried depth-charges and flares, and sophisticated electronic detection equipment. For use as either gun or torpedo craft was a new design of fast patrol boat. In the gunboat role they were able to mount a 4.5-inch gun, and in the torpedo-boat role two 21-inch torpedo tubes. 75 feet in length, with wooden hulls incorporating water-resistant plywood structural members, their 5,000 hp Packard engines gave them a speed of 40 knots. Known as the 'Gay' class, they bore such names as *Gay Bombadier*, *Gay Archer*, *Gay Charger* and *Gay Fencer*.

Another new type of mosquito craft built at this time was the 'Bold' class. These were the first warships in any navy to be fitted with gas turbines in conjunction with diesel engines, a system of light, compact propulsive machinery in which Britain had a four-year lead over other nations. 123 feet long with a beam of 20 feet and a displacement of 140 tons, they had two funnels abreast, and a speed in excess of 43 knots. As gunboats they were armed with two 4.5-inch and one 40-mm radar-controlled guns, and in the MTB role four 21-inch torpedo tubes. Their hulls were constructed of light alloy.

Helicopters were also added to the Navy's anti-submarine armoury. The value of these machines had become apparent soon after the war when, in September 1946, the first landing by helicopter on a naval escort vessel at sea was made by Lieutenant Alan Bristow, RN. In February 1947 Lieutenant K. Reed, RN, became the first man to land one on a battleship—HMS *Vanguard*—and three months later the first British naval helicopter squadron was formed to fly Sikorsky Hoverfly machines.

By 1950 a more powerful type of helicopter, the Westland Sikorsky S.51, equipped with a hydraulic winch, came into service. Known as the 'Dragonfly', the machine had a speed of 95 mph and a range of 200 miles. Later came the much larger American-built Sikorsky S.55, designated the 'Whirlwind', which was supplied by the United States under the Mutual Aid Defence programme. Powered by Wright Cyclone engines, it had a top speed of 110 mph and an operational range in excess of 400 miles.

In August 1952 two of these machines made the first transatlantic crossing, completing a journey of 3,410 statute miles in a flying time of $42\frac{1}{2}$ hours. Soon afterwards the first naval Whirlwind squadron was formed in the United Kingdom and sent out to Malaya, where it served with distinction in the long and arduous campaign against Communist terrorists. During its service the squadron transported 200,000 lb of freight across miles of jungle, lifted over 10,000 troops, evacuated casualties, landed paratroops and tracker dogs, dropped leaflets, and carried out valuable low-level reconnaissances, spending more than 3,500 hours in the air. On returning from Malaya the squadron transferred to the anti-submarine role, being equipped with dipping asdic, or sonobuoys, to enable them to detect submerged submarines.

Later on British-built Whirlwinds came into service with the Fleet, to be succeeded by a more powerful machine known as the 'Wessex', powered by Napier Gazelle gas turbine engines. Since helicopters require only a very small landing deck, they are well suited not only for anti-submarine work and various operations at sea, such as transferring men and stores, communications, and search and rescue, but also minesweeping. In 1951 their use in merchant ships to defend convoys at sea in war was successfully demonstrated in a series of trials carried out on board the fleet supply ship *Fort Duquesne* in the English Channel. Dubbed 'ugly ducklings' when they first appeared, helicopters were eventually to become an essential item of the modern warship's equipment.

Surface ships also received a new anti-submarine weapon in the early nineteen-fifties. During the war depth-charges had been used both by ships and aircraft to attack and destroy submarines. Metal canisters filled with high explosive, the detonation of which was controlled by a hydrostatic valve set to operate at the required depth, depth-charges were released in a pattern when the hunting vessel was directly over the plotted position of a submarine. But during this critical period when contact was temporarily lost by the asdic, the submarine could make a quick alteration of course or depth and thus escape destruction.

To overcome this disadvantage an ahead-throwing apparatus, known as the 'Hedgehog', was devised. The new weapon was a triple-barrelled mortar operated by the asdic which could lock on to a submarine no matter what evasive action it might take, and fire ahead of the hunting ship a pattern of underwater bombs of a destructive power hitherto unequalled in this type of warfare. Known as the 'Squid', this weapon was later to be superseded by an even more sophisticated device known as 'Limbo', giving a longer range and better spread.

In the field of research more efficient gear for dealing with the various types of sea mine was being developed. All possible means of submarine propulsion were under investigation, including systems using nuclear energy and oxygen-bearing fuels. New types of propulsive machinery were being developed for the projected fast frigates. Detection and location equipment which would be effective against the snorting and totally submerged submarine was being developed, more flexible and accurate in use and more deadly in action than any previously used. New types of anti-submarine aircraft with improved radar and sonobuoy were being tested. Another anti-submarine weapon being developed for use by aircraft as well as ships was a homing torpedo capable of seeking out and destroying its target whatever evasive measures were taken.

For offensive use in fleet actions, and for the protection of convoys from air attack, new and faster naval aircraft were in production which, with their parent carriers, were to be fitted with radar equipment enabling accurate interception to be made at effective ranges from the surface vessels. To deal with enemy aircraft which succeeded in evading these defences, new gunnery systems of greater range, accuracy and destructive power were being worked out, and gun and gun direction equipment to provide merchant ships with an effective defence being progressed. A guided weapon was to be added to the surface warship's anti-aircraft armoury, work on this being integrated with the whole programme of guided weapon defence of the United Kingdom.

Research in naval construction would enable ships' structures to be designed to closer margins of strength, and lighter materials were being embodied in warship construction. The resultant saving in hull weight would be used to increase fighting efficiency. Progress was being made in the development of high-performance steam, lightweight diesels and gas turbines for warship propulsion, and in parallel design for auxiliary machinery with the aim of obtaining the greatest efficiency in performance for the minimum of weight and space and maximum economy in fuel consumption.

As will be seen, all these things duly came to pass.

Following on the standardisation of equipment and operational doctrine which had earlier been agreed, Britain's naval research and development programme was co-ordinated with that of the United States. Thus some points were left to the Americans, who kept this country informed of advances made, and others were pursued by the United Kingdom, who told the Americans of progress and results. Unfortunately, however, this sharing of research did not at that time extend to the atomic field. In 1946 Congress had passed the MacMahon Act which prohibited the exchange of atomic information with foreign countries.

Thus excluded, Britain, whose scientists and research workers had played a vital part in the production of the first atomic bomb in the United States, decided to carry on with her own atomic weapon programme, and in October 1952 exploded her first atom bomb. Planning for this had begun in 1950, and the Navy took a considerable part in carrying out the test, being responsible for providing transport, housing and logistic support. These requirements included supplying a base ship—the escort ferry carrier *Campania* being used —three converted tank landing ships, and HMS *Plym,* a 1,450-ton frigate in which the weapon was to be exploded. Units of the Royal Australian Navy and the Royal Australian Air Force also worked closely with the project.

The object of the test was to investigate the effects of an atomic explosion in a harbour. The site chosen was in the Montebello Islands, a group of uninhabited islets off the north-west coast of Australia.

Everything required had to be brought to the islands, either direct from the United Kingdom or from the nearest supply base at Fremantle, 900 miles away to the southward.

Preparation took many months. Instruments were set up to record the effects of contamination, blast, heat flash, gamma ray flash and other factors of interest. When on Friday, 3rd October the bomb was exploded, thousands of tons of water together with mud and rock from the sea bottom were hurled high into the air, and a huge tidal wave was created. The effects of blast and radio-active contamination extended over a wide area. HMS *Plym* was completely vaporised except for a few red-hot fragments which were scattered over the islands.

Four years later two more atomic tests were carried out, one in the Montebello Islands and the other on a special desert range at Woomera, in South Australia. Experts considered, however, that the results of the tests, while stressing the overriding importance of nuclear weapons in any future conflict, did not wholly revolutionise methods of warfare. The new defence programme, which was announced at the end of 1953, was therefore centred around a strategy of deterrence by massive retaliation. Since, however, the first atomic strike might not be decisive, war could be expected to continue for some time in a 'broken-backed' form, and large conventional forces and trained reserves would still be needed. But greater emphasis would be placed on the striking power of nuclear weapons.

Britain's first atomic energy research station was set up at Harwell in 1945, and five years later the weapons research establishment which produced her atomic bomb. In the meantime British scientists had been studying the possibility of using atomic energy to drive ships. In 1950 they produced the design of an atomic propulsion unit for the submarine of the future. It consisted of a 'pile', or container, for the fissionable material encased in thick lead to protect the crew against radiation, from which intense heat would be emitted to convert water into steam. The steam would be generated in a boiler room immediately behind the reactor and fed to turbines to turn the propeller shafts. The unit was in fact a conventional engine, but using heat produced by atomic energy instead of oil burners. A submarine so powered could, if necessary, stay at sea almost indefinitely, with refuelling reduced to a minimum. The atom engineers were confident that they could build such an engine capable of powering a medium-sized aircraft carrier.

Unfortunately there were many difficulties in the way, the chief of which was the enormous cost since nothing less than a complete pilot plant would need to be built for test purposes. To build such a land-based prototype unit would involve the expenditure of a vast sum of money, certainly much more than the country could afford. In America, where a prototype atomic-powered submarine was in fact being built, the cost was estimated at well over £14 million. Thus, while work on plans for an atomically propelled British submarine continued, the Americans were to be the first in the field.

In 1951 the Admiralty announced that a medium-sized hospital ship was to be included in the re-armament programme which would be used in peacetime as a Royal yacht to replace the fifty-year-old *Victoria & Albert* which was no longer seaworthy. She was to be of some 4,000 tons displacement and take the place of the old hospital ship *Maine*. The latter was a 7,500-ton ex-Italian liner which had been captured during the war and converted into a hospital ship, and was now nearing the end of her useful life.

There was nothing unusual about having a dual-purpose vessel, since certain constructional features, such as spacious compartments, fin stabilisers, air-conditioning, laundry facilities and a comparatively high speed would be common to both hospital ship and Royal yacht. The King himself felt that a yacht was a necessity and not a luxury for the Head of the Commonwealth.

The first royal yacht for an English king in fact dated back more than 800 years, when a long fast galley was constructed for the use of Henry I. Under the Tudors royal yachts became more numerous, some being no more than gilded and curtained barges in which the Royal Family made periodic trips up and down the Thames. Yachting in the modern sense came in with the Stuarts when the famous shipbuilder Phineas Pett was commissioned to build the *Disdain*. Charles II added to the list of royal yachts, acquiring a total of some twenty vessels ranging from 22 to 166 tons. George I possessed fifteen yachts, and George II probably the most sumptuous, which also carried eight guns. Queen Victoria became interested in sailing in 1842, and twelve months later the first *Victoria & Albert*, a paddle steamer, was launched. The second ship of the name was launched in 1855, and the third and last in 1901.

Unhappily, King George VI, who had taken a great interest in the new royal yacht and made many suggestions with the object of reducing expenditure on her construction, was never to sail in the completed vessel. In April 1953 she was launched at the yard of her builders, John Brown of Clydebank, and named *Britannia*. Of

5,769 gross tons, she is 412 feet long with a beam of 55 feet, has a speed in excess of 20 knots, and is fitted with three masts so that when the monarch is embarked the flag of the Lord High Admiral can be flown from the fore, the Royal Standard from the main, and the Union Flag from the mizen. The royal apartments are situated aft, and accommodation for officers and crew forward. In the event of the *Britannia* being required to serve as a hospital ship, the royal apartments can speedily be converted into wards, operating theatre and ancillary departments. She was accepted into service in January 1954, since when she has cruised many thousands of miles, not only on royal tours, but participating as a warship in Fleet and NATO exercises.

A significant landmark of the nineteen-fifties was the setting up by the North Atlantic Treaty Organisation of a military command system. When the organisation came into being in 1949 a Military Committee of all member nations was formed, under which a standing group of permanent representatives from Britain, France and the United States was appointed to exercise control over five Regional Groups and deal with the area covered by the Treaty. These Regional Groups were composed as follows:

Western European : Belgium, France, Luxembourg, Netherlands, United Kingdom.
Northern Europe : Denmark, Norway, United Kingdom.
Southern European/Western Mediterranean : France, Italy, United Kingdom.
North Atlantic Ocean : Belgium, Canada, Denmark, France, Iceland, Netherlands, Norway, Portugal, United Kingdom, United States.
Canada/United States : Canada, United States.

Both Canada and the United States had observers in the three European Regional Groups.

Once preliminary planning was completed, a supreme commander, coming directly under the Standing Group, was needed to co-ordinate this work and to be vested with executive authority to train and weld together the forces of the various Powers, and direct military operations should necessity arise. By common consent, General Eisenhower, who had commanded the Allied forces in Europe after the opening of the Second Front, was nominated for the post. In April 1951 he set up his headquarters, henceforth to be known by the initials SHAPE (Supreme Headquarters Allied Powers Europe) at Fontainebleau, subsequently transferred to Casteau, in Belgium in 1966 after the French withdrawal from NATO.

The Supreme Allied Command, Europe (SACEUR) then set up three major sub-commands: Northern Command at Oslo under a British admiral, since important features of the defence of this area would be seapower and seaborne air power; Central Command, comprising the land mass of western Europe, at Fontainebleau; and Southern Command, at Naples under the American admiral commanding the US naval forces in the Mediterranean and eastern Atlantic. The Southern European Naval Command (NAVSOUTH) included forces from the French, Italian and US navies, but for strategic and political reasons not the British Mediterranean Fleet.

A single unified command for the whole North Atlantic Ocean was regarded as essential by the chiefs of staff of the various Treaty Powers in order to gain the advantages of speed and flexibility which could not be secured by retaining separate commands. Not only is the Atlantic of vital importance to Britain, but it is also the lifeline of Allied forces operating in Europe. Accordingly the NATO post of Supreme Allied Commander Atlantic (SACLANT) was set up to take control of the naval forces which each country would make available in the event of war. Understandably, because of the far greater overall resources of the United States Navy, this appointment went to an American admiral. A British flag officer was appointed as Deputy Supreme Commander.

SACLANT's command covers broadly the North Atlantic Ocean, from the North Pole to the Tropic of Cancer, but excluding the English Channel and British and European coastal waters. Subsequently it was divided into two areas: Western and Eastern Atlantic, the western area being an American command and the eastern one British. In addition a third major command, that of Allied Commander-in-Chief, Channel, was created, the post going to the Commander-in-Chief, Portsmouth, whose title was later altered to Commander-in-Chief, Home Station. The post of Allied Commander-in-Chief, Eastern Atlantic, went to the Commander-in-Chief, Home Fleet, in association with Coastal Command, RAF.

Subsequently further subordinate naval commanders were instituted by SACLANT. Thus the Commander-in-Chief, Plymouth, became additionally Commander of the NATO Central Sub-Area; and the Flag Officer, Scotland, NATO Commander, Northern Sub-Area. The extent of the commands of these flag officers lying within the United Kingdom Home Station command were named as the

'Western Approaches' and the 'Northern Approaches' respectively. Within this command structure a grand defensive strategy for the Atlantic Ocean and the sea flanks of Europe was evolved, and by means of joint exercises and the integration of staffs, the navies of the Treaty Powers were eventually welded into an efficient fighting machine.

When in February 1952 the admission of Greece and Turkey to NATO became effective, it was found necessary to create a fourth high command, to be known as Allied Forces, Mediterranean. The post was given to the Commander-in-Chief of the British Mediterranean Fleet, who set up the command (AFMED) in Malta in March 1953. It came directly under SHAPE and was to include in wartime naval and air forces of Britain, France, Italy, Greece, Turkey and the United States, with the exception of the US Sixth Fleet and forces needed to protect coastal waters. AFMED was divided into sub-area commands as follows: Gibraltar and the South-east Mediterranean— British; Eastern Mediterranean—Greek; and the Dardanelles, Marmora and Black Sea—Turkish. Thus in time of war AFMED and its subordinate commands would be responsible for the security of sea communications throughout the Mediterranean.

Various command changes were made as time went on.

In the following year another collective security agreement on NATO lines was established in order to strengthen the fabric of peace in south-east Asia and the south-west Pacific. Known as the South-East Asia Treaty Organisation (SEATO), the signatories were Britain, America, France, Pakistan, Australia, New Zealand, the Philippines and Thailand, with the political and military headquarters of the Treaty Powers at Bangkok. Ground forces in time of war would be provided by the Philippines, Thailand and Pakistan, with reserves coming from Australia and New Zealand, and the air defence of the area based on Singapore, Luzon in the Philippines, and Bangkok itself. The bulk of the Organisation's naval forces would be provided by the US Seventh Fleet and units of the British Far East Fleet.

Twelve months later a further development in the strengthening of collective security was the creation of the Central Treaty Organisation (CENTO). Originally a defensive and economic pact signed between Turkey and Iraq in Baghdad, Britain, Pakistan and Persia subsequently became members, while the United States agreed to participate as observer. Later Iraq withdrew, but the Organisation remained as the centre of relative stability in the Middle East and a deterrent to any expansionist drive by the Soviet Union. From the naval point of view attention was mainly directed to the Persian Gulf as the centre of Middle East oil production. The Treaty resulted in joint planning and occasional combined exercises by ships of the member countries, with Britain continuing to maintain a small squadron of warships in the Persian Gulf as part of the East Indies Station.

In 1951 a considerable change was made in the distinctive officer ranks of the Royal Naval Reserve Patrol Service. This section of the RNR first came into being in 1910 following a suggestion by Admiral Lord Charles Beresford that fishermen and their vessels could play a useful part in the Fleet in time of war in minesweeping. Fishing trawlers had been used experimentally as minesweepers with success in 1907, and from 1910 onwards the Admiralty began to earmark a certain number of trawlers from the fishing fleets for requisitioning in wartime.

When the RNR Trawler Section was created, the rank of Skipper, RNR, was instituted for its officers as being the most appropriate. Equivalent to the then Warrant Officer in the Royal Navy, entry was open to fishing skippers between the ages of 25 and 45 who were in possession of a certificate of competency as such and had held command of a trawler for not less than two years. They could serve in the RNR for periods of five years at a time up to a maximum of twenty years. The top rung of promotion for them would be the rank of Skipper Lieutenant. By the time the Armistice was signed in 1918, the RNR Trawler Section, originally a force of some 1,200 officers and men, had expanded to 39,000, manning more than 700 vessels at home and abroad. The bulk of these ships were deep sea trawlers representative of every fishing port in the United Kingdom.

In 1919 the RNR Trawler Section was reconstituted as the RNR Patrol Service, with a peacetime strength of 4,000 officers and men. By the end of the Second World War the Service had grown to some 70,000 officers and men, manning 7,000 minesweeping and anti-submarine trawlers, drifters and other minor war vessels.

Now the rank of Skipper was to disappear from the Navy List. Officers possessing the necessary qualifications would in future be entered as probationary sub-lieutenants and have the same promotion prospects to lieutenant and lieutenant-commander as their General Service brethren of the Merchant Navy. Their special small ship experience would be retained and they would not be appointed to vessels larger than trawlers in tme of war. Thus their rank and status was brought into line with their responsibilities in the fishing fleet, since modern long-distance trawlers had become big ships equipped with the latest navigational appliances, and their captains fully qualified navigators with training and experience in radar and radio. Officers on the active list of the Patrol Service were given the option of transferring to the new ranks, retaining their old ones, or retiring immediately.

Recruiting for both the General and Patrol Service sections of the RNR had been re-started in February 1950, with the aim of reaching a total peacetime strength of 3,400 officers and men in the former, and 2,600 officers and men in the latter. Skipper class officers who had held temporary commissions during the war could be considered for transfer to the permanent RNR in the new ranks. In March 1957, however, the General Service ratings' section of the RNR was disbanded, the Admiralty having decided that since most Merchant Navy seaman would not be immediately available on mobilisation, they could best serve the county by remaining in their merchant ships.

In consequence of the disbandment, the Admiralty approved that the qualification of Reserve officers to fly the Blue Ensign in merchant ships would in future be that the Master and one other officer only, irrespective of rank or branch, must be members of the Naval Reserve. A Commodore on the active or retired lists of the Reserve could, however, fly the Blue Ensign in his own right. In 1965 the regulations were again amended to allow Commodores and captains on the active or retired lists of the RNR or of Commonwealth Naval Reserves, and captains on the retired or emergency lists of the Royal Navy or Commonwealth navies, to fly the Blue Ensign in their own right without the requirement of an additional officer.

This ensign had been reserved for the RNR from 1864 when coloured squadons in the Navy were discontinued. Directions were then issued that the White Ensign should be used by the Royal Navy, the Blue Ensign by the Naval Reserve, and the Red Ensign as the national ensign by all other ships. Since 1956 the qualification for flying the Blue Ensign had been that the Master of a merchant ship and a percentage of both officers and crew should be Reservists.

In 1954 a new Air Branch of the RNR was formed, intended for professional pilots employed by civilian firms engaged on contract work for the Admiralty. Conditions of service were similar to those of the RNR, and for their periodical training they would be appointed to ships and establishments where they would have the opportunity of keeping abreast of developments in the Royal Navy.

Four years later there came a drastic reorganisation of the whole of Britain's Naval Reserves. On the 1st November 1958 the RNR and RNVR were amalgamated to form a new Royal Naval Reserve. The reasons for this unification were that the changed concept of modern warfare required reservists to be ready to join the Fleet without any further training, and—as always—the need for economy. In time of war the new Reserve would bring the ships of the active Fleet up to wartime complement, and commission ships from the Reserve Fleet. The change did not, however, affect the RMFVR or the Royal Naval Volunteer Supplementary Reserve, the latter of which was finally disbanded in 1965, by which time its numbers had declined from 7,000 to fewer than a third of that number.

The growing importance of another supporting arm of the Navy— the Royal Fleet Auxiliary Service—was recognised by the institution in October 1951 of the rank of Commodore for its senior Master, with the right to fly a broad pendant with the design of an anchor within a gold rope circle on a navy blue ground. The first officer to hold the new rank was Captain S. G. Kent, OBE, of the 8,500-ton store issuing ship *Fort Dunvegan* who had commanded RFA vessels for twenty-seven years. When he hoisted his new pendant in the presence of the Commander-in-Chief, Home Fleet, this historic occasion was suitably marked by the firing of a salvo of guns by the Fleet flagship.

Responsible for supplying the Navy's warships with fuel, stores, ammunition and food, the Royal Fleet Auxiliary was officially constituted by Royal Charter in 1911. But its origins date back many hundreds of years to the days when vessels laden with stores, known as *pinks*, accompanied the ships of Drake and Frobisher on their voyages. Supplies of beer and bullocks were carried from Plymouth to British warships off Brest during Admiral Hawke's blockade of the French in 1759. During Nelson's Mediterranean campaign, stores were brought to his ships by sea from Gibraltar.

When steam replaced sail the RFA Service was formed. At first it was mainly a coal-bunkering and store-carrying service, but as oil-burning warships replaced coal-burning vessels it was adapted to cater for this new requirement by the construction of a tanker fleet. From that time it grew rapidly, and in the Second World War its ships served in every naval theatre of operations, from the Arctic to the Pacific where warships fought and operated at considerable distances from shore bases. From a small group of only eight ships at the outbreak of the First World War, the RFA Service grew to be one of the largest British Merchant Navy fleets, flying its own distinctive flag—a Blue Ensign with vertical yellow anchor in the fly. In 1960 the Service received another mark of distinction when the rank of Commodore Chief Engineer was instituted.

In August 1952, 3 Royal Marine Commando Brigade, having completed two years' operational service in Malaya, was moved to the Mediterranean. It had been intended that two of the Commandos should be based on Malta to act as Middle East Strategic Reserve, and the third in the United Kingdom. 41 Commando, which had covered itself with glory in Korea during the grim winter retirement from Chosin to Hungnam, was disbanded. The Commando had won many individual decorations, but perhaps the most prized was the US Presidential Citation presented to them in March 1957 in the form of a battle streamer for attachment to their colours.

But the stay of the Marines in Malta was brief, for disturbing events were shaping in Egypt. When in 1953 a military *coup* finally overthrew the monarchy in that country and the safety of the Suez Canal was again threatened, the Brigade was moved to the Canal Zone and deployed along its length to keep the peace until fresh agreements could be negotiated with a stable government. In 1954 after a new treaty had been signed, the Brigade returned to Malta and 42 Commando was withdrawn to the United Kingdom.

One curious and interesting duty which was performed by two members of the Commando was annexation of the tiny island of Rockall, which lies 290 miles west-north-west of Barra Head, in the Hebrides, since it came within the orbit of a projected British guided weapons testing range.

In September 1955 Commander Richard Connell, captain of the surveying ship *Vidal*, received sealed orders direct from the Queen, which stated that:

When our ship *Vidal* is in all respects ready for sea and all necessary personnel is embarked, you are to leave Londonderry on the 14th day of September or at the earliest date thereafter. Thence you will proceed to the island of Rockall. On arrival you will effect a landing and hoist the Union Flag on whatever spot appears most suitable or practicable. You will then take possession of the island on our behalf. You will keep a record of your proceedings. With the landing effected and the flag hoisted you will cement a commemorative plaque on the rock.

HMS *Vidal* was the Navy's latest survey ship, named after a famous English surveyor of the nineteenth century who charted the coasts of West Africa and the eastern Atlantic. A prefabricated and all-welded vessel of 2,000 tons, she was the first of a new post-war type specially designed for hydrographic surveying and chart production. In addition to the latest electronic aids to surveying and a lithographic printing press, she was fitted with a hangar and a helicopter deck. Among the 'necessary personnel' for the special task which lay ahead, she carried two non-commissioned officers of 42 Commando.

On 18th September the two Marines, followed by the *Vidal*'s first Lieutenant and an ornithologist, were lowered by helicopter on to a tiny ledge at the summit of the 70-foot high granite rock. There they erected a metal flagstaff and cemented in position a brass plaque bearing the following inscription :

By authority of Her Majesty Queen Elizabeth the Second, by the Grace of God of the United Kingdom and Northern Ireland and of her other Realms and Territories Queen, Head of the Commonwealth, Defender of the Faith, &c., &c., and in accordance with Her Majesty's instructions dated the fourteenth day of September, One thousand, Nine hundred and Fifty-five, a landing was effected this day upon the island of Rockall from HMS *Vidal*. The Union Flag was hoisted and possession of the island was taken in the name of Her Majesty.

During the ceremony HMS *Vidal* steamed slowly past, firing a salute of twenty-one guns. Thus a lonely, storm-bound rock which formerly belonged to no one and whose only claim to fame had been the fact that its name identified a meteorological area in BBC weather forecasts became officially part of the British Commonwealth.

One of the less publicised of the Navy's peacetime duties was renewed when the Fishery Protection Squadron, which keeps a guardian eye on Britain's fishing fleets, was reconstituted. The origins of this naval commitment date back as far as 1586 when English fishermen paid the Admiralty of the day £100 for a 'wafting ship' to patrol the herring grounds of the North Sea.

In the seventeenth century the Royal Navy extended its fishing protection activities to Iceland and Norwegian waters, and George III allocated the first warship, on payment of £100, to look after the special interests of Scottish fishermen. Pepys received an annual payment for his efforts in this direction, and Nelson once served in the Fishery Protection Squadron when he captained HMS *Albemarle* in 1781. Ships of the squadron were also used in the repression of smuggling, and under an Act of 1893 the duty of keeping a lookout for smugglers was officially incorporated in their orders. Since 1882 all fishery protection vessels of the North Sea Convention nations, which included Norway, Russia, France, Belgium, Iceland, Denmark and Holland, have distinguished themselves from other ships by flying a special blue and yellow quartered triangular flag.

In 1905 the Royal Navy's squadron was formed into three divisions, Arctic, North Sea and Irish Sea; Scottish coastal waters, and Channel. In 1919 the squadron was designated the 'Fishery Protection and Minesweeping Flotilla', and consisted of eight trawlers for fishery protection duties and eight minesweepers. Of the trawlers, two were based at Grimsby, two at Lowestoft, two in the Channel, and two on Milford Haven. This organisation continued until the outbreak of war in 1939. After the war the squadron was re-instated under the title of the 'Fishery Protection Flotilla', and included one frigate, five minesweepers and two motor fishing vessels.

In 1951 the flotilla was again re-constituted to consist of six mine-sweepers and two motor fishing vessels, while to emphasise the increased importance of the ships' minesweeping duties, the title was altered to the 'Fifth Fishery Protection and Minesweeping Squadron'. Commanded by a captain with administrative headquarters ashore in Hull, the vessels were allocated to areas around the British Isles, two in the west, two in the east, and one in Scottish waters. Today the squadron consists of four minesweepers, four minehunters and a fast patrol boat, based on HMS *Lochinvar* at Port Edgar, in Scotland, and is commanded by an officer who is also Captain, Mine Countermeasures.

Fishery duties do not limit ships to home waters, their cruise programmes being arranged to ensure that British interests are protected wherever they may be. This involves cruises throughout the winter to Arctic waters north of Norway and Russia, Iceland and the Faroes and Greenland. They put in more sea time than any other group of ships in the Royal Navy. In home waters their duties are to keep foreign poachers out of British waters, enforce local fishing byelaws on request, and watch out for offences, non-compliance with regulations, improper marking or lighting and contravention of Customs regulations.

At sea abroad the Fishery Protection vessels warn British trawlers found poaching, and are ready to protect them from wrongful arrest. Apart from these duties, directly or indirectly connected with fishing, they render various services to the trawler fleets, carry out salinity runs for the Ministry of Agriculture, Fisheries and Food, trials in Arctic conditions on items of naval equipment, cold weather clothing and survival at sea.

Officers and ratings of the Fishery Protection Squadron are drawn from the ordinary general service personnel of the Royal Navy, and every effort is made by them to become acquainted with the many and complex problems of the fishing industry. Thus, relations of the squadron with the industry, both in harbour and at sea, remain extremely cordial.

Many years ago Professor Gilbert Murray, echoing an even older sentiment, wrote that:

> If there is slave trading in Africa, if there is piracy in the Yellow Sea, if there is plague in China, if the pilgrim routes to Mecca are endangered, if the buoys in the Persian Gulf are badly placed, at once Great Britain is expected to attend to the matter, and Great Britain always accepts the responsibility.

High on the list of these responsibilities comes the humanitarian work of rescue and relief, in which the Royal Navy has an unrivalled record. Thus when on Sunday, 9th August 1953 a series of colossal earthquake shocks devastated the Ionian Islands of Cephalonia, Ithaca, Zante and Santa Maura, off the west coast of Greece, ships of the Royal Navy were among the first to bring aid and succour to the dazed survivors.

Scarcely had the reverberations of this disaster died away than on 11th September another earthquake hit the south-east extremity of the island of Cyprus. The port of Paphos was partially destroyed, and whole villages in the mountainous forest country inland were wrecked. At once the light fleet carrier *Theseus* and the destroyer *Saintes* were diverted to the island, followed by two tank landing ships carrying stores and supplies.

In October of the following year Hurricane 'Hazel' scythed a destructive path across the Caribbean. The survey ship *Vidal* was anchored at Georgetown, in the Grand Cayman, where she had been re-surveying the area. When she returned to Jamaica after the hurricane had passed, news was received of disaster and loss of life wrought by the storm in western Haiti, and that assistance was

urgently needed. At once the *Vidal* embarked supplies of food, clothing, medical stores and a detachment of troops to help in the rescue
work and sailed for Haiti. Off-loading the bulk of the stores, and
leaving behind a small party of helpers, the *Vidal* cruised along the
coast, landing tents and food for the homeless and hungry and giving
medical aid to the injured in the stricken areas.

Not all the Navy's humanitarian labours take place overseas. In
the darkness of the night of Saturday, 31st January 1953 the worst
floods in living memory, caused by freak tides in the North Sea,
swept inland from Lincolnshire to Kent, causing damage estimated
at some £50 million and resulting in the deaths of more than 300
people. At Sheerness a deluge of water surging over high sea walls
raced feet deep through the naval dockyard, hurling a frigate in dry
dock on to her beam ends and swamping a submarine under repair.

Within a few hours the Navy, alerted as to the magnitude of the
disaster, was assisting in rescue work. Helicopters made aerial surveys to ascertain the full extent of the damage; boys from HMS
Ganges, the training establishment at Shotley, manned dinghies and
rescued women and children from flooded houses in Harwich, and
evacuated officers and men from the Royal Air Force base at Felix-
stowe which was cut off by the floods; Service divers assisted in
carrying out essential repairs to sewage systems, and Royal Marine
DUKWs were used to maintain important communications.

Then followed a week of non-stop, back-breaking work from dawn
to dusk for officers and men drawn from ships and shore establishments in a race against time to plug gaps in the sea defences along
the east coast before the next high tides. Naval lighters, harbour craft
and motor launches were used to move tons of food, transport emergency clothing, water bowsers and sandbags. When the immediate task
of saving human life was completed, the Navy turned its efforts
towards rescuing sheep, cattle and other livestock.

Meanwhile on the second day of the floods naval helicopters flew
across to Holland to assist the people of the Netherlands whose
country had also been badly hit by the floods, and rescued 750
marooned survivors. During the next high tide danger period nearly
1,000 sailors and Marines remained on stand-by alert day and night
ready to leave for any area where flooding might occur. Fortunately
their services were not required, for the work of the men who had
toiled on the sea walls successfully stood the test of the spring tides.

The naval highlight of 1953 was undoubtedly the Coronation

Naval Review which was held at Spithead on 15th June. On the occasion of the Coronation itself, which took place on 2nd June, a naval brigade nearly 4,000 strong had participated in the procession and helped to line the streets of the capital. Commanded by a flag officer, the naval contingent included units from all branches of the Navy, Royal Marines, WRNS, Queen Alexandra's Royal Naval Nursing Service, the Reserves, and representatives from the Dominion and Colonial navies. A naval guard of honour was mounted at Buckingham Palace, and a Royal Marine guard of honour at Westminster Abbey.

The last Spithead review had been held in May 1937 to celebrate the Coronation of King George VI. Although coronation naval reviews have taken place only since 1902, inspections of the Fleet by the Sovereign have been held at Spithead since the reign of Henry VIII. Sometimes these were specially mobilised squadrons of warships about to set out upon hostile operations, such as the British fleet assembled at Spithead in 1672 which was inspected by Charles II prior to sailing to fight the Dutch. It was in fact the orders issued for this occasion which laid the foundation upon which subsequent review ceremonial has been built up. Thus the ships were ordered to be made 'neat and predie' (pretty). Their decks, tops, masts and shrouds were to be 'thoroughly manned and as it were hung with men'. Upon the approach of the Royal barge the 'noise of trumpets' was to sound until His Majesty was within musket shot of the flagship, when the fanfare ceased, and 'all such as carry whistles are to whistle several times, and in every interim the ship's whole company are to hale him with a joynt shout after the custom of the sea . . .'

The first Royal review as we know it was held at Spithead by George III on 22nd June 1773. Present were twenty sail of the line, two frigates and thirty sloops, and the King cruised along the lines of warships in his yacht *Augusta*. That evening His Majesty dined on board the flagship *Barfleur*, after which he knighted two of the admirals and three post-captains. But his largesse did not stop there; the two senior admirals were promoted a step further in rank, all the sloop commanders were made post-captains, and other junior officers were promoted. When the King disembarked, he distributed £1,500 among the dockyard workmen, £350 among the crews of the flagship and royal yacht, and gave a further £250 to the poor of Portsea.

In later years there followed a succession of naval spectacles at Spithead, each marking the changing pattern of war at sea. In 1814 the fall of Napoleon and the signing of the Peace of Paris was celebrated by a review at Spithead to show the Tsar of Russia and the King of Prussia, our late allies, 'the tremendous naval armaments which had swept from the oceans the fleets of France and Spain and secured to Britain the domain of the sea'. In command of the assembled warships was Admiral of the Fleet HRH the Duke of Clarence, later to become King William IV. Amid great crowds of sightseers, the visitors, who included Wellington and Blucher, were embarked in royal barges and rowed out to Spithead, where they boarded the ninety-eight-gun flagship *Impregnable*. There the Tsar Alexander, always prone to the jovial and unconventional, sat down in a marines' mess and ate dinner with them.

During her long reign Queen Victoria held a number of reviews of the Fleet at Spithead, the earliest being in 1842. While she was being conducted round the mess decks of HMS *St. Vincent* she suddenly expressed a wish to taste the men's grog there and then. A basin of the brew was hurriedly procured and proffered to her by the captain on bended knee. The Queen took several sips and pronounced it good, which so delighted the sailors that they broke into spontaneous cheering and drank her health. Amid the uproar Her Majesty exclaimed with emotion, 'I feel today that I am indeed Old Ocean's youthful Queen and that I am indeed surrounded by those who will uphold that title in the battle and the breeze.'

Accompanied by Prince Albert, the Queen held her next review in 1845, and watched the Fleet setting all sail and then shortening in as if in expectation of a gale. Thus far there appeared to have been little change in the ships themselves, but two steam vessels were present. They were the *Rattler*, which in a subsequent tug of war staged with a paddle steamer decisively demonstrated the superiority of the screw propeller over paddles, and the Queen's new yacht *Victoria & Albert*, itself a paddle vessel. By the end of the century when Her Majesty passed for the last time between the lines of her warships, sail had vanished, and it was from armoured battleships that her final salute was fired.

In 1914 King George V, himself a sailor whose professional naval career had been cut short when the sudden death of his elder brother brought him in direct line for the throne, inspected from the bridge of the *Victoria & Albert* at Spithead the mightiest fleet the world had ever seen. Drawn up in seemingly endless lines lay 55 battleships, 14 battle cruisers, 65 cruisers, nearly 300 destroyers and torpedo-boats, 59 submarines, seven minelayers and a score of fleet auxiliaries—

493 ships in all. When they sailed from that historic anchorage it was to take up their war stations.

On 20th May 1937, a very different fleet assembled at Spithead for review by the new Sovereign, King George VI. This time it totalled a mere 140 ships, including representative vessels from Dominion navies. Among them were 10 battleships, 2 battle cruisers, 5 aircraft carriers, 14 cruisers, 55 destroyers and 20 submarines. Foreign warships present included one battleship each from the United States, France and Russia, while Nazi Germany sent her new 'pocket' battleship the *Graf Spee*, fated to be ignominiously scuttled in a second world war only two years away. A significant feature of this particular naval gathering was that it was the first time that aircraft of the Fleet Air Arm figured in a Coronation review. No less than eight different types of naval aircraft took part in a flypast, all of them biplanes, ranging from the Hawker Nimrod fleet fighter to the Fairey Swordfish torpedo-bomber. As the ubiquitous 'Stringbag', the latter was to earn undying fame in the Second World War.

Now once again a fleet assembled at Spithead for review by its Queen, and again it was with a difference. Despite the nation's economic difficulties and naval commitments unprecedented in peacetime, it was larger in number if not in size of ships present sixteen years earlier. Representing only about one-third of the combined strengths of the Royal and Commonwealth navies when fully mobilised for war, some 200 ships were present. In comparing them with earlier reviews the change of emphasis which modern conditions had brought about was clearly demonstrated. Instead of the twelve battleships and battle cruisers present at Spithead in 1937, only one was now in commission—the *Vanguard*. The aircraft carrier had become the capital ship of the Fleet. Consequently instead of the five out-dated vessels present in 1937, there were no less than nine, including the *Eagle*, largest and most modern.

As further evidence that the Navy had become a truly three-dimensional fighting force, more than 300 naval aircraft, including jet fighters and a squadron of helicopters, took part in the flypast. Appropriately enough, they were led by an admiral, who was himself a pilot, the Flag Officer, Flying Training.

There were fewer cruisers and destroyers—only thirty-two of both classes—but many more frigates, minesweepers and other smaller vessels, indicative of the attention being directed towards anti-submarine and anti-mine warfare. In 1937 the Navy's manpower strength totalled 112,000 officers and men; in 1953 the total was 150,000. The current Naval Estimates, pruned to meet minimum requirements, were still more than three times larger than those of 1937. Among ships of the Merchant Navy and fishing fleets represented were four yachts, one from each of the Home Commands, owned and manned by members of the recently created Minewatching Service, flying their own special burgee.

As in past reviews foreign warships were also present, among them cruisers from the United States, France, Spain, Holland, Sweden and Brazil. Creating the greatest interest among observers from the NATO countries was the new 12,800-ton Russian cruiser *Sverdlov*. Few remembered that this was the name of the man who had ordered the execution of Tsar Nicholas II in July 1918.

At 3 p.m. in the afternoon of 15th June the frigate *Surprise*, doing duty as Royal Yacht, and having embarked the Queen, Prince Philip and other members of the Royal Family, sailed from Portsmouth harbour to steam round the eight miles of assembled warships. As in the days of Charles II they had been made 'neat and predie', every vessel dressed overall with flags and her sides manned. As the Royal Yacht steamed past each ship her company cheered and waved their caps, while bands played the National Anthem. Earlier Her Majesty had received on board the *Surprise* all the flag and senior officers of the Fleet, British and foreign, captains of the merchantmen and skippers of the fishing vessels.

In the evening of that day, after having given a dinner on board the *Vanguard* for the senior officers, the Queen went up to the bridge of the battleship and pressed a golden Morse key, thus sending out a short signal which simultaneously illuminated the entire Fleet. Then, as if again at the touch of a master switch, the lights went out. In the darkness a rocket, also fired by the Queen, soared up from the *Vanguard*, and at once a dazzling firework display began, after which the ships were again illuminated.

Thus the review came to an end. More than a spectacular incident in the pageantry of the Coronation celebrations, it enabled the Fleet to do homage to its Queen, and demonstrate to the country and the world that Great Britain still possessed a Navy so prepared for modern conditions that it continued to be a safe shield to the Queen and her Realm.

CHAPTER FIVE

Dawn of the Thermo-Nuclear Era

In the bad old days of the Press Gangs, British sailors had been required to serve in the ships to which they were shanghai'd for years on end, usually being finally paid off only at the end of the emergency which had brought the vessels into commission.

Following the introduction of pensionable continuous service in 1853, the period of a warship's commission, wherever she was employed, became fixed at a normal length of two and a half years—although this could be exceeded if any exigency warranted it. Now at last with the war in Korea at an end the fact that such lengthy absences from home caused hardship to officers and men and their families—and, incidentally, was adversely affecting recruiting—was able to be given long overdue recognition.

Thus in order to shorten the periods of unavoidable separation from home or family, and to increase operational efficiency by keeping ships' companies together for the whole tour of service, a new scheme of 'General Service commissions' was announced by the Admiralty in 1954. Under this scheme ships would in future serve commissions of only eighteen months at a stretch, not more than twelve of which would be spent abroad.

At the same time all other forms of foreign service were reduced, so that single personnel and married men who could not be accompanied by their families would not normally be away from the United Kingdom longer than eighteen months. Married officers and men serving overseas in shore billets and various ships, such as local defence craft which were permanently based abroad, and who took their families with them might, however, be required to serve for as long as thirty months, but they would qualify for free family passages and other financial benefits.

Service in the Royal Navy would in future fall into four categories: General Service afloat, partly at home and partly overseas; Foreign Service—all overseas either ashore or afloat; Home Sea Service—afloat in home waters; and Port Service—ashore at home or in ships operating from one port, or in the Reserve Fleet. Periods of overseas service on whatever type of commission would always be separated by a period of home service, and billets on Home Sea or Port Service equitably shared.*

This new system of shorter commissions was followed by the creation in 1957 of a centralised drafting organisation, with the object of improving the methods of manning ships and establishments, and to ensure fairer shares of duty afloat and ashore. Up until then general service ratings on entry into the Navy had been permanently allocated to one of the three manning ports—Chatham, Portsmouth or Devonport, dependent upon Service requirements and largely irrespective of the actual location of a man's home. It was at his Port Division that a man's Service record was maintained, and where he served when not at sea or under training. Furthermore, he could normally only be drafted to ships and shore bases which were manned from his own port by the latter's own local drafting organisation.

This system had its advantages, since the ships in which a rating served were manned by men from his own port only, many of which were based on the latter when serving in home waters, and these factors helped him to decide where to set up his home. It also encouraged a spirit of healthy rivalry in exercises and evolutions, fleet regattas and other sporting events. But there were considerable disadvantages which had been highlighted by the war when it was impossible to maintain the Port Division system, and it became essential to man ships from all three depots. It was obviously unsound to have in peacetime a system which cannot be maintained in war.

Under the new centralised drafting organisation a man would now be able to select a depot for family welfare and holding purposes, and by a system of 'preference drafting' record his individual choice of the area in which he wished to serve when his turn came for Home Service. Otherwise he would be eligible to serve wherever men of his rating were needed. Promotion would also be effected from centralised advancement rosters, thus ensuring that promotion prospects would be the same for all men in the same category throughout the Service.

The system of cadet entry at Dartmouth also underwent a fresh

---

* In 1970 a system of 'continuous commissions' was introduced, under which warships remain in commission from the date of acceptance or after a long refit until their next long refit or eventual disposal. Men do not serve in a ship for longer than thirty months; ships are not deployed abroad for more than half that period; and the maximum length of any single deployment is nine months instead of twelve.

overhaul, the result of the changes now introduced being that for the first time in centuries midshipmen were to disappear from the sea-going Fleet.

Despite the considerably relaxed conditions of entry which had been introduced in 1948, an insufficient number of boys of the right quality were applying for cadetships. In 1953, therefore, the Admiralty set up a committee to examine the situation and consider alternative entry schemes. As a result of the committee's findings it was announced that, starting from May 1955 future cadet entry would be open to young men between the ages of 17 years and 8 months and 19 years.

At the same time the scope of the educational qualification was considerably broadened, so that candidates could either qualify through the Civil Service Commission's examination, or gain exemption by obtaining certain passes in the General Certificate of Education at Ordinary level and two passes at the Advanced level. Subsequently, a scholarship scheme was introduced whereby a certain number of boys could be selected by interview at the age of 16 and guaranteed a place at 18, receiving in the meantime considerable financial assistance to enable them to finish their schooling.

The new cadets would undergo an all-through course of training at Dartmouth before going to sea in ships of the active Fleet as acting sub-lieutenants for a period of eighteen months, at the end of which they would be confirmed as sub-lieutenants. A training squadron, in which they were to spend two periods of their Dartmouth course working as ships' companies and practising what they had learned ashore, was formed early in the following year. It consisted of a destroyer, two fast frigates and two fleet minesweepers. Both Dartmouth College and the squadron were placed under the command of a single captain and, because the new Royal Yacht now bore the name *Britannia*, the college was re-titled the 'Britannia Royal Naval College' and given the ship name HMS *Dartmouth*.

It is convenient at this point, although slightly anticipating events, to record probably the most far-reaching of post-war personnel changes brought about in the Royal Navy which, announced in 1956, came into effect in January of the following year. This was a drastic re-shaping of the officer structure, involving a break with principles and traditions that had been followed for generations. In brief, all officers other than those belonging to the Instructor, Medical and Dental Branches were divided into three lists, to be known as the General List, Special Duties List and Supplementary List, and limiting those eligible for seagoing commands to a Post List.

This change, which resulted from the deliberations of a special committee set up in 1954, was brought about by the need for the Navy to adapt itself to the revolutionary advances in ships and aircraft coming into service. Thus the seaman officer was required to know more and more about the technical features of his weapons and other fighting aids, while the technical officer needed to play a much more direct part in fighting his ship than in the past. Under the existing system the training of officers of the Royal Navy had not been designed to produce specialists in the narrow sense of the term, but they had been entered for service in a particular branch as, for example, executive or engineer officers.

It was now decided that this division of officers into branches would limit too rigidly for the Navy's future requirements the range of appointments in which they could be employed and the training and experience they could acquire. The trend had in fact already begun by appointing selected non-executive officers to senior posts formerly regarded as appropriate for Executive officers.

The new General List would consist of all cadet-entry officers of the existing Executive, Engineering, Electrical and Supply & Secretariat branches; all ex-ratings who had obtained commissions in one of those branches through the Upper Yardman scheme, and graduate entries into the Engineering and Electrical branches. These would form the main body of naval officers. They would range in rank from cadet to Admiral of the Fleet and fill all major posts of responsibility in the Navy. Because of the impossibility of any officer becoming an expert in every field, they would belong to one of four specialisations— Seaman, Engineer, Electrical, or Supply & Secretariat—but their early common training and, subsequently, their common responsibility for a wide range of general naval duties would be designed to form them into one corporate professional whole. All would be equal in status and have the opportunity of promotion to high rank.

Resulting from this scheme, successful candidates for cadetships at Dartmouth would, from May 1957, be entered as cadets for service on the General List and not as cadets in a particular branch as formerly. On completion of the first year's training they would be allocated to a specialisation according to their choice and aptitudes and the needs of the Service. While at the College they would be given a larger measure of common training than in the past, and all junior officers on the General List would, in their early training period, qualify to take command of boats and obtain a bridge watch-keeping certificate or certificate of competence.

After completion of their specialist training, General List officers would be encouraged to widen their professional knowledge as much as possible by interchange of appointments between specialisations. Thus General List officers other than seaman specialists might be appointed from time to time for seaman duties, while the range of day-to-day duties allocated to all specialists in the general running of ships and establishments would be broadened. Promotion to the rank of captain would be pooled between specialisations; officers would be appointed to senior posts of an administrative as opposed to strictly specialist nature according to their abilities without regard to specialisation; and officers of all specialisations might expect to be considered for promotion to the higher ranks on the basis of their individual merits in comparison with those of their contemporaries.

Most Seaman specialists would be required to sub-specialise in one of the following subjects: aviation, gunnery, navigation and aircraft direction, submarines, communications, torpedo and anti-submarine warfare, physical training and welfare, and surveying. About one-third would be required for flying duties as pilots, but approximately a third of these would return to general seaman duties after seven years with the Fleet Air Arm. Engineer specialists would sub-specialise in either marine, air, or ordnance engineering; and Electrical and Supply & Secretariat specialists would need to be competent in the whole range of their specialist duties.

Seaman specialists would be divided into two groups on promotion to commander—the Post and General List. Only those appointed to the Post List would be eligible for appointments in command at sea; those remaining on the General List being eligible for command of shore establishments, and for staff and administrative duties including staff appointments afloat. Like officers of other specialisations, Seaman specialists placed on the Post List and those remaining on the General List would both be eligible for promotion to captain and to flag rank. For officers on the General List promotion to the rank of lieutenant-commander would continue to be automatic after eight years' service in the rank of lieutenant.

Because of their special professional requirements the Instructor, Medical and Dental branches would continue their separate existence. Each branch had its own entry regulations and career structure, and each would continue to supply an essential service to the Navy. The Royal Marines also remained outside the new structure, except that their career prospects would be aligned as far as possible with those of

General List officers. The Corps would remain an essential and integral part of the Naval Service.

The second list of officers in the new structure would be known as the Special Duties List, replacing the Branch List (the former Warrant Officers). Promoted from the Lower Deck between the ages of 25 and 34, these officers were selected on the basis of their professional ability and personal qualities. In their new category they would play a more important part than in the past as their numbers increased and their responsibilities were extended. To mark this development their titles of rank would be changed to sub-lieutenant, lieutenant and lieutenant-commander, with a prefix or suffix to indicate the nature of their specialist duties. Opportunities for transfer to the General List would, however, only be available under very exceptional circumstances, but the great majority would reach the rank of lieutenant on their List before retirement. It was expected that a third of those reaching the rank of lieutenant would be promoted to lieutenant-commander, and some to the rank of commander. Like officers on the General List, Special Duties List officers would receive a pension and terminal grant on retirement on completion of the necessary service.

The Supplementary List would consist of officers entered initially on short service commissions in the Fleet Air Arm, and any other officers recruited in the future on a similar basis for certain specific duties. Entry on the Supplementary List as officer pilot or observer in the Fleet Air Arm would be for an initial period of twelve years, with the opportunity of leaving the active list after eight years. Prior to the completion of ten years' service these officers would have the opportunity of volunteering for selection for a pensionable career. Those selected would normally reach the rank of lieutenant-commander, but there would be only a limited opportunity for promotion beyond that rank. Transfers from the Supplementary List to the General List could be made in exceptional circumstances. Officers leaving the active list on completion of twelve or eight years' service would receive a tax-free gratuity.

An essential object of this new officer structure was to improve the career prospects of naval officers. To this end fewer cadets would be entered, subsequent deficiencies in the junior ranks being made good by the employment of officers of the Special Duties and Supplementary Lists.

Announcing the introduction of the scheme, the Admiralty also directed that two further changes were to take effect immediately.

The first was that the wearing of coloured distinction lace by all non-executive officers, except those of the Medical and Dental branches, was to be discontinued. Secondly the use of the suffixes (E), (L) and (S) for officers of the Engineering, Electrical and Supply & Secretariat branches was to cease, although officers of the Instructor branch would continue to retain the prefix 'Instructor' before their rank.

Alterations were also made in the rules governing the award of marks of respect to senior officers of the non-Executive branches to ensure that they received marks of respect according to rank and appointment comparable to those given to Executive officers. These changes in style and uniform applied to similar officer branches in the Reserves.

The Naval Estimates for 1954–55 again showed an increase, which reflected the intensive programme of research and development in which the Navy was now engaged. The fruits of this programme were to become evident over the next few years as new ships, aircraft, weapons and equipment came into operational service.

Aircraft carriers, from which a new twin-jet interceptor fighter and other new types would be operated, were to be fitted in addition to angled decks, steam catapults and other flying aids, with high-performance radar and complementary fighter-direction systems to enable simultaneous interceptions of numbers of enemy aircraft to be made at increased distances from the Fleet. To put this new equipment into existing carriers, however, necessitated considerable reconstruction, and for financial reasons only two or three would be modified in the next few years. The first to be taken in hand was HMS *Victorious*.

As to aircraft, the Hawker Sea Hawk single-seat jet fighter which had recently come into full operational service, was soon to be joined by the De Havilland Sea Venom, a two-seat, all weather fighter. The development of a twin-jet, swept wing, carrier-borne fighter capable of supersonic speed and of carrying air-to-air guided missiles, to supersede the Sea Hawk and Sea Venom, had reached the production stage. But for some years to come the Westland Wyvern strike fighter remained the Navy's standard attack aircraft.

An increasingly important part in the anti-submarine role was planned for naval aircraft, and the first to be designed specially for this work, the Fairey Gannet, came into squadron service during 1954. The machine was a three-seater, mid-wing monoplane, powered by an Armstrong-Siddeley Double-Mamba turbo engine driving contra-rotating airscrews, and to give a speed of 310 mph, and a wide operating range. Radar-equipped, it was to become the Navy's standard AEW (Airborne Early Warning) aircraft.

The Gannet was followed by the Short Seamew, a comparatively lightweight aeroplane. Simple in design and extremely manoeuvrable, it was intended to halt the trend towards larger and more complicated and expensive aircraft, and was designed for rapid production and ease of operation from small aircraft carriers.

Of the 100 helicopters in service with the Navy, an operational force of Sikorsky S.55s equipped with dipping asdic had been formed for anti-submarine duties. Another 100 British-made helicopters were on order.

Two experimental submarines, named *Explorer* and *Excalibur*, fitted with a new system of underwater propulsion, were soon to be completed. Their main propelling machinery consisted of turbines supplied with steam and carbon dioxide produced by burning diesel oil in an atmosphere of steam and oxygen formed by the decomposition of high test peroxide. They were thus able to develop full power when completely submerged independent of atmospheric oxygen. Carrying a complement of seven officers and forty-two ratings, they were unarmed, their purpose being to provide experience in the operation of this new propulsive combination, and to serve as fast underwater targets to train surface forces in the tactics which would be required to destroy submarines with high underwater speeds. Further development of those two came to a halt with the spectacular success of the nuclear submarine.

For the purpose of trials and training and to ensure that small submarine techniques should continue to be developed, five new midget submarines were also built, bearing such appropriate names as *Sprat*, *Shrimp* and *Minnow*. These 35-ton, five-man boats, each 54 feet long and powered by diesel-electric machinery, were improved versions of the wartime X-craft which attacked the German battleship *Tirpitz* and other enemy targets.

The equipment of the latest anti-submarine vessels included the new Limbo asdic-controlled depth-charge mortar; and improved weapons for anti-submarine aircraft, able to home on to submerged targets, were coming into service. A large guided missile for fleet and convoy protection was in course of development. The Admiralty considered, however, that future air defence by carrier-borne fighters and anti-aircraft guns would continue to be essential, and that the gun as a means of medium and close-range defence of the fleet and of convoys against attack was unlikely to be superseded by guided weapons for many years.

The principal medium range anti-aircraft weapon was to be a new 3-inch gun having a rate of fire comparable with that of a heavy machine-gun. An improved Bofors gun for short range protection was also being developed, both weapons being operated by a new fire-control system far more effective than any used in the war, and as accurate by night as by day. A new control system suitable for fitting in merchant ships was also being developed.

The new radar sets which were being fitted in anti-submarine ships of the fleet were capable of detecting a submarine's snort masts and periscopes at considerable ranges. Communication systems of greater speed and consequently greater complexity were being developed to keep pace with the demands brought about by new weapons, the fallible human link being eliminated wherever possible by increased automation. The latest anti-submarine vessels were equipped with greatly improved action information arrangements, which could present to the captain in an enclosed operations room a comprehensive picture of the current situation, both above, on and below the sea. The ship could thus be fought from this position rather than from the bridge as previously, where much of the information available to the captain was at second hand.

Evidence of soaring building costs was provided by the figures given for new construction. Thus the cost of a light fleet carrier had risen to £10.5 million; a *Daring* class ship £2.75 million; a coastal minesweeper £460,000; an inshore minesweeper £230,000; a surveying ship £1.3 million; a large fast patrol boat £370,000; a small fast patrol boat £123,000; and a seaward defence boat £176,000. In an era yet to come these would easily be surpassed.

During 1954 three of the four light fleet carriers of the *Hermes* class, *Centaur*, *Albion* and *Bulwark*, came into operational service. 737 feet long with a beam of 90 feet, they displaced 20,330 tons and could boast a top speed of 28 knots. They carried a complement of approximately 1,300 officers and men, were armed with eleven multiple and single-barrelled Bofors guns controlled by close-range director systems, and could carry forty-five aircraft. They were the first large warships in the Royal Navy to be completely fitted with canvas bunks for all ratings. Improved living conditions included large dining halls, and air-conditioned mess decks equipped with tubular steel furniture.

The first of the new anti-submarine and anti-aircraft frigates whose advent was mentioned earlier were also launched during the year. They set the pattern for a type of ship in the Royal Navy which would last well into the future.

The anti-submarine vessels were of two classes, designated first- and second-rates. The first-rates, of which at first sixteen were built, were named after coastal towns in Britain, such as Whitby, Torquay and Rothesay. They measured 370 feet overall with a beam of 41 feet, and displaced 2,800 tons at full load. Primarily designed for the location and detection of the most modern submarines, they were fitted with the latest underwater detection equipment and facilities for directing anti-submarine aircraft. Their armament comprised two 4.5-inch guns in a twin mounting, a twin-barrelled 40-mm gun, and two anti-submarine mortars. In addition they carried two twin and eight single 21-inch torpedo tubes. Of all-welded construction and prefabricated to allow for rapid building, they were very manoeuvrable and able to maintain a high speed in heavy seas. Powered by geared turbines developing 30,000 hp, they had a top speed of 30 knots. Complement was 160 officers and men.

The second-rates, designated the *Blackwood* class, and bearing the names of famous captains of British naval history such as Duncan, Hardy and Keppel, were smaller vessels, displacing 1,400 tons at full load. 310 feet long with a beam of 33 feet, they were armed with three 40-mm Bofors guns and two 3-barrelled anti-submarine mortars. Powered by geared steam turbines developing 15,000 hp, their top speed was 24 knots, and they carried a complement of 111 officers and men. Twelve of these vessels, later referred to as Type 14 anti-submarine frigates, were eventually built.

Designated the *Leopard* class, or Type 41, the anti-aircraft frigates were similar in construction to their first-rate anti-submarine sisters, but only four were built, for they were eventually superseded by a new class of general purpose frigates. Intended for the protection of convoys against aircraft and as small destroyers in offensive operations, they measured 340 feet overall with a beam of 40 feet, and displaced 2,450 tons at full load. They were of all-welded construction, and powered by diesel engines giving a top speed of 25 knots. They carried a complement of 200 officers and men, and a powerful armament of four 4.5-inch guns, two 40-mm anti-aircraft guns, and an anti-submarine mortar. Gun control was similar to that fitted in the *Daring* class ships.

Particular attention was given to the provision of the best possible

HMS *Hampshire* firing Sea Slug

Loading the Seacat guided weapon

Limbo anti-submarine mortar

HMS *Dreadnought* at Gibraltar

Replenishment at sea. Ships from top to bottom: RFA *Retainer*, HMS *Galatea*, RFA *Reliant*, the Commando carrier HMS *Hermes*, RFA *Tideflow* and the frigate HMS *Minerva*

Buccaneer aircraft over Aden

Guided missile destroyer replenishing from the RFA *Olwen*

The *Leander* class frigate *Andromeda*

The Polaris submarine *Resolution*

Helicopter support ship *Engadine*

K 08

accommodation arrangements in these vessels. Improvements included special schemes of furnishing and the provision of plastic table tops, interior sprung settees, patterned linoleum and other minor items. The galleys were fitted with electrically controlled oil-fired ranges, a laundry, and stainless steel washbasins with hot and cold water supply fitted in the bathrooms. The living accommodation was illuminated throughout by fluorescent lighting.

Meanwhile important developments were taking place elsewhere in the atomic field. On 21st January 1954 the world's first nuclear-powered submarine was launched. She was the USS *Nautilus*, built by the Electric Boat Division of the General Dynamics Corporation of America at Groton, Connecticut. 340 feet long, and with a submerged displacement of 3,500 tons and an underwater speed in excess of 20 knots, her cost was estimated at £18 million. Fitted with an atomic boiler using Uranium 235 to create steam to drive a turbine, her power plant was almost exactly similar to the drawing-board design produced earlier by British atomic scientists.

Ten months after her launching the *Nautilus* commissioned for service, and by January 1956 she had set up some impressive records. These included the completion of seventy-five cruises, during which the vessel voyaged over 25,000 miles, travelling submerged for more than half that distance; averaged a dive a day, sometimes to more than 300 feet; sailed for more than eight days continuously, and travelled under water for three days, seventeen hours.

Early in 1957 the uranium core of her reactor was removed and replaced by a new core of enriched uranium, by which time the *Nautilus* had covered more than 60,000 miles. Submerged, she had voyaged 34,500 miles at sustained speeds impossible of attainment by conventional submarines, and had made 859 dives. In the summer of 1958 she made history by carrying out a transpolar voyage from the Pacific Ocean to the Atlantic, travelling beneath the North Polar icecap. A true submersible, the *Nautilus* was the harbinger of the capital warship of the future.

In March 1954 while the *Nautilus* was still being fitted out at her building yard, the Americans exploded their first hydrogen, or 'megaton', bomb in the Marshall Islands, in the Pacific. Known as the 'H-bomb', the new weapon was a device designed to utilise a thermo-nuclear reaction. When it was triggered off the resultant explosion, the size of which staggered even the experts, was estimated as being equivalent to fourteen million tons of TNT—more than the total for all the bombs dropped by the belligerents during the Second

World War. It also produced much more radio-active fallout than an ordinary atomic bomb. In fact some Japanese fishing boats and their crews eighty miles away from the test area were affected by radiation and their catches destroyed; one of the fishermen eventually died.

Six months later the Russians exploded their first H-bomb. By 1957, when Britain carried out her first hydrogen test, the nuclear arms race was in full swing, with consequent effect upon weapons of war ashore and afloat.

Thus in the White Paper which accompanied the statement of the Naval Estimates for the following year, the Admiralty laid stress on the growing development of weapons of mass destruction. The coming of the hydrogen bomb had added a new and horrifying significance to the nuclear age. But while this and other similar inventions might affect maritime warfare and alter the character of the forces needed to wage it, they did not diminish the need for navies. For an island nation dependent upon seaborne supplies, the need for a navy in fact becomes all the greater.

In peacetime naval power plays a predominant part in supporting national policy overseas and in ensuring that Britain's world-wide trade continues unmolested. In wartime two outstanding qualities of sea power become more evident : mobility and relative independence of land bases. In local wars, such as Korea, the sea and air power of the Royal Navy could be brought to bear quickly and effectively in almost any part of the world. But what would be its role in a future war fought with the newest weapons of mass destruction?

This question was answered in the White Paper, which defined the role of navies as a threefold function. These were :

(a) to search out and destroy enemy ships wherever they are, and by all means within their power to prevent the enemy from using the seas for his own purposes.

(b) To protect the communications necessary to support our warlike operations and to safeguard the supply lines of the Allied countries.

(c) To provide direct air support for operations ashore and afloat in those areas where it cannot readily be given by shore-based aircraft.

No one navy, could, however, undertake all these duties alone, but Great Britain was part of a closely knit alliance of Commonwealth and NATO Powers which together could achieve these objectives.

As part of Britain's contribution to the allied navies of the future, battle groups of carriers, guided missile ships and their escorts were visualised, to replace in effect the concentrated main fleets of past wars. They would provide the strength upon which all other naval activities depend, cover the manifold activities of the escort forces protecting our world-wide sea communications, and provide a mobile offensive force which could be quickly deployed wherever required. By their ability to disperse and re-concentrate at will, they would remain in the thermo-nuclear era both an elusive and a hard-hitting fighting force.

The Royal Navy required, therefore, carriers operating the latest aircraft; powerful ships armed with guided weapons; escorts capable, in co-operation with carrier and shore-based air forces, of providing protection for our shipping; submarines and amphibious forces; and minesweepers to keep the sea lanes clear for vital supplies. All of these ships should be well equipped and efficient, and maintained in a high state of readiness. An Admiralty statement declared that 'We have already made long strides towards meeting the need for modern carriers. We have for some time been clear about the design of our smaller ships which are coming forward in large numbers. Now, after a thorough study by our sailors and scientists of the conditions and developments we shall have to face, we can see sufficiently clearly the lines on which we should build ships to take the place of the conventional cruisers.'

Thus was forecast the advent of a new kind of warship of revolutionary design, armed with a ship-to-air guided weapon system of great lethality. While at first carrying a gun armament for surface gunnery and bombardment, the vessel would be so designed that her guns could be superseded in due course by ship-to-ship guided weapons. But in fact various considerations, not least of them financial, were to delay the coming of guided weapons ships for several years.

Mention has been made of the development by Admiralty scientists of an underwater television camera in connection with the search for the submarine *Affray*. In 1954 this new and improved aid to underwater discovery played a leading role in one of the most extraordinary operations in the history of salvage ever to be carried out by the Royal Navy.

On the morning of 10th January a BOAC Comet II airliner flying from Singapore to London exploded in mid-air and crashed in the Mediterranean near the island of Elba soon after leaving Rome. All thirty-five passengers and crew were lost. After taking off from Rome the aircraft was still climbing, and had reached a height of 26,000 feet when the disaster occurred. No SOS had been sent, a wireless message which was being transmitted to another BOAC aircraft having been abruptly broken off. The actual crash was seen by a number of eye-witnesses on Elba, but their stories were confused. Fishermen who had hastened to the scene and recovered fifteen bodies were, however, able to indicate the approximate position where the aircraft hit the water.

All Comet services were promptly suspended to enable a thorough technical examination of every aircraft to be carried out, but since the lost machine was the latest of its type, it was a matter of the greatest importance to discover the cause of the accident. Admiral Mountbatten, then Commander-in-Chief, Mediterranean Fleet, was asked if he thought the wreckage could be recovered, and replied in the affirmative. Six days later he received the laconic signal from the Admiralty : 'Endeavour to locate and salve the Comet.'

The task involved exceptional difficulties, and would inevitably be long and protracted due to the great depth of water in which the aircraft had gone down, and the winter storms. The depths in the area of the crash varied from 360 to 600 feet, deeper than was considered profitable by a commercial salvage company. Furthermore, although the water in the Mediterranean is translucent enough for a diver to be able to see as far as 100 feet at a like depth, at 500 feet in the disturbed winter water, direct vision from an observation chamber or underwater television camera is only possible up to about ten feet.

But these obstacles did not deter the Navy. On 17th January the anti-submarine frigate *Wrangler* accompanied by the danlayer *Sursay* sailed from Malta for Elba. They were followed by the boom vessel *Barhill*, the Royal Fleet Auxiliary *Sea Salvor*, which was specially equipped for salvage work, and a number of trawlers. While shore parties were closely interrogating every eye-witness in an effort to pinpoint the exact position of the crash, the *Wrangler* scoured the sea bed with her asdic, and the danlayer marked out possible search areas for special attention.

On 21st January a small piece of wreckage from the airliner was recovered by one of the trawlers, and several other promising objects were located by asdic. HMS *Wakeful*, which had been equipped with an underwater television camera, then took over from the

Wrangler. With its aid positive identification could now be made of the asdic contacts, and among them were found portions of the Comet. It soon became apparent that the aircraft had been smashed into a thousand pieces. The difficulties of recovering these were immense, and made more so by periodical gale-force winds.

After six weeks of unremitting toil involving 140,000 man-hours of work and the expenditure of 2,000 tons of oil fuel which covered an area of 100 square miles, barely one-tenth of the wreckage of the crashed aircraft had been recovered. The operation was described by Admiral Mountbatten, who several times visited the scene, as being like searching for a handful of peas in a one-acre field from a helicopter on a misty day. Gradually, however, with the aid of two additional under-water cameras, more and more pieces of the airliner were identified and dredged up, until by early October when 'Operation Elba Isle' finally ended, the greater part of the wreckage had been recovered.

In a message of thanks to the officers and men of the Mediterranean Fleet who had taken part in the recovery operation, the then Minister of Transport and Civil Aviation declared that :

In the sphere of aircraft accident investigations no bigger problem has ever arisen than the determination of the cause of the accident to the Comet aircraft which crashed off Elba. In no other accident has it been more necessary to find out the cause. There can be no doubt that the evidence furnished by the wreckage from Elba will be of the greatest value to the inquiry into this accident. That more than seventy per cent of the wreckage should have been recovered is little short of miraculous.'

When the pieces were carefully re-assembled in England, the cause of the disaster was finally tracked down and found to have been due to metal fatigue, a phenomenon never previously suspected.

While 'Operation Elba Isle' was in progress, trouble had been brewing in another Mediterranean island which was to engage the attention of Britain's armed forces for many weary months. That island was Cyprus, which in 1954 was about to erupt in violence and terrorism.

A protectorate of Great Britain since 1878 and annexed in 1914, Cyprus had for long been a trouble spot, and riots in 1931 had called for naval and military intervention to restore order. For years there had been a movement among the Greek population of

the island for union with Greece (Enosis), which was always strenu-
ously opposed by the Turkish minority.

In 1946 the British Government summoned a consultative assembly
to discuss setting up a new constitution. The Cypriots, however, remained divided. Left Wing elements and the Turks were willing to
accept the British proposals, but the Right Wing, led by the Church,
rejected all but Enosis. The assembly was therefore dissolved in 1948
without having accomplished anything.

The local Communists then decided to abandon their campaign
for self-government and to back the movement for Enosis. In 1950
the Church organised a plebiscite to show the strength of the Enosis
demand, and agitation, fanned by Athens radio, began to intensify.
In 1954 the Greek Government raised the issue of the union of Cyprus
with that country in the United Nations, and when this move failed,
more serious riots broke out in the island.

Towards the end of the year, in accordance with our treaty with
Egypt to carry out a phased withdrawal of our forces from that
country, the headquarters of British land and air forces, Middle East,
were moved to Cyprus from the Suez Canal Zone. A few months
later a Cypriot terrorist organisation known as EOKA began an
active campaign of sabotage and murder. Security forces were
strengthened, and in September 1955, 3 Commando Brigade was
moved to the island, the two Marine Commandos taking up duty at
Paphos and Troodos to help in the difficult task of combating the
terrorists. Field Marshal Sir John Harding was appointed Governor,
and a state of emergency proclaimed.

From the outset of the troubles destroyers, minesweepers and patrol
boats of the Mediterranean Fleet were brought in to maintain day
and night patrols around the coasts of Cyprus to prevent the
smuggling of arms to the insurgents. Within the three-mile stretch of
the island's territorial waters fishing vessels and other craft which
might be carrying arms to be landed in some secluded cove, or assisting wanted fugitives to flee from the island, were stopped, boarded
and searched. The work was often unrewarding and monotonous.
Most of the vessels intercepted were found to be following legitimate
pursuits, but all were considered suspect until proved otherwise.

Hundreds of ships of many nationalities, both large and small, were
challenged, their crews being treated with patience and tact. But
the naval men were alert and ready to deal with all cases of illegal
trafficking. Each warship had its own clearly defined stretch of
coastline to patrol, and at night cruised without lights, using radar

bearings to assist navigation. Greek and Turkish Cypriot police officers were carried to talk to suspect craft over loud-hailers and to accompany boarding parties in the role of intepreter. Steaming hundreds of miles every month, the patrolling ships operated from Malta and, with few exceptions, their crews never set foot in a Cypriot port. But there was little gaiety to be found ashore, and opportunities for sightseeing in an island of curfews and restrictions were severely limited.

Although the emergency was to continue for several years to come —Cyprus finally becoming an independent republic within the Commonwealth in 1960—the Royal Marine Commandos were withdrawn to Malta again in August 1956. But their breathing space was only a brief one, for an even more serious situation was developing in Egypt.

Before this came to a head, however, two events of naval importance occurred. In July 1955 a 'Summit' conference between the heads of government of Britain, the United States, France and Russia was held in Geneva with the aim of bringing to an end the 'Cold War' which, following the death of Stalin in 1953, had showed signs of a thaw. In the conciliatory atmosphere of the conference the possibility of an exchange of visits by British and Soviet warships was discussed, and later these were finally agreed upon.

Accordingly, in October of that year, a Soviet naval squadron consisting of two *Sverdlov* class cruisers and four destroyers, under the command of Admiral Golovko, Commander-in-Chief of the Russian Baltic Fleet, arrived at Portsmouth. It was the first visit of this kind by a Russian naval squadron since before the first World War. At the same time a British naval squadron comprising the aircraft carrier *Triumph* wearing the flag of the Commander-in-Chief, Home Fleet, Admiral Sir Michael Denny, the minelayer *Apollo* and four destroyers, visited Leningrad.

Goodwill radiated in all directions. After Admiral Golovko had held a press conference in his flagship, the Russian ships were thrown open to the public. Russian sailors were taken to London by motor coach for sightseeing tours of the capital, and Russian naval cadets visited Dartmouth to see how the Naval College was run. Admiral Golovko was entertained to lunch by the Admiralty Board, and later received by the Lord Mayor of London at the Mansion House. Everywhere they went the Russian sailors were given a great reception.

Leningrad's welcome to the British squadron was equally warm, crowds of spectators waiting to greet the ships when they arrived.

Apart from organised sightseeing tours, the British sailors were able to wander freely about the city. Wherever they went Russians came up to talk to them, shake hands and ask for their autographs. Scores of schoolchildren gathered round them, eagerly asking questions and managing to make themselves understood. The youth newspaper *Smena* published a poem in English and Russian, which ran:

> Welcome to Russia,
> Let us shake hands,
> We were allies,
> We must be friends.

Observers recorded that it was one of the greatest spontaneous demonstrations of friendly feeling for foreign visitors seen in Russia since the Bolshevists came to power in 1917.

Unfortunately, however, the atmosphere of goodwill engendered by this exchange of naval visits was somewhat soured by an occurrence which took place some months later.

In April of the following year Marshal Bulganin, the Russian Prime Minister, accompanied by Mr. Kruschev, First Secretary of the Communist Party, paid an official visit to this country. They travelled in the Russian cruiser *Ordzhonikidze*, a vessel of the *Sverdlov* class, escorted by two destroyers. The squadron, which remained berthed at Portsmouth during the ten-day visit of the Russian leaders, was commanded by Rear-Admiral Kotov.

An extensive programme of entertainment was arranged for the officers and ratings of the Russian squadron and, as before, they were greeted everywhere they went with the greatest cordiality and friendliness. When the visit finally came to an end, Bulganin and Kruschev re-embarked, and the squadron sailed amid a flurry of signals expressing goodwill and renewed hopes of a further strengthening of Anglo-Soviet friendship.

Then on 30th April, for no adequately explained reason, the Admiralty disclosed that on the day after the arrival of the Russian warships Commander Lionel Crabb, a former RNVR officer who had won the George Medal for his work in countering sabotage operations against our ships during the war, was missing presumed dead after an underwater diving exercise at Portsmouth. The Press immediately fastened on to this, and reports became current that Crabb had been checking up on the asdic apparatus fitted to the underwater hull of the Russian cruiser. In reply to this rumour the Admiralty stated that Commander Crabb had simply been testing underwater equipment.

Speculation about the Crabb mystery continued to grow, but when the Prime Minister, Sir Anthony Eden, was questioned about the matter in the Commons, he declined to disclose the circumstances in which the commander was presumed to have met his death. This satisfied no one. A remark made by Mr. Kruschev at one of the public functions he and Marshal Bulganin had attended in London hinted that the Russians knew that British naval frogmen had spied on their ships during the previous visit. Then, seemingly taking up the story from British newspapers, the Russian press openly accused the British of 'shameful underwater espionage'. This was followed by an official Soviet Note asking for an explanation of the presence of a naval frogman near the Russian warships where he had been seen by several Russian sailors.

Replying to the Note, the British Government offered its apologies, and declared that any activity by a frogman in the vicinity of the Russian ships was entirely unauthorised. Admiral Kotov disclosed to the newspaper *Isvestia* that he had in fact questioned the Chief of Staff to the Commander-in-Chief, Portsmouth, about the presence of a frogman near his ships, and had been told that it could not have been a naval diver, and that his description of the gear worn by the frogman answered to that of civilian equipment.

At this point the affair dropped out of the headlines, but it had cast a shadow over Anglo-Soviet relations. Then, nearly twelve months later, the mutilated body of a man wearing a frogman's suit was washed up at the mouth of Chichester harbour, eleven miles from Portsmouth. The Crabb story was at once revived, and at the subsequent inquest evidence was given that the frogman's suit was not standard Navy issue. In spite of the difficulty of identifying the body, the Coroner decided that it was that of Commander Crabb, and returned an open verdict as to how he met his death. Thus this extraordinary affair passed into history as a still unresolved enigma.

By that time what has since been described as 'the last great amphibious expedition in British Imperial history' had taken place. The experience gained thereby was to influence our future naval preparedness to deal with limited, or 'brush fire', wars.

In an earlier chapter the abdication of King Farouk of Egypt, the deposition of his son, and the proclamation of a Republic under the Presidency of General Neguib has been recorded; also that in 1954, following these events, a new treaty was negotiated with Britain

under the terms of which the Suez Canal Zone was to be evacuated
by British troops and the military base at Ismailia staffed by civilian
technicians on a care and maintenance basis. But in November of
that year General Neguib was himself ousted as Head of State by
Colonel Gamel Abdel Nasser, an ardent Arab Nationalist.

It has also been related that, claiming to be still at war with Israel,
Egypt had stopped Israeli ships from using the Canal. In 1951
Britain took the matter to the United Nations, who called upon the
Egyptians to lift the ban, but they refused. Israel was also hampered
from using the port of Eilat because of Egyptian fortifications on two
small islands which guarded the entrance to the Gulf of Akaba. Arab
guerrilla raids were being made into Israel from Syria, Jordan and
Egypt, and Nasser was suspected by the French of supporting rebel
forces in Algeria who were causing them a good deal of trouble. He
tried without success to obtain arms to continue his fight against
Israel from the United States, then China, but finally managed to
secure a quantity of tanks and aircraft from Russia.

Egypt had for some time contemplated the construction of a high
dam at Aswan in order to develop the Nile valley. Both Britain and
America offered financial help with the project, but Nasser feared
that acceptance of the necessary safeguards for the loan would mean
that the economy of his country would be overseen by the United
States for a number of years. He therefore began to hedge over the
conditions, and threatened to apply to Russia for the money. The
Americans sharply reacted by cancelling the loan, and Britain
followed suit. The Egyptian leader now declared his intention to
nationalise the Suez Canal and use the money received from transit
dues to finance the Aswan dam project.

Such action was, of course, unacceptable. Nationalisation of this
important waterway, the free navigation of which had been guaranteed by Egypt under the 1954 Treaty, would affect world shipping,
and in particular the needs of Britain and France. Britain owned a
controlling interest in the Canal, and more than one-third of the ships
passing through were British. The British Government were also
worried about the threat to Europe's oil supplies coming from the
Middle East, and the future of our base and stores at Ismailia. Both
countries began to strengthen their forces in the Mediterranean.

At that time the British Mediterranean Fleet comprised one aircraft carrier, two cruisers, a fast minelayer, one squadron of Daring
class ships and two squadrons of conventional destroyers; a frigate
squadron, a submarine squadron, an amphibious warfare squadron

consisting of tank landing ships and assault craft; a minesweeping squadron, and two Royal Marine Commandos. Operational additions now made to this strength included the aircraft carrier *Bulwark* and a number of landing craft and minesweepers. The cruiser *Kenya* and the *Daring* class ship *Diana* which were *en route* to Malta from the Cape and Far East respectively, were ordered to remain at Aden. At home two non-operational carriers, *Theseus* and *Ocean*, which normally constituted the seagoing Training Squadron, were ordered to stand by for trooping duties to the Mediterranean. No reserves were called up, but officers and men due for release were informed that they would be retained until the crisis had been resolved.

Nevertheless, on 26th July 1956, Nasser went ahead and proclaimed nationalisation of the Canal, assumed control of the Company's offices in Egypt, imposed martial law on the Zone, and forbade all employees of the Company, including foreigners, to leave their jobs.

Internationalisation of the Canal was suggested as an acceptable compromise, and a conference of twenty-two major maritime Powers was held in London to consider this plan. Nasser was invited to attend, but refused the invitation. The conference supported a scheme for a board of representatives of user nations to run the Canal, and this was duly presented to the Egyptian leader. But he rejected the scheme, and in this he was supported by Russia who had suggested instead a Four-Power conference to re-cast the 1888 Treaty, making Egypt proprietor and manager of the Canal. Britain and France now proposed that international control of the Canal should be restored by force, but the Americans refused to support such action and suggested that a Users' Association should be formed. The conference on this was indecisive, and Russia did not attend it.

Meanwhile Israel was preparing to wage a preventive war against Egypt in order to eliminate Egyptian forces from the Sinai Peninsula and free the Gulf of Akaba. In this she was backed up by the French, who promised to protect her rear and Mediterranean flank, and were urging Britain to take firmer action with Egypt.

In fact when Nasser seized the Canal, plans for military intervention had been concerted by Britain and France and a scheme of operations drawn up. General Sir Charles Keightley, Commander of the British forces in the Middle East, was nominated Allied Commander-in-Chief of the invasion forces.

These were to be drawn from the United Kingdom, France, Malta,

Algiers and Cyprus. The main components were to be two aircraft carrier task groups, one British and one French; two support forces groups; two minesweeping groups, and the amphibious warfare squadrons of the respective navies. The land forces would comprise a standard division each from France and Britain, with a French airborne division and a British parachute brigade group; an additional British contribution being 3 Royal Marine Commando Brigade from Malta brought up to full strength by the arrival of 42 Commando from home, making a total of some 80,000 troops. Both countries would provide bomber and fighter/ground attack forces, the land-based aircraft to operate from Cyprus.

Of the naval forces available, the Royal Navy undertook to provide more than a hundred warships, which would include the aircraft carriers *Eagle*, *Albion* and *Bulwark* with fourteen squadrons of Fleet Air Arm aircraft embarked; the *Theseus* and *Ocean* carrying operational helicopters and Royal Marine Commando units; the cruisers *Jamaica*, *Ceylon* and *Newfoundland*; a fast minelayer; thirteen destroyers, including six *Darings*; six frigates; five headquarters and maintenance ships; five submarines; fifteen minesweepers, and a surveying ship.

The French contribution was to consist of the fast battleship *Jean Bart*, the aircraft carriers *Arromanches* and *Lafayette*, a headquarters ship and thirty other warships. Also included were a considerable number of landing craft, and some eighty store and supply ships. Since Cyprus had no adequate harbours, Malta, although nearly 1,000 miles from Egypt, was designated the assembly base for the British forces. The French would use Marseilles and Algiers.

The object of the operation, code-named 'Musketeer', would first be to neutralise the Egyptian Air Force, which was largely composed of Russian fighters and bombers; then, after a preliminary bombardment, to land troops to capture Port Said and Alexandria, occupy the Canal Zone and seize the Canal. Beyond attaining these objectives no other aim was specified. Preparations for 'Musketeer' were completed by mid-September, but action was held up pending the outcome of negotiations. When these failed the decision was taken that should Israel attack Egypt an Anglo-French ultimatum to both sides was to be presented. If this were rejected, 'Operation Musketeer' would be put into effect.

On 29th October Israeli forces invaded Sinai, and within a matter of hours had advanced to within thirty miles of Suez. On the following day Britain and France called upon both sides to cease fighting and withdraw their forces to positions ten miles from either side of the Canal, at the same time requesting Egypt to accept the temporary occupation by Anglo-French forces of key positions in Port Said, Ismailia and Suez. Israel, having attained her objectives in Sinai and the Gulf of Akaba, accepted the ultimatum, but Egypt refused. Accordingly 'Operation Musketeer' was activated, and at dusk on 31st October bombers from Cyprus and Malta attacked Egyptian airfields.

At dawn next day naval aircraft from Anglo-French aircraft carriers joined with the land-based fighters in a succession of strikes on military objectives, being careful to avoid targets which might endanger civilians. By 4th November complete Allied air supremacy had been established. Egyptian naval resistance was slight. In the Red Sea the cruiser *Newfoundland* sank the Egyptian frigate *Domiat* which had failed to answer when challenged or to stop when called upon to do so. Sixty-nine survivors were picked up by the *Newfoundland*. She was found to have been carrying mines with the intention of laying them in that area. Between Alexandria and Port Said four Egyptian E-boats were attacked by British naval Sea Hawks. One of the boats was blown up, two set on fire, and the fourth damaged but allowed to pick up survivors from her consorts. Farther east the Egyptian destroyer *Ibrahim-El-Awal*, which was bombarding the Israeli coast near Rafa, was crippled by French warships and surrendered.

Meanwhile the Allied invasion fleet was steadily converging on Port Said. The maritime movements involved not only the seaborne assault, the maintenance of naval air cover, air warning pickets, and anti-submarine escorts, but also bringing forward salvage vessels and recovery equipment in anticipation of damage to Canal installations and blocking action.

On 5th November Allied paratroops were dropped on the outskirts of Port Said, being sustained and covered for the first time in any warlike operation entirely by carrier-borne aircraft. Naval helicopters evacuated wounded, including Egyptians, and supplied the paratroops with water, medical stores and other military necessities until they could be relieved by ground forces.

Shortly before daybreak on the 6th, after a preliminary bombardment by destroyers, two Commandos of 3 Commando Brigade landed from assault craft to secure a beachhead at Port Said. It had been planned that the third Commando, No. 45 which had come from the United Kingdom, should be air-lifted in to the beachhead by a fleet of S.55 Whirlwind and other helicopters of the Army and RAF from the *Ocean* and *Theseus*. This manoeuvre, never before attempted, was a complete success, the 500 men of the Commando being transported direct from the carriers, which were lying seven miles out, in ninety-one minutes. Subsequently the helicopters were used to evacuate casualties, performing this task with such efficiency that one Commando, who had been wounded soon after landing with the first wave, was whisked back on board and in bed within twenty minutes of leaving his ship.

By the end of the day the Allied ground forces had occupied Port Said and advanced more than twenty miles down the Canal. But that was as far as they were to get.

An urgently convened meeting of the Security Council of the United Nations had been held on 30th October, at which the United States sponsored a resolution calling on Israel to withdraw her troops and urging all UN members to refrain from the use of force. The resolution was vetoed by Britain and France who, however, undertook to cease military action if certain conditions affecting Egypt, Israel and the Suez Canal could be agreed upon. But five days later the UN General Assembly decided to set up an emergency international force to secure and supervise the cessation of hostilities. Accordingly a cease-fire was ordered at midnight on 6th November. The 'war' had lasted 6 days 18 hours, in which Britain lost 22 killed, the French 10, and 10 Allied aircraft had been lost, 4 of them by accident, for a total of 260 Egyptian aircraft destroyed. From the naval point of view this brief campaign had given an effective demonstration of a carrier group's mobility and strength. On 15th November the first unit of the United Nations peacekeeping force arrived at Ismailia.

The fighting was over, but the Navy's work was by no means at an end. As soon as the Allied air attacks had begun, President Nasser gave orders for the Canal to be blocked. Six vessels filled with concrete and scrap iron were moored in the Great Bitter Lake ready to be sunk as soon as the Anglo-French invasion started. Although they were bombed by British aircraft, only one had been damaged. They were promptly scuttled and formed an effective barrier.

At Port Said itself and along almost the whole length of the Canal the process was repeated, a total of fifty-one ships and craft ranging from 100 to 4,000 tons being hurriedly sunk by high explosives. They included floating cranes, dredgers, merchant vessels, tugs, barges, and the wreckage of two bridges blown up by the Egyptians. Twenty-two obstructions were sunk in Port Said harbour alone. Thirteen foreign merchant vessels found themselves marooned in the Canal.

On 6th November the surveying ship HMS *Dalrymple* entered Port Said and commenced a survey of the harbour and the wrecks. On the following day two British salvage vessels entered harbour and started work to open a channel. Meanwhile the Admiralty began mobilising all available salvage craft, and by mid-December the number of salvage vessels operating in the Canal area had risen to fourteen British, three French and two large German lifting craft which had been chartered by the Admiralty. Eleven more salvage vessels were on their way through the Mediterranean, and eight others were held at Aden and Djibouti ready to move to Suez. Altogether forty were employed or held in readiness. By 24th November a deep draught channel had been cleared in Port Said, and the way was open for the Anglo-French salvage fleet to proceed with the clearance of the rest of the Canal.

By the middle of December all Allied troops had been withdrawn. 3 Commando Brigade went back to Malta, and 42 Commando returned home to be reduced to a training complement. The number of salvage vessels was reduced to eleven and, with certain support ships, were placed under United Nations control, their crews wearing plain clothes and the ships flying the United Nations flag. By early April 1957 clearance of the Canal was complete.

In the summer of 1967 war again broke out between Egypt and Israel after the latter had provocatively mined the Gulf of Akaba, Syria, Iraq, Jordan and Lebanon allying themselves with Egypt. After only six days of fighting the war ended in a complete Israeli victory. But once again the Egyptians closed the Suez Canal, trapping fourteen ships belonging to various nations in the Great Bitter Lake. This time it was to stay closed.

CHAPTER SIX

The Way Ahead

The explanatory statement which accompanied the Naval Estimates for 1956 announced a 'New Deal' for the Royal Navy and Royal Marines. This included another welcome rise in pay—the third since the end of the war—to come into force from 1st April, and the introduction of a new form of Service engagement.

Called the 'New Regular Engagement', this was for nine years' service over the age of 18 with the Fleet, with no obligation to join the Royal Fleet Reserve on discharge. Both the old Continuous Service engagement of twelve years with the Fleet from the age of 18 which had functioned for many years, and the Special Service engagement of seven years with the Fleet and five in the Royal Fleet Reserve were abolished. Engagements for artificer apprentices, however, remained unchanged at twelve years from the age of 18 because of their long and expensive training.

Men nearing completion of their first nine years' service over the age of 18 could volunteer to re-engage for a further five years. By then they would have had a fair opportunity to make a good start in the Navy. They would be old enough to know if they wanted to make a career of the Service and, if not, still be young enough to begin again in a new job. During this second period they could then apply to re-engage to complete time for pension, the normal qualifying time being twenty-two years' service from the age of 18.

Since it was the Government's declared intention that men serving in the armed forces should be able to earn a financial reward comparable with that earned by equivalent grades in civilian life, the new pay structure showed considerable improvements over the former pay code. In some cases the old rates were practically doubled. Seamen boys and other junior ratings received an additional fourteen shillings (70p) weekly, but the pay of able seamen went up by as much as two pounds, twelve shillings and sixpence (£2.62½) a week. Leading rates and their equivalents received a similar amount, and chief and petty officers three pounds three shillings (£3.15). Men serving on seven-year engagements likewise benefited by 'the new pay rates, although on a slightly lesser scale, but were given the opportunity of transferring to the new nine-year engagement.

To these substantive rises could also be added various financial increments such as length of service pay; good conduct badge pay; marriage allowance; kit upkeep allowance; ration allowance; lodging, subsistence and local overseas allowances; trade pay for skilled ratings; charge pay; and for engine room artificers, watchkeeping certificate allowances. Submarine, flying and parachute pay went up by amounts ranging from fourteen shillings (70p) to two pounds, six shillings and sixpence ($£2.32\frac{1}{2}$) weekly. Long service pensions were proportionately increased, as well as the tax-free terminal grants payable after twenty-two and twenty-seven years' service.

For officers the increased pay scales were equally generous. Thus the pay of a naval sub-lieutenant and lieutenant, Royal Marines, went up by £119 annually; a lieutenant by amounts ranging from £146 to £155, dependent upon seniority; commanders from £155 to £219; captains from £365 to £511 per annum, and admirals by £1,186. Branch officers, soon to be re-titled Special Duties officers, received rises of from £146 per annum to £319, dependent upon rank and length of service. Flying and submarine pay rates were proportionately increased. Retired pay went up according to rank by sums ranging from £100 annually for lieutenants to £200 for admirals, and terminal grants from £500 for lieutenants to as much as £4,700 for a senior flag officer.

Rates of pay for National Service officers and men were also increased—although somewhat less dramatically since they had always been lower than those of personnel serving on regular engagements—as were those of WRNS officers and ratings. The latter, rather unfairly perhaps, were still paid only slightly more than half the rates received by their male counterparts.

From 1st April the rating of Boy was abolished in the Navy; in future they were to be known as Junior Ratings. As well as changing their title, the Admiralty also extended this method of entry into the Service, which had previously been limited to the seaman branch, to include the engineering and electrical branches and the Fleet Air Arm. Young ratings entering the training establishments at the age of 15 would in future be entered as Junior Seamen 2nd class, Junior Engineering Mechanic 2nd class, Junior Electrical Mechanic 2nd class, and Junior Naval Air Mechanic 2nd class. Communications ratings (Signalmen) would be selected from volunteers in the seamen branch at an early stage in their training.

Engineering and Naval Air Mechanics would be entered in HMS *Ganges,* the training establishment at Shotley Gate, near Ipswich; while Electrical Mechanics would go to HMS *St. Vincent,* a new entry training establishment at Gosport. Seamen could be entered in either of the two establishments. The first half of the course of training at both HMS *Ganges* and HMS *St. Vincent* would be common for all branches, but during the latter half there would be a bias towards the specialist technical requirements of the branch to which each rating belonged. Further specialist training would be provided at the technical training establishments. Junior ratings entered above the age of $16\frac{1}{4}$ years would go directly to the appropriate adult new entry establishment.

Thus another link with the old Navy was severed, for the rating of Boy had been in use in the British Fleet for well over three centuries. An early reference to it occurs in an official order of 1625 setting out their pay as seven shillings and sixpence ($37\frac{1}{2}$p) per month. Two hundred years later the pay of a Boy 3rd class had risen to only ten shillings and ninepence (54p) a month. Under the latest pay code the basic rate for a junior rating varied from one pound, eleven shillings and sixpence (£1.57$\frac{1}{2}$) to £3 a week.

In the past 100 years only a handful of Boys had managed to reach flag rank, notably Rear-Admiral Sir Thomas Spence Lyne, Admiral Sir Philip Enwright, and Vice-Admiral Sir Benjamin Martin. Probably the Boy Seaman best known to the public was Jack Cornwell, who was posthumously awarded the Victoria Cross for gallantry in action at the battle of Jutland when he was 16 years old. In the days of the old 'Wooden walls' Boys, by virtue of their station in action, were known as 'powder monkeys', since their task was to maintain the flow of ammunition from the magazines below to the crews at the guns.

Unhappily, in the view of many traditionalists, the 'New Deal' was also to involve at no distant date certain drastic economies.

Provision was made in the 1956 Naval Estimates for a maximum personnel strength of 128,000 officers and men, this figure to include both the WRNS and Queen Alexandra's Royal Naval Nursing Service, since the latter formed an integral part of the Royal Naval Medical Service. It represented a reduction of 5,000 over that for the previous year, and conformed to the Government's decision to reduce the overall armed manpower in the three Services. Fewer National Servicemen were to be entered in the Navy, since it was expected that the higher rates of pay and an increase in regular recruiting would reduce the requirement.

The White Paper stressed the Government's determination to maintain an effective fleet capable of supporting Britain's influence and interests as a world-wide Power and a member of the Commonwealth and NATO. Further development of new weapons and techniques would enable it to strike back at whatever might threaten by sea in the future, whether in limited or global war. But long-term plans for the Navy would be based on the deployment of fewer but more powerful ships.

A survey had been made of the Reserve Fleet, and only those vessels capable of putting to sea at short notice and fighting effectively in a modern sea war would be retained. Of the rest, obsolete vessels or those that had reached the end of their useful life would be disposed of. The structure of the Navy's shore support was also to be overhauled to ensure that it could meet the changed requirements of the active and reserve fleets now in the process of being re-shaped.

Current naval strength was shown as 5 fast battleships, but by now all of them were in reserve. Seven aircraft carriers were in commission, with a further 7 in reserve and 1 under construction. Ten cruisers in active commission with 12 in reserve or refitting, and 3 (*Tiger* class) building. Two fast minelayers were operational and 1 in reserve. Eight *Daring* class ships were in service. Twenty-four destroyers were in active commission, 44 in reserve, refitting or undergoing conversion to fast frigates. Fifty-one frigates were operational, of which 31 were converted destroyers, and another 110 in reserve or refitting, with 24 building. Forty-four submarines, with 15 in reserve and 2 under construction; and 65 minesweepers, plus 189 in reserve, with 70 coastal and inshore types building. In addition, there were 70 coastal craft (fast patrol boats and seaward defence craft); 8 large tank landing ships; 7 surveying ships; and 115 fleet support vessels, such as ferry carriers, destroyer and submarine depot ships, headquarters ships, repair ships, submarine rescue ships, controlled minelayers, boom defence and de-gaussing vessels.

Included in the building programme for the coming financial year were four 'Fleet Escorts', the first of a new and bigger type which would embody all the latest advances beyond the very successful *Daring* class design. Significantly, they would be fitted with guided weapons instead of anti-aircraft guns. They were in fact to be designated, most inappropriately, guided missile destroyers. But to close the gap before these vessels could come into service, the three *Tiger* class ships were to be completed and equipped with the new radar-controlled, automatic 3- and 6-inch guns which were being tested in the trials cruiser *Cumberland*.

In the event, however, HMS *Tiger*, first of the class, was not ready until late in 1959; the *Defence*, renamed *Lion*, in 1960; and the *Blake* in 1961. Destined to be the last of the Navy's conventional all-gun cruisers, they had been laid down in 1945, work on them suspended in 1946, and all three subsequently laid up in a state of preservation.

The decision to complete the *Tiger* class had in fact been taken in 1954, but so much new equipment had been developed since they were first designed that considerable re-planning was necessary in order to incorporate the new generation of equipment in the existing hulls. Originally intended to be 8,000-ton vessels carrying nine 6-inch guns, they eventually emerged with a displacement of 9,550 tons (11,700 at full load) and a main armament of four automatically loaded and fired 6-inch guns in twin turrets, and six 3-inch mounted in three twin turrets. The rate of fire of these guns was more than twice as fast as that of any similar weapon. The ships' main machinery of four geared steam turbines was largely automatic and capable of being remotely controlled, and gave them a top speed in excess of 30 knots. The cost of the three *Tigers* on final completion was over £40 million, and they were to have a comparatively short life in the cruiser role.

Meanwhile, in July 1956, a very different type of trials ship commissioned at Devonport. Marking the Navy's entry into a new era of weapon power, the design of the 'Fleet Escorts', or guided missile ships, to be ordered by the Admiralty would largely depend upon the results of the tests she was scheduled to conduct.

The new 'floating laboratory' was HMS *Girdle Ness*, originally a tank landing ship which had been built in Canada. In October 1953 she was taken in hand at Devonport dockyard to be completely stripped and reconstructed in preparation for her new role. Displacing 10,000 tons, she was fitted with accommodation for 80 officers and 536 men. Her normal naval complement was, however, 30 officers and 370 men, the additional living space being intended for scientists and technical representatives from the Admiralty, Ministry of Supply, and various civilian firms who had manufactured the equipment under trial and would go to sea in her. The main task of the *Girdle Ness* was to prove ship-launched guided weapons for service in the Fleet, and to gain experience in handling and maintaining and the tactical uses of these weapons.

The latter were extremely complex. Their equipment consisted of radars, displays and communications systems to enable a target to be selected and to control the missiles in flight, magazine and handling gear for stowing and transporting the missiles, and finally a launcher. In addition there were elaborate facilities for obtaining instrumental data from the trials. Research and development trials of a surface-to-air missile had been taking place ashore since the early nineteen-fifties, some at the Ministry of Supply's research establishment at Aberporth, in Wales, and some at the Weapons Research Establishment at Woomera, in Australia. Considerable advances had been made since the commencement of these tests, which endowed the new weapons with a greater performance and certainty of hitting the target than anything previously attempted. One of the most important was the development of a radar able to lock on to one aircraft in a formation and follow it until it had been destroyed.

In her trials programmes the *Girdle Ness* was to test operational guided missiles against 'drones'—small pilotless aircraft able to fly at great heights at supersonic speeds. The finned missiles, fired from triple mountings in the trials ship, would be equipped with a homing device and a proximity fuse. Fired roughly in the direction of the target, the missile would be controlled on its flight by an electronic 'brain'. Explosive warheads would not, however, be used, the space provided for this in the missile being packed instead with instruments for transmitting data back to the ship.

Within a few months the Navy's new ship-to-air guided weapon had successfully passed its initial seagoing firing tests, and fuller details were made public. Christened with the unlikely name of 'Seaslug', it was revealed that the weapon was propelled by a solid fuel rocket motor, assisted at take-off by four booster rockets which were jettisoned after accelerating it to supersonic speed. Its target detected by ship-borne tracking radar, and 'illuminated' by a narrow beam of radiation which locked on to and automatically followed the target regardless of any evasive manoeuvres, the Seaslug rode along the axis of the beam until the point of interception. Guidance equipment in the missile, comprising radio and radar-receiving serials and other detecting devices, produced appropriate fin movements to keep the missile in the centre of the beam.

Although maintenance of the missile equipment and its firing preparations required the servicees of a large number of officers and men, the number engaged in the actual operation of firing was far smaller than the crew of a conventional gun turret in a major warship. The weapon could be operated and fired from positions within the ship without exposing any deck personnel, and without the operator ever seeing the target. It was confidently claimed to be the best shipborne surface-to-air missile at sea in the western world.

As a corollary to the launching of the *Girdle Ness* trials, a Guided Weapons Group was formed at Whale Island Gunnery School (HMS *Excellent*) in Portsmouth. Comprising an office, lecture and model rooms and a cinema, its purpose was to teach officers and men the techniques, operation and technical capablities of the new weapons. This was in line with the policy earlier adopted of charging the Gunnery Branch of the Royal Navy with responsibility for guided weapons, airborne gunnery in all its forms, including rockets and bombs, and such atomic weapons as might be developed within their sphere. Similarly the Torpedo Anti-Submarine Branch had become responsible for all weapons which function under water.

Although failing to score an actual 'first' with the introduction of the Seaslug, the United States Navy having earlier produced an air-to-air missile called the 'Sparrow', the Royal Navy had been a leading protagonist of the guided weapon from the very beginning. As far back as 1945 an Admiralty committee had been set up to investigate means of providing the British Pacific Fleet with a short-range guided weapon to deal with Japanese *kamikaze* suicide attacks. But Japan was defeated before the project was sufficiently advanced. Thereafter the demands of post-war economy had further restricted research and development. Now at last guided missiles had been advanced in Britain to the stage where they could play an effective part in the nation's ordnance.

It has already been mentioned that the Government's 'New Deal' for the Services involved a general tightening up of available resources and a fresh wave of economies. In a special statement on defence published early in 1956 the list of priorities for the armed forces in the light of the continuance of the Cold War was for the first time set out in detail. They were :

(*a*) To make a contribution to the Allied deterrent commensurate with Britain's standing as a world Power, by not only building up and maintaining a nuclear stockpile and the means of delivery, but also contributing to the maintenance of NATO's defensive effort by land, sea and air;

(b) to play their part in the Cold War; by their mere presence contributing to the stability of the free world and the security of overseas territories whose peaceful development was threatened by subversion, whether overtly Communist or masquerading as nationalism;

(c) to be capable of dealing with limited wars should they occur;

(d) to be capable of playing an effective part in global war, should it break out, to include support to the civil authorities.

The statement warned, however, that the burden of defence could not be allowed to rise to a level which would endanger the country's economic future. The claims of defensive research would have to be balanced against competing claims on the nation's limited resources of scientific manpower; also the size of the forces since they inevitably affected the manpower available for the tasks of civil industry.

Because of the increasing costs of new weapons, any long-term defence programme based on the maintenance of forces at their existing level would also step up expenditure. Since this could not be allowed to rise beyond a certain point, the consequence of equipping the armed forces with new weapons would be a decline in their numbers. The total manpower in the Forces was accordingly to be cut to some 700,000 by March 1958.

This concept of smaller and better equipped forces placed a premium on the highly skilled long-service regular. Apart from the advantages in terms of morale and stability of a predominantly long-service force, the newer weapons would demand for their proper use increasingly high standards of training and maintenance. Hence the substantial improvements in pay and other inducements. Against this background the Government ordered a review of the future development of the Services.

The first results of the Admiralty's survey under this directive, which was conducted by a number of committees set up by the First Lord and known as 'The Way Ahead', were announced in the following August. Its principal objects were to effect a radical reorganisation of the Navy's shore structure to bring it in line with modern conditions and eliminate waste.

Heading the list of bases and shore establishments to be closed was the famous naval base at Scapa Flow, from which the Grand Fleet operated in the First World War and on which the Home Fleet was based in the Second. The importance of the decision to close it was not so much in the actual installations to be dispensed with, but the changed strategic view which led to the abandonment of a base considered vital in two world wars.

Scapa Flow, a magnificent natural anchorage in the Orkneys, had been selected as the main coaling base for the Grand Fleet in 1914 by Admiral Sir George Callaghan, who preceded Jellicoe as its Commander-in-Chief. With the advent of the U-boat menace its defences had to be hastily improvised. The surrendered German Fleet was interned there in 1918, and scuttled by its crews on 21st June 1919. In later years a number of the sunken ships were raised by a British firm and broken up to be sold as scrap.

The base fell into disuse between the wars except for occasional visits by the Atlantic Fleet. It was re-activated in 1939, and was the scene in October of that year of the torpedoing of the battleship *Royal Oak* by a U-boat which managed to penetrate the defences. The ship went down with the loss of 833 officers and men. Subsequently the entrances were protected by blockships and anti-submarine booms. The White Ensign was finally hauled down over the base at Lyness in March 1957. Also closed was the small naval base at Invergordon.

Training establishments recommended for closure by the 'Way Ahead' Committee included the gunnery schools at Chatham and Devonport and the anti-aircraft range at Sheerness. All gunnery training was henceforth to be concentrated in HMS *Excellent* at Portsmouth and HMS *Cambridge* at Wembury, near Plymouth. The signal schools at Chatham and Devonport were to be absorbed by HMS *Mercury*, the RN Signal School at Leydene, near Portsmouth; the Supply and Secretariat School known as HMS *Ceres* and situated at Wetherby, in Yorkshire, to be housed in the Royal Naval Barracks at Chatham; and HMS *Raleigh*, the training establishment for Engineering Mechanics at Devonport, brought into the Royal Naval Barracks at that port.

HMS *Phoenix,* the Damage Control School, was to be greatly reduced. HMS *Alaunia*, a hulk at Devonport used as a mechanical training and repair establishment, was to be paid off and its functions transferred to HMS *Sultan*, the Marine Engineering School at Gosport, and the Mechanical Training Establishment at Chatham. HMS *Defiance*, the Torpedo and Anti-Submarine School at Devonport, was to be closed and its functions absorbed in other establishments. Two naval air stations, at Anthorn in Cumberland, and

Fearn near Invergordon—the latter used for storage only—were also closed.

Of storage and production establishments, the Royal Naval Armament Depot at Woolwich was to be shut down; the Royal Naval Cordite Factory at Holton Heath reduced to care and maintenance; and the Naval Ordnance Proofing Range at Kingsclere, in Berkshire, disposed of. In addition a considerable number of minor establishments, which included store depots, engineering depots, boom defence depots, camps, etc., were also to be closed.

In March of the following year a second list of closures and reductions of naval shore establishments was announced, their rundown to be spread over a period of up to ten years. They included HMS *Harrier*, a naval air navigation and direction training establishment at Kete, in Pembrokeshire. The Royal Naval Medical School at Alverstoke, in Hampshire was to be moved into the Royal Naval Hospital, Haslar, early in 1958 and the Alverstoke building sold. This was later rescinded. The Royal Marines Small Arms School was to be closed. Of research and development establishments, the Admiralty Materials Laboratory at Holton Heath, in Dorset, was to be closed by 1959; also the Admiralty Experimental Establishment at Perranporth, and the Underwater Launching Establishment at West Howe, Bournemouth, by 1960.

A large number of naval store depots were scheduled for closure between 1957 and 1961. They included depots at Chatham and Rochester, six in the Portsmouth area, one in Devon, one in Scotland and two in Northern Ireland. One of the largest depots, at Risley in Lancashire, which boasted over 2.25 million square feet of storage space and was used for victualling, general and engineering stores, was to be closed in the early nineteen-sixties. Fifteen naval armament depots situated in various parts of the British Isles—and even one as far afield as Durban, in South Africa—were ordered to be closed by 1959.

The closure of the Royal Marines barracks at Chatham has already been mentioned in an earlier chapter, also the transfer of the pay and records office to Portsmouth, which were all part of the 'Way Ahead' economies.

Following this extensive pruning of the Navy's shore support, mainly in the United Kingdom, attention was then turned overseas. The first actual naval station to be abolished, the America and West Indies, was probably the oldest. The base at Bermuda had already been closed down in 1951. On 30th October 1956 Vice-Admiral

Sir John Eaton, the last Commander-in-Chief of this historic station whose waters had known many famous British sailors, from Drake to Nelson, struck his flag and that command ceased to exist.

There was a twofold purpose behind the abolition of this command: to ensure the most efficient deployment of our naval forces in more important strategic areas, and to integrate our command arrangements with our NATO allies in the vital North Atlantic zone. Admiral Eaton accordingly became Deputy Supreme Commander, Atlantic, taking up his post in the NATO Headquarters ashore at Norfolk, Virginia, and a Commodore, flying his broad pendant in a frigate assumed the title of Senior Naval Officer, West Indies. His 'parish' was limited to British possessions and interests in the Caribbean. Responsibility for the southern part of the old America and West Indies station was transferred to the South Atlantic, whose Commander-in-Chief assumed the new title of Commander-in-Chief, South Atlantic and South America.

In June 1962 the Senior Naval Officer, West Indies assumed the additional title of Commander, British Forces, Caribbean Area. He also held the NATO appointment of Island Commander, Bermuda. Three years later a small naval base was established on Ireland Island under the revived ship name of HMS *Malabar*.

In April 1957 as the result of a defence agreement made with the Union of South Africa the Royal Naval Base at Simonstown was handed over to the Union Government, which from thenceforward became responsible for its upkeep. The agreement, however, did not affect the use by Royal Navy ships of its facilities either in peace or war, even if South Africa herself was not engaged in hostilities.

Except for transfer of control of the base, the position of the British naval Commander-in-Chief remained unaltered. Indeed, he acquired additional functions. One of these was his designation as Commander-in-Chief in wartime of a maritime strategic zone on the lines of the NATO command structure, within which he would operate all ships, both Royal Naval and South African, by agreement placed under his command for control of the sea routes round southern Africa.

Simonstown first became the principal British naval base in southern waters when the 'Cape of Good Hope Station' was formed in 1795, and a number of naval storehouses were established on shore there. By 1814 the base had expanded to include an Admiralty House, dockyard and a naval hospital. Subsequently victualling, store, chart and cash depots were set up, and a dry dock built which was

capable of accommodating the largest cruisers and other warships up
to the size of a light fleet carrier. After the end of the Second World
War the naval hospital which in 1915 had dealt with casualties from
the Coronel and Falkland Islands battles, and in 1939 tended
wounded from the River Plate action, closed down.

At the time of the handover of Simonstown base in 1957 the
South African Navy, based on Durban, comprised two destroyers,
three frigates, two ocean minesweepers and a survey vessel, all former
Royal Navy ships; a controlled minelayer, two boom defence vessels,
and a number of seaward defence craft. Considerable expansion of
this force was planned by the Union Government.

On 31st May 1961 as the result of a referendum among the white
voters, the Union of South Africa became a Republic and withdrew
from the Commonwealth. But the facilities of the Simonstown base
remained available to the Royal Navy, and the Commander-in-Chief,
South Atlantic continued to fly his flag over the base.

Among the subjects discussed at the Commonwealth Prime
Ministers' conference held in London in June 1956 was Britain's
future naval strategy and the vulnerability of her world-wide chain
of static bases in a nuclear war. Since their dockyards and installations
would become top priority enemy targets, a new role for them was
visualised. Instead of offering facilities for repairing and refitting
ships, they would become places where ships could refuel and their
crews rest between spells at sea. Alternatives considered were the provision of operational 'fleet trains' to supply warships at sea, and secret
anchorages where damaged ships could be patched up before more
permanent repairs could be effected in safer areas and bases likely
to be far removed from the immediate scene of hostilities. Growing
co-operation between the navies of the Commonwealth would facilitate
the extension of the use of permanent 'fleet trains' such as served
with the British Pacific Fleet during the Second World War.

In their offensive roles it was intended in future to deploy ships
of the combined navies of the Commonwealth and NATO Powers in
battle groups formed round aircraft carriers and guided missile
cruisers. Carrier-borne long range aircraft would deliver thermo-
nuclear attacks deep inside enemy territory. In order to remain at sea
for long periods, each battle group would require to be accompanied
by its own replenishment force.

In fact there were already indications that 'fleet trains' for the
Royal and Commonwealth navies were on the way. The current

Naval Estimates for the first time listed repair, supply and other such vessels under the heading 'Fleet Support and Auxiliaries', and the Admiralty announced that a policy of building up the forces of ships needed to support the Fleet at sea was to be pursued. A programme of modernising ships to maintain escorts and minesweepers would begin with the conversion of the light fleet carrier *Triumph* into a heavy repair ship, the carrier *Perseus* into a submarine depot ship, and the hull of a cargo vessel to be bought for conversion into a store issuing ship.

When, therefore, the Government of Ceylon declared their wish at the conference to take over the naval base at Trincomalee under the Defence Agreement of 1947, Britain willingly recognised their right to do so. 'Trinco', as it had long been known to generations of British sailors, is one of the finest natural harbours in the world, its huge expanse almost entirely enclosed by palm-fringed beaches, and well sheltered from the turbulent waters of the Bay of Bengal. Used as a naval base since 1795 when Ceylon was taken from the Dutch, Trincomalee's port facilities were built up over the years by the British Navy. Although not a dockyard, it became a harbour and fuelling base with the largest naval oil reserves outside the United Kingdom, its installations including an armament depot and wireless stations. It achieved its greatest importance as a key base in the war against Japan when hundreds of ships were based there. When Japan surrendered a large British fleet had assembled at Trincomalee under orders to invade enemy-held Malaya.

Under the transfer arrangement the Ceylon Government agreed to make available certain facilities in the island for communications, movements and storage. In return Britain would provide assistance for the expansion, development and training of Ceylon's armed forces.

Accordingly, on 15th October 1957, as a Royal Marines band played 'God Save the Queen', the White Ensign was duly hauled down over the shore establishment which had for long borne the ship name HMS *Highflyer*. In its place a Ceylon Navy signalman hoisted a Ceylonese White Ensign. On the following day the British cruiser HMS *Ceylon*, flagship of the East Indies Station, sailed out of Trincomalee for the last time.

Along with the naval base, the RAF airfield at Katunayake, on the western side of the island, was also handed over to the Ceylon Government, the transfer agreement providing that its facilities, like those of Trincomalee, would be made available to Britain if required.

But when Anglo-French forces attacked Egypt in October 1956, Ceylon's Prime Minister at once sought and obtained from the British Government a guarantee that neither Trincomalee nor Katunayake would be used for any purpose connected with the operations. Subsequently he declared that a similar ban would be imposed in any future crisis.

Since these bases thus became useless to Britain in any conceivable war, an alternative was sought to bridge the communications gap with Australia and the Far East. The island of Gan, in Addu Atoll, was eventually leased for the purpose from the Sultanate of the Maldive Islands, at that time a British protected State, to which the atoll belongs. Addu Atoll itself also contains a large natural harbour where during the war various installations had been built, and which in emergency could replace Trincomalee. Peripheral fuelling stations already existed at Mombasa and Aden.

Five years later a naval wireless station commenced operating on the island of Mauritius. Equipped with the latest radio and electronic switching apparatus, the new station under the ship name HMS *Mauritius* took over the task formerly performed by HMS *Highflyer* to form an important link in the Royal Navy's world-wide radio chain.

Here may also be recorded the final dissolution of the East Indies station itself, whose headquarters had originally been at Trincomalee, and was soon to follow its transfer.

In the explanatory statement which accompanied the Naval Estimates for 1958–59, the Admiralty policy of increasing the ability of the Fleet to operate over longer periods independently of bases was again stressed. In order to contribute to the support of British and Commonwealth interests in the area stretching from Aden to Hong Kong and from Mombasa to New Zealand, a battle group comprising an aircraft carrier and supporting ships was to be continuously maintained east of Suez. Like the Far East Fleet, its operational base would be Singapore.

Accordingly the East Indies command was to be abolished, and the Senior Naval Officer, Persian Gulf, based on Bahrain and formerly responsible for the Persian Gulf Squadron on behalf of the Commander-in-Chief, East Indies, would become an independent commander. Taking the title of 'Commodore, Arabian Seas and Persian Gulf', he was to be responsible for the operations of British naval forces in the Arabian Sea, Persian Gulf, Gulf of Aden and Red

Sea. The remainder of the responsibilities of the Commander-in-Chief, East Indies, would be divided between the Commander-in-Chief, Far East, and the Commander-in-Chief, South Atlantic and South America.

Thus another chapter of the Navy's history, lit with famous names and daring deeds, came to an end when at nine o'clock in the morning of 7th September 1958, the flag of the one-hundredth Commander-in-Chief of the East Indies station, Vice-Admiral Sir Hilary Biggs, was hauled down over HMS *Jufair*, the naval base at Bahrain.

It was in 1744 that the first British warships were sent to the East Indies at the request of the Honourable East India Company, whose foothold in India was being threatened by the French. In command was Commodore Curtis Barnet, who later died on the station. Successive Commanders-in-Chief included such naval heroes as Boscawen, Hughes, Byron and Cornwallis and, during the Second World War, Admiral of the Fleet Sir James Somerville, who had commanded the famous 'Force H' when the war was going badly for Britain in the Mediterranean.

Two months after Admiral Biggs struck his flag at Bahrain, the Queen's Colour of the station was ceremonially laid up in the church of St. Martin-in-the-Fields. In the presence of the Board of Admiralty and nine former Commanders-in-Chief, Admiral Biggs handed the flag over to the vicar of the Admiralty's church with the time-honoured words :

'Reverend Sir, this, the last of the Queen's Colours carried in the service of the Queen's Commonwealth by the East Indies Station, Royal Navy, I now deliver into your hands for safe custody within these ancient walls.'

By then the days of another eastern outpost of the Royal Navy had become numbered. For in November 1957 the Government announced that the naval dockyard in Hong Kong was to be closed, its rundown to be spread over two years.

First used as a base by British warships in the Opium War of 1839–42, Hong Kong became a British possession in 1842 under a clause in the Treaty of Nanking. This declared that :

It being obviously necessary and desirable that British subjects should have some Port whereat they may careen and refit their ships when required and keep stores for that purpose, his Majesty the Emperor of China cedes to her Majesty the Queen of Great Britain, etc., the island of Hong Kong to be possessed in perpetuity by Her Britannic Majesty, Her Heirs and Successors.

A naval dockyard was constructed between 1908 and 1911. Since then the China Station had become the second largest of the Navy's overseas stations. But its closure did not mean the disappearance of British warships from Far Eastern waters. A number would still be based on Hong Kong for the protection of British shipping and the security of the Colony. A small naval base from which they could be serviced and operated would be retained, and units of the Far East Fleet would continue to visit Hong Kong from time to time.

In pursuance of the policy of re-shaping Britain's naval forces and their shore support, Malta was now scheduled as the next overseas dockyard to come under the axe, and more shore establishments—and even commands—in the United Kingdom were to disappear as the 'Way Ahead' committees continued their survey.

Since the end of the war British atomic scientists had been studying the possibility of using nuclear energy for marine propulsion. By 1955 when the American nuclear submarine *Nautilus* was commissioned, Britain possessed the know-how but not the resources to build her own nuclear-powered boats. In October of that year Admiral the Earl Mountbatten, the First Sea Lord, visited the United States to discuss atomic propulsion with Admiral Strauss, Chairman of the Atomic Energy Commission, and Admiral Burke, Chief of Naval Operations, but found that his inquiries were greatly hampered by the rigid restrictions imposed on the release of US atomic information. So unbending were these that Admiral Burke was unable even to obtain authority for Mountbatten to inspect the *Nautilus*. Relaxation of these restrictions would have enabled Britain to speed up her own programme for atomically propelled warships.

Fortunately, however, in the following year there came a change of heart on the part of our NATO Ally, and in June 1956 an agreement was signed in Washington under which provision was made for the exchange of information between Britain and America on atomic propulsion for naval vessels, aircraft and land vehicles and packaged power units. The exchange was to be entirely discretionary, neither Government being required to provide all the information requested by the other, but only such as it deemed suitable. Nevertheless, the agreement swept away much of the secrecy which had caused unnecessary duplication of effort in this field by both Britain and America.

When nuclear power was first mooted as a future main source of propulsion for both naval and merchant ships, the Admiralty declared its intention to employ it in the first instance in submarines. Accordingly, in September 1956, a research reactor to assist in the development of a nuclear propulsion unit for British submarines was started up at Harwell. Appropriately, it was named Neptune.

In February of the following year the Admiralty created the post of Rear-Admiral, Nuclear Propulsion. His task was to act as focus of the operational and material aspects of nuclear propulsion and to keep in touch with developments by the Atomic Energy Authority and by industry on the application to ships of nuclear power. He would be in charge of the work of the Navy Section at Harwell, and also act as the link between the Admiralty and other Government departments, Ministries and Services, and between Commonwealth navies and foreign navies. The first holder of this important post was Rear-Admiral G. A. M. Wilson, an experienced engineer officer.

Two months later the name *Dreadnought* was earmarked for the Royal Navy's first nuclear submarine when it should be built. It was chosen because the eighth *Dreadnought*, built in 1906 as the brainchild of the legendary Admiral Fisher, was of a design which revolutionised battleship construction at that time. The ninth vessel to bear the name would be equally revolutionary.

At the same time as this name was chosen the Admiralty Ships' Names Committee also selected names for the first guided weapon fleet escorts. It was decided to revive the old county names, many of which had been made famous in the last war. Accordingly the first to be selected were *Hampshire, Devonshire, Kent* and *London*.

In May 1957 it was announced that Britain's first atomic submarine engine was to be built at Dounreay, the Atomic Energy Authority's reactor proving station in Caithness. But in the event Dounreay did not after all produce the power unit for the *Dreadnought*. Instead a complete nuclear submarine propulsion plant was purchased from the United States under the Anglo-American agreement for co-operation on the uses of atomic energy for mutual defence purposes Thus much valuable time was saved, and the limited number of nuclear scientists and engineers in this country did not have to be diverted from their vital work on fundamental research and power stations.

Oceanographical survey ship *Hecla*

Board of Admiralty in session in the old Board Room. Note the famous wind gauge over the mantelpiece

The aircraft carrier *Ark Royal* with Phantom and Buccaneer aircraft ranged

Below: one of her engine rooms

Main engine controls in a
guided missile destroyer

Control room of the
nuclear Fleet submarine
Warspite

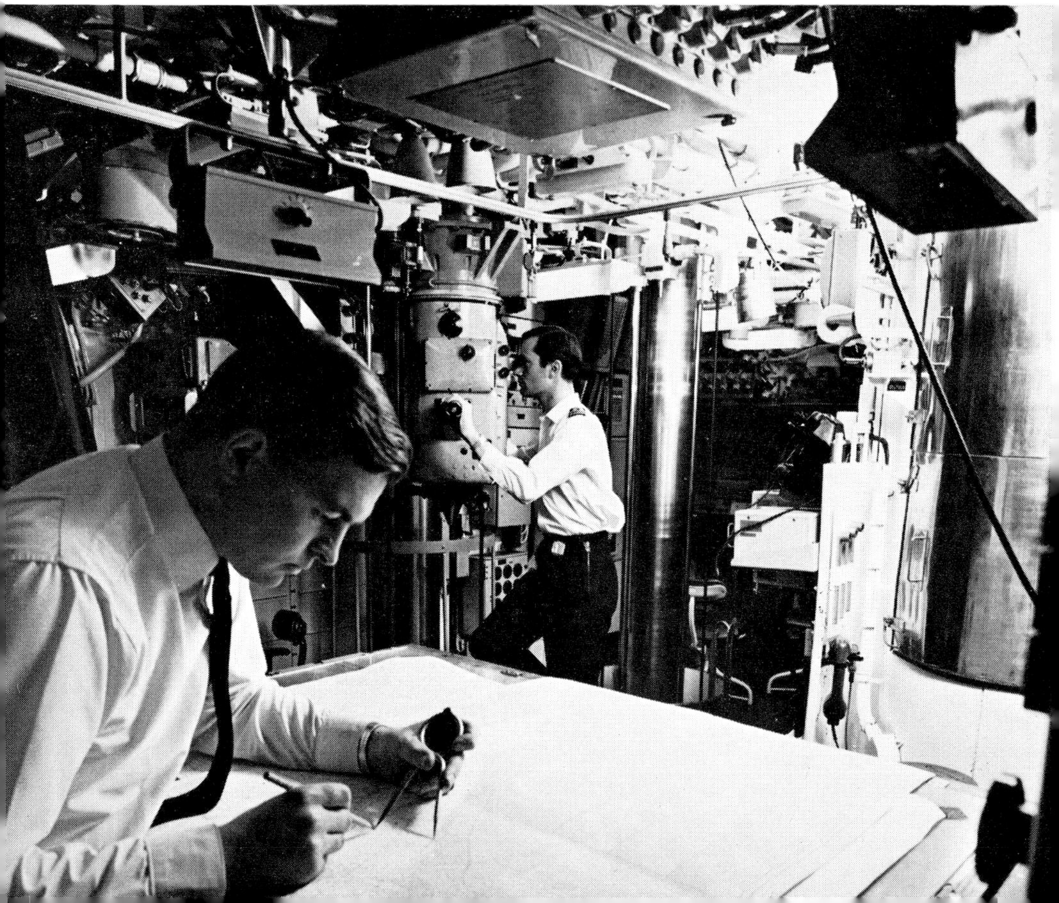

Wasp helicopter landing on board a frigate

The helicopter cruiser HMS *Tiger*.

Wessex helicopter refuelling from a *Rothesay* class frigate. The ship's Wasp can be seen to starboard

Meanwhile in the building yard of Messrs Vickers Armstrongs at Barrow-in-Furness, which firm was already engaged on a design project for a set of nuclear submarine machinery, the hull of the new submarine began to take shape. On 12th June 1959 Prince Philip officially laid its 'keel' by moving a handle which caused a gamma ray to operate a winch which drew a 30-feet high cylindrical section of the vessel into position. Thus was opened, in the words of Queen Elizabeth herself, 'A new chapter in the history of the Navy.'

The commanding officer-designate of the *Dreadnought* and other key personnel were already undergoing courses of special training. Officers were given theoretical instruction in nuclear physics, electronics, metallurgy, chemistry, mathematics and related subjects at the Royal Naval College, Greenwich, where a Chair of Nuclear Science and Technology had been established. Ratings underwent special training at HMS *Collingwood*, the Naval Electrical School, and in the Mechanical Training Establishment at HMS *Sultan*. On completion of these courses both officers and ratings were to go to America to receive practical instruction and gain experience in handling a nuclear power plant and its associated machinery. Further training would then be given in seagoing nuclear submarines of the US Navy.

Despite a confident prediction by the First Sea Lord, Admiral Mountbatten, that Britain's first nuclear submarine would be in the water by the end of 1961, four years were in fact to elapse before the *Dreadnought* actually commissioned.

Not all the emphasis at this time was on nuclear submarines. For at Vickers' yard a new type of conventional operational submarine was about to come into service. The first to be designed since the war, she was HMS *Porpoise*, and gave her name to a class of eight Porpoise, or 'P' class vessels. 295 feet long, with a beam of 26½ feet, the hull and superstructure of this class were designed to give high underwater speed and great diving depth. Propelled on the surface or when snorting by diesel-electric drive from two Admiralty Standard Range 16-cylinder diesel generators, and from a large battery when submerged, they were capable of voyaging round the world at a steady 8 knots without refuelling. Alternatively, they could travel a total of 187,000 miles at 5 knots and remain submerged for 100 days at a stretch. Other performance data included a speed in excess of 17 knots submerged, and the ability to dive to 220 feet in less than a minute. The snort equipment was designed to give maximum charging facilities even in rough seas, and the submarines carried air and surface warning radar which could be operated at periscope depth as well as when surfaced.

General habitability was of the highest standard, the living quarters of the boats being furnished with strip lighting, nylon curtains and panelling in laminated plastic and wood. To combat boredom on long periods of submerged patrol, a cinema projector and tape recorder were among the amenities provided. Each of the six officers and sixty-four ratings forming the crew had his own pull-down bunk with foam latex mattress. An air-conditioning plant provided drying and either heating or cooling of the air for Arctic or tropical service. Oxygen replenishment and carbon monoxide elimination made it possible for the boat to remain totally submerged without use of the snort apparatus for several days on end. Distilling equipment providing fresh water from salt, and stowage for large quantities of stores and provisions enabled these submarines to remain on patrol for months without any outside support. Probably their most important strategic advantage, however, lay in the fact that because all working machinery was mounted on rubber seatings, they became the world's most silent submarines.

Sister ships of the *Porpoise* were named *Sealion, Cachalot, Pinwhale, Grampus, Narwhal, Rorqual* and *Walrus*. Of 1,700 tons displacement—later increased to 2,030—and 2,500 submerged, they were armed with eight 21-inch torpedo tubes, and constituted a formidable underwater threat. Designated patrol submarines, they were followed between 1961 and 1967 by thirteen more of an improved type, which were known as the *Oberon*, or 'O' class, since their names all began with that initial letter.

The growing emphasis on underwater warfare, coupled with the advent of the deep diving submarine, gave impetus to the necessity for increased knowledge and experience of the effects on the human system of working at greater depths beneath the surface of the sea. Considerable attention was therefore directed in the post-war years to the techniques of deep sea diving.

Curiously enough, up to about the middle of the nineteenth century, all diving done for the Royal Navy was carried out by the Army's Royal Corps of Sappers and Miners. One of their tasks was the dispersal by explosives in 1839 of Admiral Kempenfelt's flagship, the *Royal George*, which capsized at Spithead in 1782. The wreck had become dangerous to navigation and an obstruction in the anchorage. Colonel Pasley, the officer in charge of the operation, asked the naval Commander-in-Chief at Portsmouth for additional labour, and was duly provided with a working party from HMS *Excellent*, the gunnery training ship.

During the operations, which took several years, a number of the sailors were taught the techniques of diving, and soon became as proficient as their military instructors. The upshot was that HMS *Excellent* was eventually given the responsibility for all naval diving. A Royal Naval Diving School became part of the gunnery training establishment, and in due course naval divers formed part of the complement of every capital ship, cruiser, depot and repair ship.

Men have practised natural diving in search of food or treasure from early times. But the invention of equipment to enable a diver to remain under water for more than the normal human limit dates only from 1778 when Smeaton, of Eddystone lighthouse fame, devised a type of diving bell which contained the elements of modern appliances. In 1837 Augustus Siebe invented the close diving dress which, with various improvements, was eventually adopted for general use. In essence this equipment consisted of a copper helmet and heavily weighted canvas suit and boots, the diver being supplied with air by a team on the surface operating an air pump and tending the air pipe and safety line.

Little progress was made during the first part of the twentieth century, except in such equipment as the Davis Submarine Escape Apparatus. But this was primarily intended for men coming up from below and not the reverse. Articulated metal diving suits and observation chambers were, however, developed abroad and successfully used in various salvage and recovery operations. But these, although enabling greater depths to be reached, did not improve the individual diver's capacity to work.

The advent of the Second World War and the introduction of the influence mine and underwater sabotage and their associated problems brought about a complete renaissance in the diving world. The self-contained equipment using pure oxygen which was developed made it possible for a swimmer to be completely independent under water, and enabled the X-craft operators and divers in the port parties to do much successful work during the war.

In 1944 naval diving became a torpedo commitment and was transferred to HMS *Vernon*, which two years later set up an experimental diving unit to conduct research into deep diving.

In 1949 a Clearance Diving Branch was formed, composed of men who were not only expert divers and underwater swimmers, but were fully trained in the technique of bomb, mine and missile disposal. In its early days the branch was heavily committed to the clearance of mines, bombs and explosives which had been dropped in our ports and harbours during the war. Clearance Diving Teams were attached to naval commands abroad as well as at home, and their services were constantly in demand. During 1957 the Mediterranean Fleet Clearance Diving Team alone dealt with 900 missiles of various kinds, including large influence mines and bombs. The Far Eastern Fleet team was chiefly occupied with unexploded Japanese bombs and shells round Singapore, also ship salvage and the demolition of underwater hazards.

Using improved equipment giving wider underwater vision and increased air supply, and breathing different mixtures to enable them to work at various depths down to 180 feet, Clearance Divers are today attached to all naval commands and to NATO. Their duties include wreck salvage, investigation of underwater obstacles, mine identification, and explosive ordnance disposal work.

Important advances were also made in deep diving techniques. Up to the end of the war the deep sea diver, breathing air pumped down to him from the surface, could descend to, work at, and ascend safely from about 300 feet. But tests carried out at the RN Physiological Laboratory found that at depths of 200 feet a diver's reactions began to slow down. The nitrogen in the air pumped to him produced a narcotic effect, while its oxygen content reached toxic pressure at just under 300 feet.

Accordingly a new breathing mixture of oxygen and helium was introduced, by means of which the working depth for the deep diver became almost limitless except for lengthening the decompression time of ascent. Controlled decompression is necessary, since the percentage of oxygen is reduced as the diver goes deeper, and must be replaced while ascending to prevent hypoxia. Nitrogen and other inert gases in the blood can also cause decompression sickness, known more popularly as the 'bends'.

Experts found that these delays could be overcome by lowering a submersible decompression chamber to meet the ascending diver. A vertical cylinder with a door at the lower end, the chamber is supplied with air from the surface and contains an attendant. When lowered into the water with the lower door opened, air pressure keeps the chamber clear of water on the diving bell principle. At a depth of some 200 feet, or preferably just clear of the bottom, the depth being controlled by available air pressure, the ascending diver enters the chamber. The attendant removes his heavy gear, disconnects his supply pipe and breastrope and closes the door, so locking in air pressure equivalent to its depth. The chamber is then hoisted inboard and decompression effected in safety by pumping in oxygen to eliminate the helium.

In 1948 Petty Officer William Bollard of the Royal Navy's Experimental Diving Unit set up a world record when he dived to 535 feet. Ten years later Commissioned Boatswain George Wookey broke this record when he descended to a depth of 600 feet from HMS *Reclaim* wearing a helmeted flexible diving suit. Both were breathing an oxy-helium mixture. In the same series of trials Wookey also dived to a depth of 1,060 feet in the *Reclaim*'s observation chamber, remaining for an hour without discomfort at this depth. Breathing oxy-helium, divers from the *Reclaim* and the submarine rescue ship *Kingfisher* were able to carry out routine dives to a depth of 430 feet and work at this depth for a maximum period of twenty minutes with ease.

By means of these improved techniques, important salvage operations were made possible, notably in the recovery of crashed aircraft such as 'Operation Elba Isle', to enable the cause of such accidents to be determined by experts. In 1966 a considerable portion of the wreckage of a Royal Air Force Shackleton aircraft was recovered from the bed of the Moray Firth into which it had plunged with the loss of all the crew. During this operation a new underwater communication system between surface and diver was successfully used for the first time. Instead of a microphone and handset, a bone transceiver combined the functions of transmitting and receiving. Two years later naval divers from the *Reclaim* set up new endurance records by salving important parts of the wreckage of a Viscount airliner which crashed into the Irish Sea. They carried out ninety-one dives in twenty-six days at depths of 250 feet in hazardous tidal conditions.

Apart from salvage work, submarine rescue and ship husbandry—which involves carrying out urgent repair work below a ship's waterline, and even changing a propeller to save docking—the Navy's divers are also trained in measures necessary to recover costly secret weapons which may accidentally fall into the sea. Since it may be necessary to dive beneath the Polar icecap or in the tropics, their training includes acclimatisation to working in all water temperatures.

Equipment produced by the Admiralty Experimental Diving Unit, a Royal Naval Scientific Service research organisation which works closely with the Superintendent of Diving, includes warm lightweight garments of foam rubber composition for divers, thus obviating the need for bulky woollen underclothes; and a new lightweight diving suit which dispenses with most of the impedimenta associated with the old-fashioned deep diving gear.

Known as Surface Demand Diving Equipment, a fabric hood with wide-angled face window replaces the helmet and, except for certain special tasks, flippers instead of heavy boots to give a greater radius of movement over the sea bed. Linked to the surface ship by a neutrally buoyant air hose which serves also as a lifeline able to withstand a pull of 1,000 lbs, the diver carries a supply of breathing mixture on his back in alloy bottles which can be automatically fed to him if the surface supply should fail. The Unit also produces breathing apparatus, compasses, depth gauges, and compression chambers.

A special chamber in which diving pressures equivalent to more than 1,100 feet can be simulated has been installed in the RN Physiological Laboratory. With its aid advanced research work is being continually carried on in co-operation with diving research enterprises in other countries, to enable men to reach great depths and stay there under free diving conditions working with their hands on a variety of tasks.

Early in 1957 the economy axe fell upon the Navy's Reserve Air Branch when all RNVR Air Squadrons were ordered to be disbanded by the weekend of 9th/10th March.

This decision, which came as a great blow to the hundreds of enthusiastic volunteer airmen, was forced on the Admiralty by financial and manpower considerations. But although taken chiefly on the grounds of economy, it was also a recognition that the operational flying of ever faster and more complex aircraft had become a job for the professional naval aviator.

In the ten years which had elapsed since the RNVR Air Squadrons were formed, naval aircraft had changed from the piston-engined types in use at the end of the Second World War to jet and turbo-jet machines of near supersonic speed. In the same decade pilots who were in their early twenties when the war ended had in many cases passed beyond the normal span of combatant flying and were now well into their thirties. For some time the ex-Second World War pilots of the RNVR had been giving place to post-National Servicemen, and if the squadrons were to continue, their personnel would before long have contained no one with war experience.

As mentioned earlier, the first units of the RNVR Air Branch came into being in the summer of 1947 with the formation of three fighter and one anti-submarine squadron. These were No. 1830, based at Abbotsinch, in Renfrewshire; No. 1831 at Stretton, near Warrington, Lancashire; No. 1832 at Culham, near Abingdon in Berkshire; and No. 1833 at Bramcote, near Nuneaton in Warwickshire. Personnel were recruited from Scotland, the Midlands, North-West England, North Wales and Yorkshire, and London and South-Eastern England respectively.

The age limit for entry was between 20 and 30, but for those who had commanded a front line squadron during the war the upper age limit was extended to 33, but not over 35. Pilots and observers were required to carry out fourteen days' continuous training annually, 100 hours' non-continuous training, and twelve weekends. During this time they had to log between 75 and 125 hours' flying time. The initial period of service in the Reserve was for five years, which could be extended by further periods of similar duration. Of the four squadrons, Nos. 1831, 1832 and 1833 flew fighters and were equipped with Seafire 17s; No. 1830, the anti-submarine squadron, flew Mark I Fireflies.

Nothing could exceed the keenness and enthusiasm of these 'weekend pilots', as they were called. By 1950 the squadrons had flown a total of more than 7,000 hours. 1832 Squadron logged the most, the pilots being airborne for 2,479 hours. But Culham, being within easy reach of London, was the largest. They were also the first post-war squadron to go to sea, being embarked in the carrier *Theseus* for ten days in 1949, when they made 176 accident-free deck landings.

No. 1830 Squadron, which was largely Scots manned, won the Boyd Trophy in the same year for making 205 deck landings with only one minor accident while embarked for training in an operational carrier. This achievement was all the more remarkable since nearly all the eighteen pilots had been trained during the war, and had not done any deck landings for five years. All four squadrons took part in full scale operational exercises with front-line carrier groups at home and with the Mediterranean Fleet. By the end of 1953 they had logged more than 10,000 flying hours.

In April 1951, a second anti-submarine squadron, No. 1840, was assembled at Culham, then shortly afterwards moved to Ford, near Arundel. Later that year all were re-equipped with more modern aircraft. The fighter squadrons received Sea Furies in replacement of their Seafires, and the anti-submarine squadrons were given Firefly Mark VIs which were equipped with more up-to-date radio and radar gear. Personnel was also strengthened by the addition of 200 ex-service pilots and 115 observers, entered mainly from the Royal Naval Volunteer Supplementary Reserve. The establishment of Engineer, Air Traffic Control, Medical, Supply, and Electrical Officers was increased, and entry opened for the Reserve's own Air Intelligence, Meteorological and Photographic Officers. Ex-rating pilots could also be entered in commissioned rank.

An important administrative change came about in June 1952 when, in order to facilitate rapid expansion in an emergency, the RNVR Air Branch was reorganised into four Air Divisions. These were constituted at Donibristle, Stretton, Culham and Ford, and were officially titled Scottish, Northern, Southern, and Channel Divisions respectively. Twelve months later a fifth, the Midland Air Division, was formed. New squadrons were also created, bringing the total number to twelve.

RNVR Air squadrons provided about one-fifth of the Fleet Air Arm aircraft which took part in the Coronation Review fly-past at Spithead in June 1953. That year also happened to mark the fiftieth anniversary of the formation of the Reserve itself.

Naval volunteers have served as far back as Edward the Confessor under such names as Sea Fencibles, River Fencibles, Coast Volunteers, and Royal Naval Artillery Volunteers. The London Corps of River Fencibles escorted the funeral procession of Nelson by river from Greenwich to Westminster in 1806. On 30th June 1903 Parliament sanctioned the formation of the RNVR with 4,200 men in five Divisions, the earliest of which were designated as London, Scottish, Mersey, Tyne and Bristol. Later eight more were formed.

In the two world wars the Reserve expanded beyond all recognition and rendered magnificent service. At the end of the First World War some 6,665 officers held commissions, and there were 45,000 men serving in the Royal Navy and 15,000 in the Royal Naval Division. In the Second World War 80 per cent of all the officers serving in the Navy at one time held RNVR commissions, 48,000 in all. Ninety-two per cent of the pilots in the Fleet Air Arm were members of the RNVR.

Because their anniversary fell in Coronation year, arrangements were made to hold a special Jubilee parade in the following year. This duly took place on Horse Guards Parade on 12th June 1954, when the Queen inspected some 2,000 officers and ratings of the RNVR, its associated Reserves and Commonwealth Naval Volunteer Reserves, and included representatives from the five Air Divisions. The parade was held in drenching rain which caused the postponement of a fly-past of the air squadrons. This took place, however, on the following Saturday, when nearly 100 aircraft from the twelve squadrons flew past her Majesty at Windsor Castle. It was the first time they had flown together on their own, and because of their civilian commitments they did so without full-scale formation rehearsal. But it was in fact to be their swansong.

There was little indication of the coming axe when in 1955 approval was given for the RNVR Air Branch to convert within the next two years to jet aircraft. All piston-engined fighters in the Northern and Midland Divisions, and half in the Southern Division, were to be replaced, first by Attackers and subsequently Sea Hawks. But then came the decision that the RNVR establishment of these costly aircraft was to be reduced by about one-fifth; also that one fighter squadron of the Southern Division was to be disbanded. Finally came the order for total disbandment.

Another Reserve which was drastically cut at the same time was the Royal Fleet Reserve, which in March 1957 was reduced from 30,000 to 5,000. This Reserve, originally brought into being by the Naval Reserves Act of 1900, had been chiefly recruited from ratings and Royal Marine other ranks serving on the old Special Service engagements of seven years with the Fleet followed by five in the Reserve. Other ex-naval and Marine personnel not in receipt of pensions could also enrol in this Reserve. Because of their former service they were considered to be more highly trained than any of the volunteer bodies.

The Royal Fleet Reserve had greatly expanded during the post-war years, mainly because of the low rate of re-engagement of the seven-year men. Those now to be discharged who were under the age of 45 would be enrolled in the appropriate emergency reserve, but with no training liability or retainer, and subject to recall only in a national emergency by Royal Proclamation. The inference to be drawn from this reduction of a trained Reserve was that the Navy did not expect to have to deal with more than minor emergencies in the foreseeable future.

Not least momentous among the many changes brought about in the Royal Navy during the decade which followed the end of the

Second World War were certain overdue amendments to the Naval Discipline Act, which defines the offences and procedure of naval law and governs the naval court-martial system. They resulted from the impact of events in another of the armed Services.

Thus in 1946, as a result of the quashing of sentences passed on a number of British paratroops for 'mutiny' against their living conditions in Malaya, a committee was set up under Mr. Justice Lewis which recommended far-reaching changes in the court-martial systems of the Army and Air Force. Probably the most important was the recommendation for the creation of a court-martial appeal tribunal. Before implementing the recommendations, however, the Minister of Defence set up a new committee in 1949 under the chairmanship of Mr. Justice Pilcher to examine the naval system, since it was obviously desirable that as far as possible similar principles should apply to all three Services.

The naval court-martial had been gradually developed over the centuries. In early times there were no regular tribunals for the trial and punishment of offenders afloat. The captain of a ship awarded punishments according to the 'laws and custom of the sea'. Over him the commander of an expedition or squadron held a commission from the Sovereign to make ordinances and inflict punishments. To advise him the Admiral or 'Generall' usually had a 'Council of War' which could call accused persons before it and try them for offences against the 'Articles or Ordinances of War'.

These latter had their origins in an Ordinance of Richard I (Coeur de Lion) which he drew up for the discipline of the fleet he took on the Great Crusade in 1190. Richard appointed certain high ranking officers as justiciaries, and for their guidance set out a scale of offences and punishments. Thus a proven murderer was to be tied to the corpse of his victim and hove into the sea. For stabbing another, or even drawing a knife with the intention to do so, the culprit was to lose a hand. A convicted thief was to have boiling pitch poured over his head, followed by a shower of feathers, and to be cast ashore at the first point of land.

This code, in somewhat milder form, received Parliamentary sanction for the first time under the Commonwealth. It was re-enacted as the Articles of War under Charles II in 1661.

Under the Act the Lord High Admiral was given power to grant commissions to commanders of squadrons to call and assemble courts martial consisting of commanders and captains, usually to number not less than five and not more than nine. In 1866 the Naval Discipline

Act was passed which codified the Articles of War. The constitution of courts-martial, whose numbers had been increased to thirteen, was re-established on the earlier basis, but all officers of or above the rank of lieutenant were made eligible to become members, providing that they were 21 years of age. Normally the president was to be a captain, but if a flag officer was being tried the president had also to be a flag officer, and the members of the court captains or higher ranks.

There was no appeal from a court-martial, but the Admiralty could amend or annul a sentence, except for the death penalty which could only be remitted by the Sovereign. There was a Judge Advocate, but he was originally the prosecutor until 1884 when that duty was transferred to the captain or executive officer of the accused's ship. The duty of the Judge Advocate was to examine witnesses on oath and record their depositions; take minutes of the proceedings, and give his opinion on doubtful points. He also drew up the sentence and, under the direction of the president, pronounced it. The prisoner had to defend himself, but from 1884 onwards was allowed to have a friend or legal adviser. Various changes in procedure were made from time to time, until in all essentials a naval court-martial differed little from that of an ordinary criminal court—in some respects being more favourable to the accused.

The original Articles of War had numbered thirty-six, which ranged from mutiny, failing to pursue the enemy, quarrelling or fighting on board and profane swearing, to embezzling public stores. No less than twenty-two of the listed offences carried the death penalty, and for ten of them this was mandatory. As time went on more offences were added, but fewer carried the death penalty. In fact, the last official yardarm execution in the Royal Navy took place at Talienwan Bay in 1860 during the second Chinese War, the culprit being a Royal Marine who was convicted of trying to murder his captain.

As a result of its deliberations the Pilcher Committee made a large number of recommendations, which also included the setting up of an appeal tribunal. Other recommendations were that the constitution of future courts-martial should not include the captain of the accused's ship; that the title 'defending officer' should be used instead of 'prisoner's friend'; and that the section of the Naval Discipline Act which provided for the trial without specific charge of the surviving officers and crew of a ship lost, destroyed or captured, should be repealed. It speaks volumes for the modern naval court-martial, which had been evolved from the harsh regimes of past centuries, that the Committee found it enjoyed a high degree of prestige in the twentieth-century Navy, and was considered to administer justice satisfactorily.

Most of the proposals of the Lewis and Pilcher Committees were embodied in subsequent legislation, and a court-martial appeal court duly set up.

In 1956 another Select Committee was appointed to examine the Naval Discipline Act itself and to re-write it to meet modern conditions of life in the Royal Navy. As a result of the Committee's recommendations many penalties were reduced or abolished, and for the first time various forms of flying offences were added. The death penalty for all specifically naval offences was abolished, except for certain treasonable acts and the worst kinds of mutiny. New additions to the list of misdemeanours included surrendering a ship while it was still capable of being destroyed, aiding the enemy while a prisoner of war, and careless talk. The revised scale of punishments also included for the first time fines for officers, to be limited to thirty days' pay.

Impressed by the *esprit de corps* of the WRNS, the Committee recommended that they should continue to remain outside the Naval Discipline Act, considering that 'a code of discipline designed for service at sea was inappropriate to women'.

Two important amendments were made to the Naval Discipline Act. Up until then, in order to be subject to its provisions, a person had to be borne on the pay ledger of a warship or naval shore establishment. This requirement dated back some 200 years when an Act was passed that when a ship was lost or captured by the enemy the men's pay was to be continued in order to make them liable to naval discipline. Previous to this, all pay had ceased on the date of loss or capture, and the Articles of War no longer applied to the crew. But because the application of the Naval Discipline Act to naval reservists and pensioners recalled to duty was now dependent upon other Statutes, the existing connection between the application of naval discipline and ships' books was finally severed. In future every officer on the active, retired or Emergency Lists when ordered on any duty or service, and every rating of the Royal Navy, reserves or pensioners, whether borne on ships' books or not, became subject to the Act.

The second amendment altered the wording of the historic preamble to the Act. Ever since 1864 this preamble had referred to 'His Majesty's Navy whereon, under the good providence of God, the wealth, safety and strength of the kingdom chiefly depend'. The 1956 Committee recommended that this should be abolished altogether on the grounds that there was no such preamble in the other two Services. The Admiralty, however, desired it to be retained for traditional reasons, and upon reconsideration the Committee, which included a number of former naval officers, agreed that it should be retained as a source of inspiration. But they re-worded it so as no longer to claim that the 'wealth, safety and strength' of the kingdom chiefly depend on the Navy. For the word 'chiefly' they substituted 'so much depend'.

Although there were protests that this diminished the importance of the role of Britain's first line of defence, the alteration in fact brought this famous and oft misquoted preamble more into line with that of the original Act of 1661. For the wording had then referred to 'His Majesty's navies, ships of war and forces by sea, wherein under the good providence and protection of God, the wealth, safety and strength of this Kingdom *is so much concerned*'.

To round off this reference to post-war changes in the Naval Discipline Act, it is appropriate to mention that in 1971 the Act ceased to be a permanent Statute. Along with the Army and RAF Discipline Acts, it has thereafter to be brought up for Parliamentary scrutiny at five-yearly intervals.

CHAPTER SEVEN

The First Five-Year Plan

The work of streamlining the Navy's shore organisation begun by the Way Ahead Committee anticipated still further and more drastic cuts to come. In a White Paper published in April 1957 setting out future policy, the Government announced that a complete reorganisation of the armed forces was to be carried out over the following five years.

The plan outlined represented the biggest change in military policy ever made in normal times, and constituted an admission that Britain could not be adequately protected against nuclear attack. 'The overriding consideration in military planning must be to prevent war rather than prepare for it'.

Accordingly National Service was to be abolished, the armed forces made wholly regular, and manpower strength cut to little more than half the existing total of 690,000 by the end of 1962. Defence expenditure was to be kept strictly within limits prescribed by current strategic needs and the economic capacity of the country. For this purpose the functions of the Minister of Defence were re-defined, giving him increased authority to take decisions on matters of general defence policy affecting the size, shape and equipment of the armed forces, and to secure reductions in expenditure and manpower.

To assist him in this task and to deal with inter-Service problems, a Defence Board was set up consisting of the three Service Ministers, the Minister of Supply, the Chiefs of Staff, the Permanent Secretary, and the Chief Scientist of the Ministry of Defence. The chairman of the Chiefs of Staff Committee, at that time Marshal of the Royal Air Force Sir William Dickson, was given the new title of Chief of the Defence Staff. In 1959 he was succeeded in this post by Admiral the Earl Mountbatten, formerly First Sea Lord.

Within the limits of the policy determined by the Minister of Defence, the Service Ministers, working through the Board of Admiralty and the Army and Air Councils, were made responsible for the efficiency and administration of the three Services. The

Minister of Supply was given responsibility for the efficient execution of approved programmes of defence, research, development and production, while the Chiefs of Staff Committee remained collectively responsible to the Government for professional advice on strategy and military operations and the military implications of defence policy generally.

The Navy was to be smaller and more compact, and armed and organised on the most up-to-date lines. A start had already been made on cutting down the Reserves and the Reserve Fleet, and increasing the emphasis on afloat support to replace conventional shore bases. Peacetime overseas commitments would be met by organising the seagoing Fleet into Task Groups built around the fleet carrier.

Naval manpower was to be reduced from the current figure of 121,000 to between 90,000 and 100,000 by 1962, the major part of the rundown to be effected in 1958 and 1959. No drastic alterations in the policies for recruitment or re-engagement were contemplated, but re-engagement would become more selective in certain categories. Further to reduce the Reserve Fleet, the four *King George V* battleships were to be scrapped. The *Vanguard*, however, would be retained and earmarked for assignment to NATO in an emergency.

Of the 14,000 officers then serving in the Royal Navy and Royal Marines, some 2,000 were to be prematurely released, together with about 1,000 ratings. Categories affected were General List officers of the Seaman, Engineer, Supply & Secretariat, and Electrical Branches, mostly of the rank of lieutenant-commander. Officers of the Special Duties List earmarked for reduction included Seamen, Shipwrights, Electrical, and Supply & Secretariat specialists. Royal Marine officers to be released would be lieutenant-colonels, majors and captains on the General List, and Quartermasters and Bandmasters on the Special Duties List. About 25 per cent of flag officers were to go, the reductions being met by retiring officers after they had held one appointment in the rank, and reducing the numbers to be promoted.

The reductions in ratings would be met largely by the cessation of National Service and the normal termination of engagements. But in the meantime some senior rates would have to go, mostly men who had completed seventeen years' service. Categories affected included engine room artificers and mechanicians, shipwrights and artisans, Masters-at-Arms and regulating petty officers, chief air fitters, and Royal Marine bandsmen. As in the case of officers, the majority to be prematurely released would be volunteers, the required numbers being made up where necessary by compulsory discharge. All those selected would be given six months' notice before the actual date of discharge.

Financial compensation to those being axed was fairly generous in the light of prevailing standards. Thus officers with more than ten years' qualifying service were given tax-free capital payments of up to £6,000 for captains, £5,500 for commanders, and £5,000 for lieutenant-commanders and below. Those nearer normal retirement age received smaller sums. In addition they received retired pay and a terminal grant, the qualifying age for both being reduced from twenty to ten years. Both General and Special Duties Lists officers who were within a month of completing ten years' service and did not qualify for retired pay and terminal grant, received a special capital tax-free payment of £5,000. Others were paid lesser sums. Since they were not eligible for retired pay, they also received a service gratuity of £100 per annum for each year of qualifying service. Permanent officers retired at the normal age limit during the rundown period were given a special resettlement grant of £500.

For ratings and other ranks of the Royal Marines the minimum period of service qualifying for pension was reduced from twenty-one to ten years from the age of 18, and five years' credit for pension and terminal grant was added to the actual qualifying service, providing it exceeded ten years. In addition they received tax-free capital sums of up to £1,250.

Discharge of those selected for release—and in the event all were volunteers—was smoothly effected within two years. The officers included 50 captains and 300 commanders; and of the remainder some two-thirds were lieutenant-commanders or its equivalent rank in the Royal Marines. Of the ratings discharged, all had served for seventeen years or over. This rundown, however, brought problems later on when new ships with more sophisticated and complex weapons and equipment came into service. But at least the 1957 version of the 'Geddes Axe' was wielded much less harshly than its notorious predecessor of the nineteen-twenties.

In February 1957 there were some 400 ships in reserve, being refitted or undergoing modernisation. Forty vessels had been sent to the breakers since the last statement, among them two wartime fleet carriers—*Illustrious* and *Indefatigable*—two cruisers, *Phoebe* and *Sirius*; four destroyers, and thirty-one frigates and ocean mine-sweepers. By July 1958 a further eighty-five vessels, including some of the fast patrol boats of post-war construction, were on their way to the scrapyards.

It was felt by many observers, however, that the continued selling and scrapping of ships in the Reserve Fleet constituted a danger to national security. In fact, at that time the Reserve Fleet was made up of three categories. The first and most substantial was the Operational Reserve consisting of ships able to put to sea, and capable of being fully equipped and manned in a very short time. The second category, known as the Supplementary Reserve, consisted of ships in good condition but mothballed and no longer at notice for service. The total of destroyers and frigates in these two categories equalled the number of those in the seagoing fleet. None of these were being scrapped.

The third category was known as the Extended Reserve, and consisted wholly of vessels of wartime construction which were unmaintained. They included cruisers of from eighteen to twenty years old, destroyers from fourteen to seventeen years old, and frigates and ocean minesweepers which had been built during the war. None had been refitted and they were gradually deteriorating. Both on the grounds of expense and shortage of manpower it was impracticable to modernise any of the ships in this category; nor could the laid-up aircraft carriers be used either as helicopter carriers or transports. No other country wanted them, and there was no alternative, therefore, but to break them up.

Warship scrapping is a melancholy business, but the departure of the *King George V* class battleships for the breakers' yards, followed by that of the *Vanguard*, was even more sadly notable because it marked the end of a splendid but outmoded era. As late as 1952 ten battleships were still in commission in the navies of the world. Of these America possessed three, France two, Italy two, and Russia two. Alone in the British Navy, while her sisters lay mothballed in 'Death Row', the *Vanguard* proudly flew the flag of the Commander-in-Chief, Home Fleet. But in the autumn of 1955 the Admiralty announced that she would be placed in reserve at the end of her current refit.

After twelve months spent in mothballs the *Vanguard* was reactivated to become flagship of the Flag Officer Commanding Reserve Fleet. Then, in October 1959, the decision was taken that she, too, must go. Accordingly in mid-summer of the following year Britain's last battleship was towed away to be broken up on the Clyde. On the way out of Portsmouth harbour she went aground and could not be budged for an hour, as if she were protesting at this ignominious departure from the Fleet in which she had served so briefly and without the opportunity to demonstrate her immense potential.

The Fleet's carrier strength, however, was greatly augmented by the emergence from her seven-year refit and modernisation pro-gramme at Portsmouth dockyard of HMS *Victorious*. Built by Vickers Armstrongs on the Tyne and completed in May 1941, the original displacement of the *Victorious* had been 22,600 tons. During the war she had taken part in actions against the German battle-ships *Tirpitz* and *Bismarck*, sailed on Malta and Arctic convoys, and supported the North Africa landings. From 1943 to 1945 the *Victorious* served in the Pacific and Indian Oceans. While working with the Americans she was hit and severely damaged by a Japanese *kamikaze* aircraft, but was back in action after a few hours. Of our wartime carriers she was the only one to be modernised.

Her modernisation was the biggest task of its kind ever undertaken by a Royal or commercial dockyard, the ship being completely re-built above the hangar deck and fundamental changes made to her structure. Nearly 15,000 tons of plating, machinery and internal fittings were removed, while the weight of items added brought her new displacement up to 30,530 tons, 35,500 at full load. Equipped with angled deck, steam catapults and mirror deck landing aids, she was thus rendered capable of handling the latest and heaviest Fleet Air Arm aircraft.

Powered by three sets of steam turbines, operated by hydraulic remote controls, giving her a speed in excess of 30 knots, and fully equipped with up-to-date 'ABCD' arrangements, the most outstanding feature of the 'new' *Victorious* was her Type 984 three-dimensional radar mounted in a giant 'dustbin' above the island superstructure. Described as the best shipborne air defence radar in the world, this combined early warning and high discrimination of an aircraft's position in plan and height simultaneously. Associated semi-automatic data-processing equipment collected and displayed the information produced by this radar, enabling the admiral or captain to see at a glance the tactical situation in any sector of the sky for miles around. Air control was effected by computer, and a computer-operated, high-discrimination radar was fitted to enable aircraft to be talked down safely in all weathers. These items of her equipment alone cost over a £1 million.

In the battle for internal space between the volume of new tech-nical equipment required and the needs of ship's company accommodation, an effective compromise was reached which set the standard for later construction. Thus single-berth cabins for all officers were provided, occupying less overall space than the old two-berth and dormitory cabins. Bunks were provided for all ratings, dining halls for junior rates and separate messes for senior ratings. There was even a chapel capable of seating forty-five persons. Panelled in oak, it actually boasted a stained glass window. This lengthy and expensive face-lift enabled the *Victorious* to operate as a front-line carrier until well into the sixties.

The reorganisation of the Navy ordered under the new five-year plan was made slightly less painful for serving personnel by still further increases in pay which came into force on 5th April 1958. Thus a midshipman was now to receive a daily rate of from 75p to 95p; a lieutenant from £1.70 to £2.40, dependent on seniority; a commander from £4.25 to £4.85; captain £5.30 to £6.30; while the daily pay of an admiral of the fleet went up to £14.30.

Every man in the Royal Navy and Royal Marines over the age of 18 serving on a nine-year engagement or longer received an increase of at least £1.05 in his weekly basic pay; bigger increases being paid according to length of service. New entries at the age of $17\frac{1}{2}$ now started at £6.12$\frac{1}{2}$ weekly, all found. Marriage allowances were increased by between 70p and £1.40 a week. The pay for the WRNS was also substantially improved. Officers received basic additions of from £82 to £292 a year, and ratings between £1.05 and £2.54 a week according to rating and length of service. Overall, however, their pay still remained below that of equivalent male ranks and ratings.

Indicative perhaps of the growing affluence of the post-war British Serviceman was the abolition in June 1957 of the traditional naval custom of junior ratings removing their caps at pay musters. This was not only a form of salute : the cap had then to be placed on the pay table for the money due to be tipped on to its crown from a wage envelope by the paying officer.

In pre-war days fortnightly payments to the average junior rating frequently consisted of little more than a handful of silver coins. Now because of greatly increased post-war pay rates the sums due were more likely to consist of a wad of banknotes. The old custom of tipping the money on to the cap was therefore considered impracticable, and from thenceforth all ratings attending pay musters were ordered to give the hand salute only.

The long-standing rule, however, that sailors must remove their caps when being formally inspected by the captain or other senior officer remained unaltered. Similarly, caps are still removed during the reading of his commission by a newly appointed commanding officer —itself the post-war revival of an old custom—when a rating is appearing at the defaulters' table, or when any section of the Articles of War relating to punishments is officially read. This last has been a naval custom since 1644.

Until Queen Victoria came to the throne, doffing the cap was in fact the only form of personal salute in the British Navy. Thus whenever addressed by an officer, a rating removed his headgear, and junior officers similarly saluted their seniors. Her Majesty, however, objected to seeing men in uniform standing about bareheaded, and so the salute with the hand was instituted.

As mentioned earlier, efforts were begun soon after the war ended to improve living conditions for ships' companies. Various amenities had been introduced from time to time, but not on any large scale. Now that new construction ships were coming forward in increasing numbers it was possible to implement this policy more fully. Detailed investigations and trials had shown that centralised messing and bunks for ratings provided more efficient, economical and habitable accommodation than the old-time broadside messing and hammocks. Accordingly this form of accommodation became standard in all future construction ships down to ocean minesweepers. The layout of messdecks was designed to retain traditional mess life, bunks and lockers being arranged to leave communal space. Chairs and plastic-topped tables were provided, and a proportion of the bunks were made convertible into settees during the daytime.

New types of lockers for suitcase storage were supplied, the suitcase having completely ousted the old-time naval rating's canvas kit-bag. Coat cupboards and bookcases were built in, ship's side settees with upholstered backs installed, drinking water coolers, electric irons and ironing boards provided—even sockets for electric razors. Messdecks were illuminated by fluorescent lighting, covered with coloured linoleum, coloured paints and plastic wallpaper on bulkheads, and overcases supplied for stool and settee cushions for use in hot weather.

Senior ratings' messes now boasted table covers, easy chairs with patterned overcases, and door and scuttle curtains, in addition to coloured linoleum and coloured plastic-topped tables. Fireplace surrounds with panel-type electric fires and club fenders were fitted, and carpets provided.

Three standard furnishing schemes designed by civilian specialists for wardrooms and senior officers' messes were adopted for cruisers and above, and three for smaller ships. Where space admitted, fire-proofed wooden furniture was supplied for officers' quarters, all of which, whether of wood or metal, being given a cheerful light-coloured wood grain finish in place of the dark mahogany fittings of the past which had tended to make living spaces appear small and gloomy. Where practicable all cabins were fitted with hot and cold running water washbasins, sockets for electric razors and, for use from a common aerial, sockets for private wireless sets. Improved types of louvres and air distributors were fitted, and tobacco smoke and dust filters for air-conditioned spaces.

Attention was also given to shore accommodation in the naval barracks at the three home ports of Chatham, Portsmouth and Devonport, and various instructional establishments with large 'floating populations', such as the gunnery, signal and electrical schools, and HMS *Dolphin*, headquarters of the Submarine Branch.

The naval barracks had changed but little since their first erection in the early part of the century. Thus they had become overcrowded and unsuitable for requirements accompanying the post-war rise in general living standards. In addition the barracks at Portsmouth and Devonport had been badly damaged by enemy action.

A seven-year scheme of reconstruction and modernisation was put in hand in 1952 which soon began to show results. Planned on hotel lines, new high rise accommodation blocks arose in the naval barracks and technical training establishments. As well as providing comfortably furnished dormitories for junior ratings, they included many single 'bed-sitter' type cabins for chief and petty officers. Decorated in pastel colours, these were equipped with such refinements as built-in ward-robes, linen closets, h & c washbasins and bedside lamps and, instead of numbers, were given the names of warships of the Royal Navy past and present. Each new block included games rooms, television rooms, guest rooms, lounges, bars, and reading and writing rooms furnished in considerable comfort; also all-electric galleys, dining halls, bathrooms, showers and drying-rooms.

Naval catering underwent a remarkable transformation, both ashore and afloat. In pre-war years officers' messes were catered for by private contractors known as 'Messmen', many of these being Maltese who served in the nominal rating of Chief Steward. Sailors were still fed on a 'standard' messing system, which involved the issue on an individual scale of certain staple articles of diet such as meat, potatoes and bread, sugar, tea, cocoa and tinned milk. These basic rations had to be supplemented by mess caterers out of a small daily victualling allowance by the purchase from the canteen of such 'luxuries' as eggs, bacon, sardines, tinned meats, jams, soups, etc.

The preparation of all meals had to be undertaken by the ratings themselves, the actual cooking being merely supervised by the ships' cooks using small, cramped, coal-fired galleys as had been done by their notoriously incompetent predecessors. Since few sailors had any real knowledge or experience of the culinary arts, the results of their efforts were generally lamentable.

In 1907 a Naval Victualling Committee recommended the adoption of a form of 'general messing' which had been originated a few years earlier in the American Navy. Under this system the planning and preparation of meals for both officers and men was placed under the supervision of one accountant officer, who was also responsible for drawing up a weekly menu and arranging the purchase and provision of all food stocks.

But the United States had fewer warships, and Congress was lavish in its appropriations for food, mess traps and cooking appliances; furthermore, the Americans welcomed changes, whereas the British were conservative. Nevertheless, a modified form of the 'general messing' system was tried out in the new battleship *Dreadnought* and in certain training establishments. It was extended only very gradually, and the standard messing system remained in force for many years in most seagoing ships.

In the nineteen-thirties an improved form of general messing was adopted in all naval shore establishments and warships of new construction, but the standard system still lingered on in destroyers and smaller craft which lacked the facilities of their larger sisters. Then, as part of the promised post-war improvements in naval amenities throughout the Fleet, came the introduction of cafeteria messing, to be followed by the provision of self-service dining halls in the larger ships and shore establishments, placed close to modern electrically equipped galleys and serving rooms.

Along with these innovations the quality of cooking was immensely improved. A Central School of Naval Cookery was set up in Chatham, the syllabus comprising basic cookery training to a standard equivalent to City and Guilds qualification. Advanced courses were subsequently introduced to enable naval cooks to obtain full membership of the Cookery and Food Association, and even of the Hotel and Catering Institute.

Catering Officers were introduced into the Navy during the war to replace Messmen in the running of wardroom messes; and in the early nineteen-sixties a Catering Branch came into being, consisting of senior ratings with cookery experience to plan the daily menus for men of the Lower Deck, exercise cost control of food, and order provisions, fresh food and luxury items. The result has been the introduction of gourmet-style meals in all naval ships and establishments, and a wide variety of dishes for the sailor to choose from on his daily menu. A far cry indeed from the bad old days when pamphlets addressed to Parliament by senior naval officers complained that, 'Where we had one man died by shot we had ten died by means of bad provisions.'

Early in 1958 the Fishery Protection Squadron was strengthened and equipped with ships possessing better sea-keeping qualities. The six wartime-built *Algerine* class minesweepers which had constituted the squadron since 1951 were replaced by four *Blackwood* class frigates and four of the new coastal minesweepers. Service in the squadron was designated Home Sea Service. A few months after this changeover was effected the first of the so-called 'Cod Wars' with Iceland began.

In 1952 that country unilaterally extended the fishing limits off her coast to four miles, this measure being designed it was claimed, to conserve the fisheries. Indignant British trawlermen, however, regarded it simply as a means of affording economic protection to Icelandic inshore fishermen. The resulting dispute between Britain and Iceland was eventually referred to the United Nations where it dragged on for several years, but ended in deadlock.

Then, in September 1958, Iceland suddenly announced an extension of her territorial waters to twelve miles, thus banning all foreign vessels from fishing within that limit. Efforts to persuade the Icelandic government to alter the decision failed, and the latter was therefore informed that Britain intended to protect her vessels fishing within the new limit.

Accordingly the Fishery Protection Squadron organised three 'havens' within which British trawlers could be given reasonable protection. Code-named 'Butterscotch', 'Toffeeapple' and 'Spearmint', these havens were located between the four- and twelve-mile limits.

All remained quiet at first. Then one day sailors from the Icelandic gunboat *Thor* boarded the British trawler *Northern Foam*. At once the frigate *Eastbourne* went to the trawler's assistance and put her own boarding party on board. As the Icelanders refused to leave, they were removed to the British frigate who landed them at Keflavik. Thereafter the Icelandic gunboats confined themselves for the most part to steaming among our trawlers informing them that they were inside territorial waters and threatening arrest if they put into an Icelandic port. But when our warships were out of the way, they proceeded to harass the trawlers and sometimes attempted to board. As the weather deteriorated with the approach of winter, tempers began to fray.

Subsequently for many weary months the Fishery Protection Squadron, supplemented by ships of the Home Fleet, provided constant protection to trawlers from Hull, Grimsby, Fleetwood and Aberdeen. Steaming monotonously up and down the thirty-mile long 'safe' areas, each warship spent an average of eighteen days on station, often in appalling weather. Fog frequently persisted for weeks, and breakaway ice from the Greenland icefields constituted an additional hazard.

Royal Fleet Auxiliary ships played an essential part in maintaining the patrols, five 10,000-ton tankers being detailed to refuel the warships at sea. Prevailing weather conditions made this operation difficult, but only once was it found impossible. During a Force 11 gale one tanker had to remain hove-to for eighteen hours. In a seventeen-day trip made by a sister ship constant gales were experienced for fifteen and a half days, followed by dense fog. Sick and injured trawlermen were treated by medical officers from the warships, whose technical staffs also gave assistance in the repair of engine defects.

This first 'Cod War' eventually came to an end when a compromise settlement was reached in 1961. Under this agreement Britain no longer objected to the twelve-mile limit around Iceland, while the Icelandic Government agreed that British vessels could continue to fish in the greater part of the zone between six and twelve miles off shore at certain times of the year. Finality on this vexed question was not, however, to be reached.

But if the 'Cod War' had been temporarily settled, the Cold War showed few real signs of thawing. Poised between the hope of total peace and the fear of total war, the Western nations and the Soviet Union continued to face one another with deep-seated mutual distrust. Each feared that the other had aggressive intentions, and no amount of pacific assurances in both directions had so far succeeded in removing these suspicions.

In October 1957 the Russians gave awesome proof of the remarkable progress they had made in the development of a science capable of immense military potential when they successfully launched an earth satellite which they called 'Sputnik I' A month later 'Sputnik II' soared into space, this time carrying a dog on board. These achievements were greeted with admiration and general disquiet in Western countries.

The Americans had been experimenting with artificial satellites since 1946 but had not yet successfully launched any. Britain had also been trying out space-exploring rockets, the first of which was successfully fired in February 1957 from the Woomera range in Australia. Their main purpose was to probe the upper atmosphere for information on winds, meteorites, cosmic radiation, and other information which could aid future space travel.

Nevertheless it was not felt in Britain that the temporary Russian lead in rocket development had upset the balance of military power, since the overall superiority of the West was likely to increase rather than diminish. While the Western nations would never start a war against Russia, it had been made abundantly clear that if Russia were to launch a major attack on them, even with conventional forces only, they would hit back with strategic nuclear weapons. The protection of the free world against the Communist threat in all its forms was regarded as an indivisible problem to be undertaken by the collective effort of all the countries concerned, a policy particularly applicable to those forming the North Atlantic Alliance.

Russia's formidable submarine fleet did however constitute not only a world-wide threat, but one of special concern to an island nation dependent upon sea communications for food supplies and economic life in peace and war. In a White Paper published in March of the following year, the Government therefore emphasised that the efforts of the Royal Navy would continue to be concentrated to an increasing extent on the anti-submarine role and other measures to safeguard ocean communications. For economic reasons, however, the earlier idea of maintaining a number of independent task forces grouped around carriers, and including guided missile cruisers, was abandoned in favour of forming groups of ships, with or without carriers, to be known as composite squadrons. These squadrons, whose composition would vary with local requirements, would form the focal points of the re-shaped Navy.

In the Atlantic and Mediterranean the Royal Navy would continue to play its part in NATO. Since, apart from fulfilling certain colonial responsibilities, the Royal Navy would be operating in conjunction with other allied navies, our aim would be to make the most effective contribution to the combined forces of the Alliance, not necessarily to provide a fully balanced, all-purpose British Fleet. British naval forces in the area would include two carriers, two cruisers, and a number of destroyers, frigates and submarines. The carriers, while including strike and fighter aircraft, would be predominantly equipped with anti-submarine aircraft and helicopters.

East of Suez a balanced, all-purpose fleet of appreciable strength would be maintained in order that British obligations to the South-East Asia and Central Treaty Organisations could be discharged, and independent military commitments in the area fulfilled. This Eastern Fleet would be based on Singapore, and would consist of an aircraft carrier equipped with strike, fighter and anti-submarine aircraft, a cruiser and a number of destroyers, frigates and smaller vessels. It would also include a converted carrier equipped to accommodate a Royal Marine Commando and capable of operating helicopters in either the troop-carrying or anti-submarine role. These ships would operate singly or in groups, assembling at intervals for training.

In addition to these main operational fleets, a small number of frigates would be stationed in the Persian Gulf to discharge British responsibilities in that area. Some light craft were to be stationed in Hong Kong for local defence, together with a frigate patrol to protect British shipping along the China coast. A few frigates or destroyers would be kept on the West Indies and South Atlantic stations.

Formerly only larger ships of the Fleet had carried Royal Marine detachments. It was now decided that Marines should be embarked in lieu of seamen in frigates stationed in those parts of the world where landing parties were likely to be required. A frigate of the Persian Gulf squadron was the first to include twenty Marines in her complement, and the ruling was later extended to frigates of the West Indies station.

Continuing the curtailment of dockyard and base facilities, Sheerness and Portland dockyards were now to come under the axe. The tasks of the Home Air Command were to be concentrated in larger groups at fewer bases. Consequently the aircraft repair yard at Donibristle was to be closed by the end of 1959, also the RN Air Stations at

Ford, Bramcote and Eglinton. The air station at Brawdy, in Pembrokeshire, would be kept in reserve, and the Air Electrical School at Worthy Down closed. Most important of the new reductions was the announcement that the Nore Command was to be abolished in April 1961, its remaining functions being transferred to other authorities. Overseas, Malta dockyard was to be transferred to civilian ownership, since the smaller Navy would not require all the facilities which for generations had been necessary to maintain control of the Mediterranean; but the dockyards at Gibraltar and Singapore were to be retained.

In consequence of the achievement of independence by the newly created Federation of Malaya, the appointment of Flag Officer Malaya, formerly a separate subordinate command under the Commander-in-Chief Far East Fleet, came to an end in March 1958. In July of that year the Royal Malayan Navy was transferred to the Federation as part of the new State's armed forces. Since its inception in 1952 this small colonial navy had been based at Singapore, administered and paid for by the Singapore Government. Five years later, in 1963, the Federation of Malaya, the State of Singapore, and the colonies of North Borneo—renamed Sabah—and Sarawak merged to form the new independent State of Malaysia. Under the earlier defence agreement the headquarters of the British naval Commander-in-Chief Far East continued to be based in Singapore island.

The transfer of Malta dockyard to the private ship-repairing firm of Messrs C. H. Bailey of South Wales, took place on the morning of 30th March 1959, the changeover being marked by a ceremony enacted on the previous day in the Red State Room of the Palace in Valletta. Before a gathering of senior Service and civilian personalities, the Fourth Sea Lord handed over a key on a red plush cushion to the Governor, who in turn presented this symbol of transfer to the chairman of the Company. While the principal aim of the firm was to develop the dockyard for commercial purposes, the yard would continue to be supplied with naval repair work, which would diminish as commercial activities expanded.

From 30th March therefore the post of Admiral Superintendent Malta lapsed, all remaining Admiralty departments and naval activities hitherto administered by him coming under the authority and general direction of the Flag Officer Malta. The Navy would continue to use Malta as a naval base and remain responsible for certain functions carried out in the dockyard. A new Admiralty organisation, operating under the authority of the Flag Officer would act as overseer responsible for work placed with Messrs Bailey by the Admiralty, and for the continuing commitments of the dockyard professional departments which were unaffected by the transfer.

Twelve months later an even more historic link with the Navy's past was severed. In a simple ceremony which took place at sunset on 31st March 1960, when the White Ensign was hauled down for the last time, Sheerness Naval Dockyard ceased to be. The sixty-acre yard with its docks and basins passed from the Admiralty to a civilian firm who had purchased the area with the object of developing it as a trading estate.

Sheerness had been extensively used for shipbuilding and repair work for more than a century, new construction ranging from brigantines used in the suppression of the slave trade to 4,000-ton cruisers of the First World War. But the origins of its dockyard date back to the middle of the seventeenth century. Samuel Pepys, then Secretary of the Admiralty, noted in his diary in 1665:

> To Sheerness where we walked up and down, laying out the ground to be taken in hand for a yard, to lay provision for cleaning and repairing ships, and a most proper place it is for the purpose.

During the next few years Sheerness was equipped to clean ships' hulls to save having to work them up to Chatham, but it remained an adjunct to Chatham until the beginning of the nineteenth century. In those days there was no shore accommodation for the civilian workmen and they had to live in hulks. Since they were compelled to serve there, and because the surrounding marshland and bad drainage gave rise to ague and fever they dubbed the place 'Sheernasty'. In 1823 it was made a complete and independent establishment with its own Resident Commissioner, a title later changed to that of Captain Superintendent. Between 1818 and 1823 a basin had been built with three docks opening into it at a cost of £2.5 million. The Duke of Clarence, later William IV, opened the yard to celebrate the completion of the work, and the largest ship of her day, HMS *Howe*, was floated into No. 1 Dock.

Sheerness had first been suggested as a naval yard as far back as 1572. At that time it was feared that Spanish warships, then lying in Flemish ports, might make a sortie to destroy ships in the Medway. British warships assembled at Sheerness after the Battle of Gravelines in 1588, the port being used as a defence outpost at the time of the Armada.

The second of the home dockyards to be closed was Portland, which was run down by July 1959. This small yard could boast little of the colour and history of Malta or Sheerness, having originally been constructed as a harbour of refuge by the Admiralty between 1847 and 1862. Sheltered by a system of breakwaters facing Weymouth Bay, it provided an extensive enclosed anchorage. Ships of the Home Fleet concentrated there in 1914 and left Portland to proceed to their war stations at the outbreak of the First World War. During the inter-war years part of the Reserve Fleet was kept at Portland, and submarine and anti-submarine training became a feature of the base activities.

But if its dockyard had closed down, Portland was to acquire a new importance when in October 1960 the Admiralty Underwater Weapons Establishment was set up there under a Captain Superintendent. The new centre was formed by the amalgamation of four separate research and development establishments, all concerned with underwater weapons. They were the Underwater Detection Establishment, the Underwater Launching Establishment, the Underwater Countermeasures and Weapons Establishment, and the Torpedo Experimental Establishment.

Chiefly concerned with the development of asdic and underwater fire control equipment, the first-named had originally been set up in Portsmouth in 1919 as part of the Signal School. In 1927 it became a technical department of HMS *Osprey*, ship name of the Portland Naval Base; was moved to Scotland during the war years, and returned to Portland in 1946.

The Underwater Launching Establishment originated as the Torpedo Tube Design Section of the Engineering Department in Portsmouth dockyard. When its buildings were destroyed by bombing in 1940 the department moved to Bournemouth, where it remained until the amalgamation.

The Underwater Countermeasures and Weapons Establishment first started life in 1917 as a Mining School accommodated in three old hulks in Portsmouth harbour. In 1925 it became the Mine Design Department of HMS *Vernon*, the naval torpedo school. Moved to Havant in 1940 as the Admiralty Mining Establishment, it was renamed again in 1951 prior to the new amalgamation.

Oldest of the four was the Torpedo Experimental Establishment, which dated from 1891 when the manufacture of torpedoes for the

Navy was first started at Weymouth. From 1902 to 1936 the torpedo range at Portland was used for experimental purposes, when the experimental department was moved up to Greenock, transferring to Portland in 1959.

Thus the most important aspects of research and development in the underwater weapons field, previously carried out in widely separated parts of the country were concentrated in one establishment, with a resultant saving of manpower, reduction of expenditure and improvement in efficiency and technical co-ordination.

Portland also became the working-up base for newly commissioned ships of the Fleet, a concept which had proved of value during the Second World War when the crews of newly manned escort vessels were trained in anti-submarine warfare at a special base in Scotland. Under the system of Home Service, General Service and Foreign Service commissions which was introduced in 1954, warships required to be re-manned with completely new crews more frequently than in the old days of 'running' commissions. Thus in September 1958 under a Flag Officer Sea Training, special 'shakedown' or settling in courses lasting seven weeks were started to train the crews of newly commissioned ships in operating their equipment and give them experience in dealing with every eventuality likely to be met with in subsequent service at home and abroad. So successful has been the innovation that warships of other NATO and Commonwealth countries and from foreign navies now include the Royal Navy's work-up course at Portland as a final test of sea and war worthiness.

In 1957 the material requirements of the Admiralty were reviewed by a specially appointed committee. As a result of their recommendations, responsibility for the Royal dockyards and maintenance of the Fleet, which had formerly come under the charge of the Controller, were transferred to the Fourth Sea Lord who in the following year assumed the additional title of Vice-Controller.

The rest of the many material departments under the superintendence of the Controller, which had proliferated over the years as the Navy progressed from the 'wooden wall' era into the technological world of the twentieth century, were re-grouped into three, each with its own Director-General. They comprised a Ship Department, made up of five divisions engaged in the design and production of ships, propelling machinery and electrical installations; a Weapons Department, also comprising five divisions responsible for the design and production of weapons and radar and communications equipment; and an Aircraft Department, made up of two divisions and two independent sections, responsible for exercising the Admiralty's material responsibilities for aircraft, their weapons and equipment, including maintenance and repair.

The aims of this reorganisation were to attain a higher measure of co-ordination and control below Board level; to provide effective delegation of authority to the larger departments below Board level; and to relieve the Controller of certain of his responsibilities and thereby enable him to concentrate more on major problems of policy and development.

Historically one of the oldest Admiral Board officials and originally known as the Surveyor of the Navy, the duties of the Controller were at first confined exclusively to shipbuilding. In 1860 management of the Royal dockyards was added and his title changed to that of Controller. Nine years later the office was merged into that of Third Sea Lord with responsibility for the building and repairing of ships, guns and naval stores.

By the end of the First World War the responsibilities of the Third Sea Lord and Controller, exercised through eleven Admiralty departments, covered the extensive field of ships and machinery, armour, guns and mountings, torpedoes, mines, etc., appliances and stores and docking facilities; including their design, manufacture, inspection, repair and maintenance, and any alterations and additions made to them. By 1945 the number of his departments had risen to more than twenty.

The committee responsible for streamlining the Headquarters Organisation also recommended changes in the administration of the Royal dockyards themselves. Adoption of these recommendations resulted not only in transforming the management structure of the yards from a professional to a functional character, but also developed improved techniques for production, planning and financial control.

The traditional structure of three professional departments working directly under the Admiral Superintendent, each with a considerable degree of autonomy, was replaced by the appointment of a general manager under the direction of the Admiral Superintendent with full authority for the administration and organisation of production work. Under his direction and control the existing organisation of professional departments was replaced by a functional and integrated organisation, each headed by a manager, to cover planning, production, yard services, and personnel. The Captain of the Dock-yard became the Naval Assistant and Queen's Harbour Master, his responsibilities being confined to mooring and berthing ships, boom defence matters and marine salvage and the yard servicing craft. The latter were re-titled Port Auxiliary Services.

The Admiral Superintendent continued to be generally responsible for the whole dockyard, ships coming into the yard, and the discipline of Service and civilian personnel, and to ensure that its facilities could meet the work requirements of the Fleet. Since it took time to become fully operative, the new system was introduced in gradual stages with the end result of increased productivity and a quicker turn-round of ships under repair.

Despite the reduction in the size of the Fleet, the task of the Royal dockyards was increasing due to the growing complexity of modern warships and their equipment. An extensive programme of moderni-sation was necessary to keep ships up to date and fit for modern war. Many of the docks and refitting basins were out of date, and some of the principal buildings quite unsuited to modern industry. Portsmouth and Devonport in particular had suffered major war damage due to enemy bombing which had not been made good.

Shortage of labour and restrictions on finance and material resources had delayed rehabilitation of the dockyards. In 1954 a modernisation plan had been started, covering capital plant and equipment, but there was a limit on the extent to which existing dry docks and refitting basins could be modernised due to the layout of the yards. The primary need was for new workshops to handle the latest radio, radar, and gunnery equipments. By 1957 new electrical shops had been completed at Chatham, Portsmouth and Devonport, and new gunnery equipment shops at Devonport and Chatham. The modernisation schemes, which were spread over a number of years, also provided for better premises for apprentice training, better work-ing conditions in the shops, and improved shore amenities for the crews of ships refitting.*

The continuing drive for economy and maximum efficiency brought into being a new concept known as the Fleet Work Study Organisa-tion, which was set up as an Admiralty department in the autumn of 1957. Modelled on the lines of time and motion study in industry, the aims of the organisation were to bring about more effective

---

* In 1970 new plans to modernise the Royal dockyards were announced, the task to be completed by the nineteen-eighties.

'Ton' class coastal minesweeper at speed

SRN 5 Hovercraft in Sarawak

Fast patrol boats

HMS *Bristol* (Type 82) firing a Sea Dart

The Ikara anti-submarine missile

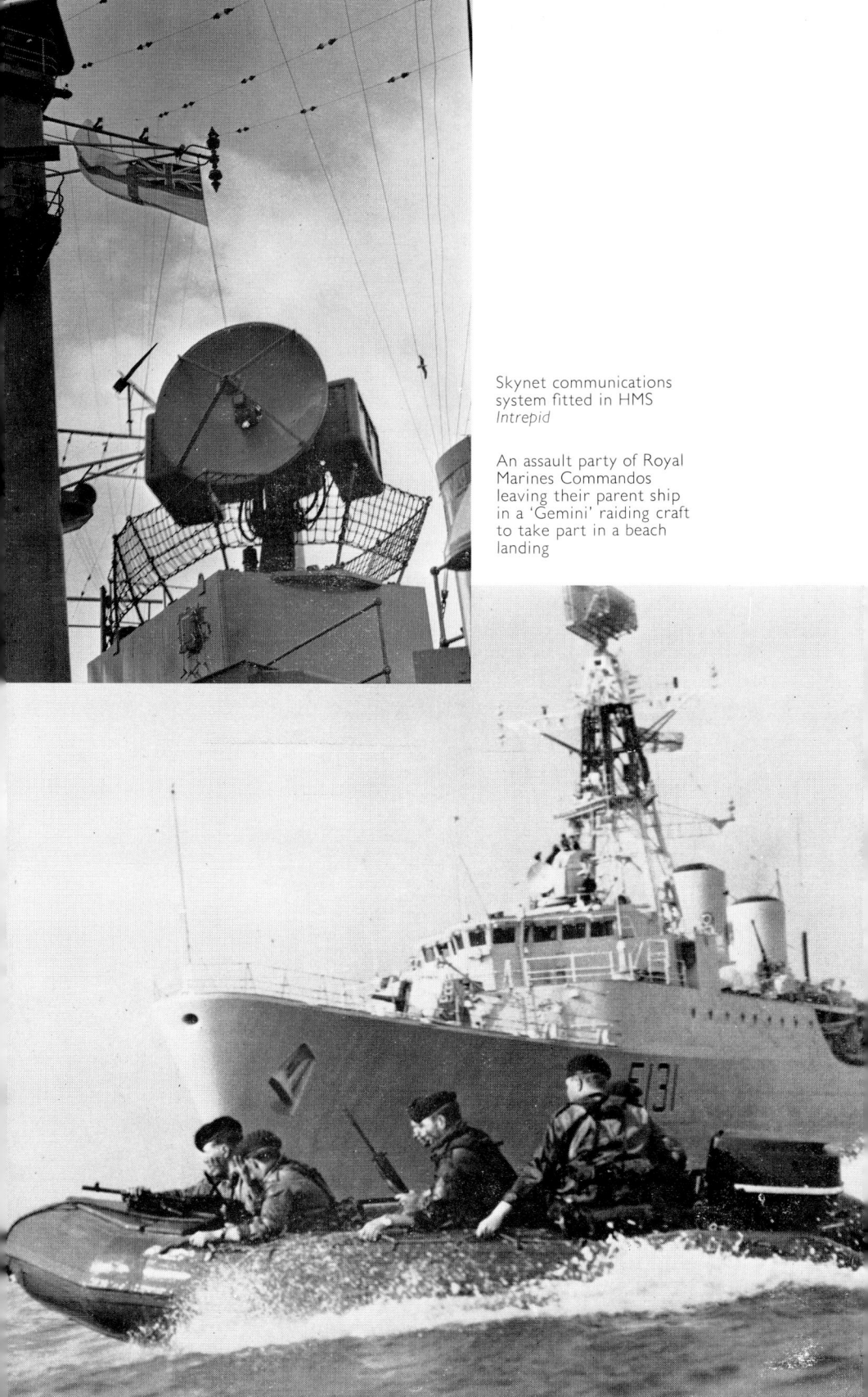

Skynet communications
system fitted in HMS
Intrepid

An assault party of Royal
Marines Commandos
leaving their parent ship
in a 'Gemini' raiding craft
to take part in a beach
landing

Junior rates' mess in a *Leander*. class frigate

Petty Officers' mess on board a guided missile destroyer

spending of public money, increased operational and administrative efficiency, and the gradual elimination of unnecessary 'chores', with essential routine tasks carried out quickly and smoothly by fewer men. An organisation of this kind had in fact existed in embryo in the Admiralty since 1948.

Four officers trained by the RAF in work study techniques were appointed to the staff of the Commander-in-Chief, Portsmouth, in June 1957, charged with the tasks of examining conditions and making suggestions to improve efficiency with available resources. From this small beginning four permanent teams were quickly established, with more under training. By the end of the following year twelve naval work study teams, each consisting of two officers and a senior rating acting as recorder-analyst, were in operation.

Results were speedy and impressive. Thus an engine change refit for a fast patrol boat was reduced from between seventy and ninety hours to twenty hours, cutting the time the vessel was in dockyard hands from two and half weeks to two and a half days. Adoption of the recommendations of a work study team increased the rate of fire of twin 4-inch anti-aircraft guns by more than half again, while reducing the crews needed to serve them by 25 per cent.

By re-planning the layout and making a small number of alterations in routine, a galley servery was made to run with its usual efficiency with twenty-one fewer staff. Routine at a naval mail depot was so re-adjusted that a quarter of the men previously employed produced the same results with an annual saving of £10,000.

Work study in aircraft carriers brought about a reduction in the time needed to rig a crash barrier from seven minutes to two, and an emergency barrier in fifteen minutes instead of the previous ninety. During the process a new and safer type of crash barrier was devised, using nylon ropes instead of steel cables. As a result both the new equipment and the revised rigging procedure became standard in all NATO carriers. A study of air traffic control at naval air stations resulted in a simplification of procedure, increasing the safety margin for pilots and reducing the number of operators from thirty-eight to eighteen. By reorganising the drill for reloading torpedoes in submarines, the time taken was reduced by 30 per cent with two fewer men needed.

In July 1958 a Royal Naval School of Management and Work Study was opened at Portsmouth for the purpose of training teams of officers and senior ratings as work study practitioners. Modelled on the work study institutional department of an international commercial undertaking, it instituted appreciation courses for middle rank officers, and provided lecturers to spread the new gospel ashore and afloat.

Within ten years the school had become a flourishing concern. In addition to maintaining work study teams throughout the Navy's ships and shore establishments, it had trained in work study techniques more than 5,000 Service and civilian students from twenty-six nations, including officers and men from the navies of Australia, New Zealand, Canada, the United States, South Africa and Sweden.

In 1804 Nelson, complaining of a shortage of ships at the siege of Toulon, wrote to the Admiralty:

'I have but five ships and keep them out absolutely by good management.'

This quotation, printed and suitably framed, was hung in the entrance hall of the Work Study School at its opening, proving that, like so many 'modern' ideas, work study is not really new at all!

Another innovation, introduced with the object of promoting a better understanding of Lower Deck problems, was the appointment to the Mediterranean Fleet in May 1958 of a chief petty officer as 'Fleet Personnel Rating' to act as a link between naval ratings and the Admiralty. His task was to visit individual ships on the station to explain Admiralty policy to their crews, and submit to the Commander-in-Chief Lower Deck views on Service conditions, accommodation and clothing. These in turn were passed on to the Admiralty.

Before the war the only channel of communication between Lower Deck and Admiralty through which representations about grievances and other matters affecting Service conditions could be officially made had been periodical 'Welfare Conferences'. First started in 1923, these were irregularly held meetings of rating representatives from ships and establishments at the three home ports. But they were so hedged about with restrictions as to the subjects for discussion that they caused more discontent than they were designed to cure. In 1935 the conferences were replaced by the institution of periodic, but equally unsatisfactory from the Lower Deck point of view, Admiralty reviews of Service conditions. These lapsed at the outbreak of the Second World War.

So successful was the 1958 experiment that a two-man body, consisting of an officer and a senior rating, was subsequently set up to visit all ships and commands. Known today as the 'Second Sea Lord's Personnel Liaison Team', the two appointees carry out regular tours of ships and establishments at home and abroad. The team takes about two years to cover its widely extended 'parish', lecturing on personnel subjects and noting views expressed and constructive criticism. At the end of each tour a report on the subjects discussed is made to the Second Sea Lord—who is the Chief of Naval Personnel—and appropriate Ministry of Defence departments for subsequent consideration in detail at the highest level. Although recommended changes may take time to put into effect, the concept provides an important link between the Admiralty Board (now known as 'the Management') and the Fleet, and a useful safety valve for the airing of grievances.

Exemplifying the working of this new channel of communication between Whitehall and Lower Deck was the introduction at their own request in August 1958 of new titles for the Navy's communications ratings.

Since the introduction of wireless telegraphy into the Fleet early in the twentieth century, the communications branch had consisted of two distinct specialisations: visual signalling and wireless. Now in order more clearly to reflect the nature of their respective duties and the common aspects of their training, signalmen were to be designated 'Tactical Communication Operators', and the telegraphists 'Radio Communication Operators'. While a chief yeoman of signals thus became a 'Chief Communications Yeoman', retaining the traditional title of 'Yeoman', the chief petty officer telegraphist became a 'Chief Radio Communication Supervisor', the term 'supervisor' denoting charge of a watch and thus bringing the Navy's higher grade radiomen into line with civilian-manned communication centres.

Within five years, however, these titles were altered again. The new change was brought about by the gradual reduction in the Fleet's use of flag signalling and the abolition of semaphore in the Navy except for emergency use, and the increasing range of advanced types of technical communications equipment which highlighted the need for a single branch to handle the Navy's communication systems.

From 1st January 1963, therefore, all communications ratings became 'Radio Operators', specialising in one or other of the three divisions of the re-structured branch—Tactical (T), General Radio (G), or Electronic Warfare (W). Of the old titles, that of Communications Yeoman and Chief Communications Yeoman were retained, these ratings continuing to wear the traditional crossed flags badge. All other ratings of the branch wore the wings and flash of the former radio specialist.

Two other branches whose rating titles had earlier been changed were the engineering and electrical specialisations. Thus in 1955 the old name of Stoker finally disappeared from the Navy, being replaced by that of Engineering Mechanic. Similarly, electrical ratings became Electrical Mechanics, those specialising in radar and radio including the word 'Radio' in their title. Subsequently as the Navy's technical equipment became more advanced and complex the two branches amalgamated to cover marine engineering, air engineering, and electrical engineering in all its aspects.

Following the decision to abolish National Service by the end of 1962 and rely thereafter on regular forces, the Government set up a committee under the chairmanship of Sir James Grigg, a former Secretary for War, to examine the factors bearing on the willingness of men and women to serve in the armed forces, and to make recommendations.

The committee's terms of reference covered pay, pensions, discipline and training, equipment, uniform, accommodation, food, public relations, recruiting organisations, promotion, the problems of married men, the education of children, the frequency of posting, and re-settlement in civilian life after service.

Factors bearing on recruitment were the coming of the Welfare State which intensified the competition faced by the Services from civilian life; the deprivation of manpower caused by the loss of Britain's colonial territories; and the impression that with the advent of push-button warfare conventional forces were no longer needed.

Although their enquiries showed that pay was not the major issue, the first of the committee's conclusions and recommendations—the majority of which were accepted by the Government—was that there should be an automatic biennial review of Service pay, to take into account movements in civilian earnings over a range of occupations to be determined by agreement between the Treasury and the Service departments. Pensions should also be included, and the first review carried out in time to bring new rates into force by 1st April 1960.

Other financial recommendations affecting the Navy, whose general conditions of service came in for less criticism than those of the Army and Air Force, concerned such forms of remuneration as disturbance allowances for officers and ratings going into Service and private accommodation; education allowances for children boarded out either at schools or with friends and relatives; and a general simplification of the code of allowances.

As regards pensions, the committee considered that those for ratings should be increased; and that while the existing level of officers' pensions did not constitute a deterrent to recruitment, their career structure should be re-designed to allow of increments after thirty years' service. Thus officers should be given the option of retirement before the age of 40 when their resettlement problems would be least, or engagement to age 60 when the latter would not exist.

This suggestion was not, however, accepted in its entirety, but in 1960 the career structure for naval officers was amended to assure a career to at least the age of 50 for all General List officers. The retirement age of Post List officers continued to be somewhat earlier since they were promoted at a younger age. For General List officers who entered the Navy before 1st May 1957, the retiring age of lieutenant-commanders and commanders would gradually be raised towards the higher limits included in the new career structure.

In general, the Government's decisions on the Grigg Committee's recommendations also applied to the WRNS. Women's pension rates, both for officers and ratings, were raised to 85 per cent of male rates, as also were gratuities and bounties for the Women's Services. One recommendation which did not, however, receive approval was that the engagement structure for women should be altered to allow them to leave at six months' notice after completing their initial engagement. The Government considered that this would have an adverse effect on morale and manpower planning. Nevertheless, the principle was accepted that the engagement structure for women should be related to the needs of the Women's Services and not based too closely on that for men. The greatest importance was attached to the role of the Women's Services in peace and war, and opportunities for women to serve overseas would be increased.

Recognising that family separation was one of the main deterrents to naval recruiting and a contributory factor to the unwillingness of many skilled senior ratings to re-engage, the Admiralty had decided in 1946 to provide married quarters at remote establishments and air stations in the United Kingdom and at the main naval bases abroad. But the urgent post-war need for economy and a general shortage of labour and materials delayed implementation of the programme. By 1953, however, some 1,800 houses had been built at home and abroad. Of this total 1,542 had been built in the United Kingdom, 252 for officers' families, and 1,290 for the families of ratings.

The second phase of this building programme extended naval housing facilities to cater mainly for men in the home ports of Portsmouth, Plymouth and Chatham and at Lee-on-Solent, headquarters of the Home Air Command. Until it was completed, furnished houses and self-contained flats were hired, this accommodation being relinquished as the new houses were built.

Those intended to benefit by the extension of the housing programme and hiring schemes were married men serving in shore establishments at the home ports, ships of the Reserve Fleet, local squadrons based at home ports, and ships of the Home Fleet; accommodation for the latter being at the ports on which their ships were based. To qualify for married quarters during the initial stages of the scheme officers had to be at least 25 years of age and ratings 21, with the proviso that there must be an expectation of occupying the quarters for at least six months. No family could occupy the same accommodation for more than three years.

By July 1955 the first batch of quarters under the Home Ports scheme had been completed at Portsmouth. Constructed on a pleasant site overlooking Portchester Creek, they comprised 130 three-bedroomed houses and 60 two-bedroomed flats. Five months later a block of 15 flats and 5 houses for officers was opened at Portsmouth. By 1959 a total of 1,250 houses had been completed.

Two years after completion of the first part of the Portsmouth scheme, a large naval housing estate was opened on a 57-acre site near Chatham. It provided 230 semi-detached three-bedroomed houses, and a similar number of two-bedroomed flats. Rents charged were 85p weekly for the houses, and 77½p for the flats. The Admiralty aim was ultimately to complete 4,500 additional married quarters by the end of 1960. In fact, by 1970 more than 9,000 naval families were housed in Service accommodation, none of which existed at the end of the war.

Besides attractive homes to live in, naval families wherever possible have also been provided with a wide range of recreational facilities and amenities. NAAFI shops, private businesses, community centres, clubs, and children's amenities have been established in the more major projects. As well as continuing the married quarters schemes, the Admiralty instituted a system of providing interest-free loans by which ratings could put down deposits on their own homes, and take advantage of private lettings through rent-assisted allowances.

CHAPTER EIGHT

The Pattern Emerges

The Suez operation highlighted the need for a new strategic concept, particularly in view of the progressive reduction of Britain's overseas naval bases as newly self-governing Commonwealth nations assumed responsibility for their own defence: in brief, the formation of a mobile naval task force capable of being speedily deployed to deal with limited, or 'brush fire' wars.

From this stemmed the idea of a 'Commando ship' carrying a highly mobile amphibious force on board which could be put ashore by helicopter as advance troops, or deal with localised outbreaks of trouble itself. In 1958 it was decided to put this concept into effect, and on completion of her second commission in the spring of the following year the 23,000-ton light fleet carrier *Bulwark* of the *Centaur* class was ordered to be taken in hand for conversion.

The notion of a mobile naval task force, however, was by no means new; the Americans already had something similar. But in the Royal Navy it went back even farther, for in 1909 when there was unrest in the West Indies, the old second-class cruiser *Indefatigable* was renamed *Melpomone* and commissioned for special service in the area. Instead of carrying the normal authorised complement of twenty-seven Marines, she embarked five and a half times that number, commanded by a major with a captain and two subalterns. The Navy provided only the ship's captain, first lieutenant, gunnery officer and navigator, steaming and skeleton upper deck crews. All the Royal Marine officers were in possession of watchkeeping certificates, and the bulk of the everyday work of the ship was performed by their men. Once arrived at a trouble spot the Marines were landed to restore order ashore.

Few basic changes were required to prepare the *Bulwark* for her new role other than removal of the arrester wires and catapults fitted for her fixed wing capability, and the provision of built-in gantries to carry a number of assault landing craft. The necessary alterations were mostly internal, concerning the Commando's living quarters and office space, the stowage of transport, storerooms and workshops. The ship retained her guns, radar and radio equipment and her capability for directing fighter aircraft. She was also fitted with a comprehensive air-conditioning system throughout to enable her to operate in the most exacting Arctic and tropical climates. Initially she was to be based east of Suez.

The troop embarked was No. 42 Royal Marine Commando, numbering some 600 officers and men with their guns and vehicles, which had been undergoing special training in the United Kingdom. The unit had previously served in the Far East as part of 3 Commando Brigade. In order to maintain military efficiency and fitness the Commando was to be based ashore in Singapore, embarking in the carrier for exercises and operations. The alterations which had been made to the ship rendered her capable of embarking a second Commando, or an Army unit of equivalent size, for short periods and of landing them ashore for operations.

The helicopter complement was provided by a naval air squadron equipped with sixteen Westland Whirlwind helicopters, plus another five in reserve. Eventually the *Bulwark* was to take up to twenty of the larger gas-turbined Wessex helicopters when they superseded the Whirlwinds. These machines were not only for use by the Commandos during initial landings, but a proportion of them were intended to operate tactically in the field. Thus they would provide the surprise, mobility and flexibility to enable the Commandos to be really effective, especially in open warfare or light operations.

Altogether more powerful and appreciably faster than the old light fleet carriers, and able to maintain a steady 28 knots, the *Bulwark*'s primary role was to be in the Cold War, extinguishing the 'brush fire' before it could spread. As a Commando ship she might well operate alone without fleet or land support in limited wars of all kinds. By virtue of the considerable variety of stores and equipment carried, she was also particularly well suited for providing speedy assistance in cases of civil disaster, such as earthquake, typhoon and flood.

Her conversion was completed by the spring of 1960, and with helicopters and Commando embarked, the *Bulwark* sailed for the Mediterranean for work-up and subsequently for Singapore. Twelve months later her sister ship *Albion* was similarly converted, and began her new task in the summer of 1962. By then the capabilities of the *Bulwark* had been put to practical test.

42 Commando was replaced at home by re-forming No. 41 Commando. No increase in Royal Marine strength was involved, the

re-formation being made possible by substantial reductions in the numbers of Marines serving afloat and elsewhere.

Originally constituted in 1942, No. 41 Commando had fought in Sicily, at Salerno, the Normandy landings, at Walcheren, the river Maas and Western Germany. It was disbanded in 1946 as part of the post-war reorganisation. In 1950 the unit was re-formed as No. 41 (Independent) Commando to take part in the Korean War, and disbanded again in 1952.

In April 1961 the headquarters of 3 Commando Brigade were moved from Malta to Singapore. Five months later a fifth Marine Commando, No. 43, came into being.

Meanwhile the first of the new class of general-purpose frigates earlier foreshadowed had been launched. Named *Ashanti* after the outstanding Second World War fleet destroyer of the same name, she was speedily followed by six more, all bearing 'tribal' names, such as *Eskimo*, *Nubian*, *Tartar* and *Mohawk*.

Designated Type 81, they represented a reversal of former Admiralty policy which had considered that to embrace all frigate desiderata in a single hull would result in too large a vessel. Hence the appearance of the earlier specialised anti-submarine, anti-aircraft and aircraft-direction types. But as the Navy contracted in size, the situation had to be envisaged when a fully balanced escort force could not always be assembled for every contingency. The decision was then made to return to the concept of building a type of ship fully competent to fulfil equally well all the duties of an escort vessel.

The new Tribals had an overall length of 360 feet, a beam of 42 feet and a standard displacement of 2,500 tons. Their armament included two 4.5-inch guns in single mountings, two Bofors 40-mm anti-aircraft guns, and a triple-barrelled Limbo anti-submarine mortar. Equipped with a small flight deck aft, they were the first warships designed from the start to carry a helicopter. In due course each was provided with a gas-turbine powered Westland Wasp anti-submarine helicopter able to fire homing torpedoes and depth charges. Subsequently the Bofors guns were replaced by a newly developed, close-range, ship-to-air guided missile known as the 'Seacat'. This was a small but highly manoeuvrable weapon powered by a solid fuel motor with a rapid rate of fire.

Capable of being operated completely by remote control, propulsion machinery was of a novel design, incorporating a gas turbine for the first time in larger surface warships. Thus a steam turbine provided the power for normal cruising and manoeuvring, while a gas turbine coupled to the same propeller shaft provided boost power at high speeds. Because gas turbines can develop full power from cold within a few minutes, ships so fitted can get under way quickly in emergency without having to wait to raise steam. These combined steam and gas turbine installations were known by the initials COSAG.

The prefabricated hulls of the new Tribals were of all-welded steel, developed from the earlier frigate designs and specially treated to resist corrosion during service. Denny Brown stabilisers were fitted to reduce rolling, and the hull shape so designed to allow high speeds to be maintained in rough seas.

Living accommodation for their complements of 13 officers and 240 men, including a detachment of 21 Royal Marines, was of the latest high standard; with bunks for all, fluorescent internal lighting, and electric galleys providing cafeteria style meals eaten in a roomy dining hall. All living spaces, offices and manned compartments were air-conditioned, as was the totally enclosed spacious bridge.

With their two funnels, 'bedstead' air warning radar and helicopter hangar, the ships' outlines were by no means as graceful as were those of their illustrious predecessors. But, designed for the many different roles visualised for the modern frigate, they undoubtedly packed more punch.

At roughly the same time, although separately developed from the Tribals, came the first of another type of general purpose frigates which proved the most successful yet to come off the drawing board. Designated the *Leander* class after the name ship of the type, twenty-six of them were built, the last of the class being launched as recently as 1971. Using the same hull form, they were evolved from the *Whitby* and *Rothesay* classes of anti-submarine frigates, which were noted for their manoeuvrability, performance at high speed, and seakeeping qualities.

Designed to hunt down and destroy high speed submarines in all weathers, and to engage ships, aircraft and shore targets, the *Leanders*, which are all now in operational service, include every form of weapon and detection device that can be packed into ships of their size.

With a standard displacement of 2,200 tons, they have a length of 370 feet and a beam of 41 feet. Their main armament includes two 4.5-inch guns in a twin mounting, directed by a fully automatic radar fire control and gun-direction system; two 40-mm anti-aircraft guns in single close-range mountings were originally fitted, but these were later replaced by a Seacat ship-to-air launcher with its own director; and a triple-barrelled anti-submarine mortar aft. Like the Tribals, they also carry a Westland Wasp helicopter, operated from a hangar and platform sited abaft the mainmast. Centralised control of the weapons systems and other equipment is exercised from an operations room below decks.

The main propelling machinery of the class consists of two controlled superheat boilers and two sets of steam turbines driving twin screws through double reduction gearing to give a high service speed. Stabilisers with non-retractable fins are fitted.

Living accommodation includes bunk sleeping throughout for the complement of 17 officers and 245 ratings, with the now customary electric galleys, separate dining halls and cafeteria messing. For service in tropical climates all essential working spaces and living compartments are air-conditioned.

Backed up by the earlier classes of anti-submarine and aircraft-direction frigates, the *Leanders* have today become the workhorse of the modern Fleet in much the same way as the destroyers of former years. Now a much larger and more powerful type of 'destroyer' was to make its appearance.

First foreshadowed in the 1956 Estimates, but delayed to await the results of the tests of the Seaslug guided weapon being carried out in the trials ship *Girdle Ness*, the first of the four guided missile vessels ordered was laid down in the Birkenhead yard of Messrs Cammell Laird in March 1959. Named *Devonshire*, she was launched by Princess Alexandra fifteen months later. Although designated a 'destroyer', she was in fact the first of the Navy's light cruiser type ships to be designed for sea warfare in the atomic age.

Still in service with her later sisters, she can be described in the present tense. With a standard displacement of 5,000 tons, she has a length of 520 feet and a beam of 54 feet. Streamlined to give a low uncomplicated silhouette, she has two stumpy funnels, two small lattice masts, and upper deck structures enclosed as far as possible to enable the crew to remain under cover while operating in an area contaminated by nuclear 'fall-out'. There are no portholes, all living and working spaces being fully air-conditioned.

She is armed with four radar-controlled, fully automatic 4.5-inch guns in twin turrets forward, one Seaslug guided weapon system mounted on the quarterdeck, and two quadruple Seacat launchers sited on either side of the after funnel. For anti-submarine work she is fitted with the latest underwater detection equipment. Above the quarter-deck is a helicopter platform from which to operate a Westland Wessex helicopter, the first of this type of aircraft to be fitted as a complete hunter-killer with a homing torpedo and dipping asdic, or sonar.

Equipped with the latest air and surface warning radars, the *Devonshire* and the rest of her class are provided with an operations room forming part of an enclosed citadel in the bowels of the ship and furnished with the most sophisticated electronic plotting facilities. From this nerve centre the captain can exercise tactical control without going up on to the bridge, for easy access to which an electric lift is fitted.

As with the Tribal class frigates, the *Devonshire*'s propulsion machinery includes gas turbines to provide additional boost and enable her to get under way speedily in an emergency. Developing 60,000 shp, it consists of two sets of geared steam turbines for normal cruising, with four gas turbines geared to the same shafts. Equipped with a large degree of remote and automatic control, her turbines can be accelerated to a maximum speed of 32.5 knots. Stabilisers are fitted to provide a steady platform for weapon firing, and for operating the helicopter in adverse weather conditions.

The space complications created by the new armament equipment and propelling machinery have in no way reduced the comfort of the ship's company of 36 officers and 450 ratings. The messdecks are fitted with bunks so positioned as to allow a maximum recreation space, and the provision of card and writing tables, games cupboards, and sockets for personal electrical equipment. Other domestic features include a twenty-four-hour laundry, education facilities, film shows, a NAAFI 'shop' selling luxuries and other needs and, with the advent of television afloat, a TV studio to produce internal programmes and relay external programmes to the messdecks. Self-service meals are prepared in all-electric galleys from a wide and varied menu, to be consumed in air-conditioned dining halls.

The principal role of these guided missile destroyers is to provide long-range air defence from the heart of a task force and augment its anti-submarine capability. As part of a smaller task unit they can bombard in support of ground forces and attack other light surface craft with gunfire. Lastly they are admirably suited to carry out police duties in peacetime in any part of the world.

The *Devonshire* commissioned in November 1962, and her three immediate sister ships, *Hampshire, Kent* and *London*—also laid down in 1959—followed her into service in 1963. Three years later two more guided missile ships, *Fife* and *Glamorgan*, were commissioned, and early in the nineteen-seventies the total number of these vessels was brought up to eight by the building of the *Antrim* and *Norfolk*, which incorporate further technical improvements.

The year 1959 also saw the addition to the seagoing Fleet of the fourth and last of the *Hermes* class of light fleet carriers, thus bringing the operational carrier fleet up to six. The seventh new carrier to be built since the war, she was HMS *Hermes* herself, name ship of the class.

Built and engined by Vickers Armstrongs, she had been launched in 1953 but work on her delayed so that she could be fitted with all the latest aids to naval flying then being developed. Thus the ship had to be re-designed to incorporate the angled deck, steam catapults, mirror deck landing aid, and the Type 984 Comprehensive System Display radar similar to that installed in the modernised *Victorious*, of which she represented a more up-to-date version.

For the requirements of nuclear warfare she was fitted with a remote control system for the engine and boiler rooms to enable the ship to operate without any personnel being present in these compartments, and pre-wetting equipment for exposed decks. Among other innovations was a liquid oxygen plant for supplying high altitude flyers. Living accommodation for her complement of 2,100 officers and men was of the high standard now current in all new construction warships.

With a displacement of 27,800 tons, her overall length was 744 feet and beam 153 feet. She was armed with ten 40-mm anti-aircraft guns in twin mountings, all radar-controlled. Later these were removed and replaced by Seacat missile systems. Her aircraft complement included strike and all-weather fighters, anti-submarine helicopters, and a flight of Gannet AEW (Airborne Early Warning) aircraft.

Uncertainty over the development of long-range guided missiles had affected the future of naval aviation and delayed the production of new aircraft for the Fleet. But in the late nineteen-fifties the decision was taken that, at least for some years to come, shore-based and carrier-borne aircraft would still be needed.

The *Hermes*, therefore, included in her squadrons two new transonic types of naval aircraft which were just coming into operational service. To supplant the Sea Venom was the 600-mph De Havilland Sea Vixen. Formerly known by its type number of DH.110, this was a two-seater, twin-boom night and all-weather fighter. Powered by

two Rolls-Royce Avon turbojet engines and having supersonic capabilities in the dive, the machine possessed exceptional powers of
manoeuvre at very high speeds. The Sea Vixen was armed with four
Firestreak air-to-air missiles, and a battery of 2-inch rockets for use
against both air and ground targets. The Firestreak was a guided
weapon working on the principle of attraction by infra-red rays
emitted from an aircraft, and also fitted with a homing device
immune from jamming.

Powered like the Sea Vixen with two Rolls-Royce Avons and
intended to succeed the Sea Hawk, was the Vickers Supermarine
Scimitar. A single-seat, swept-wing strike fighter with a maximum
speed of over 700 mph at 10,000 feet, the Scimitar was at first armed
with four 30-mm Aden guns, each firing 100 rounds per second, and
also possessed nuclear capability. Later the guns were replaced by the
American Sidewinder air-to-air weapon.

But although at that time the Scimitar was the fastest aircraft
in service in Britain, it did not have a very long life, for another new
strike aircraft was already undergoing intensive trials. This was the
two-seat, all-weather Blackburn Buccaneer. The Mark I version was
powered by two De Havilland Gyron Junior engines, but the Mark II
was given Rolls-Royce RB.169 Spey jet engines. The Buccaneer was
designed for high speed, very low altitude, long-range strikes. Capable
of penetrating deep into enemy territory with little risk of being
intercepted by fighters or missiles, its weapons system enables precision
attacks to be carried out below the detection height of hostile radars,
and automatic release of conventional or nuclear weapons. Considered to be perfection plus, the machine is still in service today.

An event of far greater importance to the Navy than the appearance of its new surface ships and aircraft was the launch, on
Trafalgar Day 1960, by Her Majesty the Queen of Britain's first
nuclear submarine, *Dreadnought.*

Under grey skies and before a crowd of 12,000 assembled in
Vickers Armstrong's yard at Barrow-in-Furness, the Queen pulled
the handle of a ship's telegraph to release a bottle of Empire wine
which shattered against the vessel's curiously bulbous bow. With
Her Majesty on the launching platform in addition to Prince Philip,
Lord Carrington, the First Lord of the Admiralty, and Earl Mountbatten, Chief of the Defence Staff, was Vice-Admiral Hyman
Rickover, US Navy, the 'father' of nuclear-propelled submarines. His
invitation to attend this historic ceremony was in recognition of the

help received from the United States in the provision of the *Dreadnought*'s power plant and machinery.

Since she, too, forms a unit of our present fleet her dimensions and details can also be described in the present tense.

With a length of 266 feet, a beam of 32 feet, and a surface displacement of 3,500 tons—1,000 more submerged—the hull of the vessel is of all-British design both as regard structural strength and hydrodynamic features, although based on the pioneering work of the US Navy. Chiefly intended to be a hunter-killer of other submarines, the whale-shaped hull and tapering stern of the *Dreadnought* have been designed to enable her to achieve high underwater speeds.

Another innovation to the eye of the conventional submariner is her outsize 'sail', or conning tower, rising to some 30 feet from the waterline, beneath which is the control room from whence various periscopes and other extensions of her control equipment can be raised. The control room itself resembles the flight deck of a jet airliner, displaying a complicated array of dials, valves and switches, with powered control columns set before aircraft-type seats from which operators work her rudders and hydroplanes. For this submersible and her sister vessels are able to dive and bank like an aircraft under water, and even perform aquabatics.

The *Dreadnought*'s propulsion machinery consists of a pressurised-water type reactor driving a single shaft through steam turbines. Almost every electrical and mechanical part is duplicated so as to minimise the inconvenience of breakdowns, as also is every control feature of the power plant and the boat itself. The purpose of these innovations is to ensure a high standard of reliability. Combined with the necessity to refuel only at very long intervals, the submarine can undertake patrols of extended endurance at continuous high underwater speeds.

For navigation she has an automatic pilot and, employing a device called 'SINS' (Ship's Inertial Navigation System) can find her way about the depths of the oceans with unerring accuracy. Using this electronic 'magic eye' there is no need for her to surface periodically to obtain a 'fix' of her position by visual observation. But she also carries a periscope sextant system so that her position can be fixed by astronomical methods at persicope depth. Inverted fathometers and other instruments enable her to measure her depth so accurately that when necessary she can operate freely beneath the Polar ice.

Her main armament consists of a large outfit of 21-inch acoustic homing torpedoes of greater accuracy and explosive power than any

used in the Second World War, master-minded by the most sophisticated fire-control equipment. The *Dreadnought* is also fitted with
long-range sonar capable of locating enemy vessels on or below the
surface.

The accommodation for her complement of eleven officers and
seventy-seven ratings is of a standard formerly undreamed of in
submarines. Separate mess spaces are provided for senior and junior
ratings, sited on either side of a large galley equipped for serving
meals on the cafeteria system. Galley fittings include pressure cookers,
potato peeler, infra-red grill, breadmaking machinery, and dishwasher,
worked by atomic power. A water distilling plant provides unlimited
fresh water for shower baths and the fully equipped laundry.

The ship's interior comprises three deck levels; the top deck housing
the wardroom and officers' quarters alongside the control room, and
on the deck below the ship's company messes. There are bunks for
all, and the living quarters are tastefully decorated. Recreational
facilities include cinema equipment, an extensive library, and tape
recordings to offset the monotony of prolonged underwater voyages.

Special air-conditioning plant and air purification equipment
enables the *Dreadnought* to stay below the surface for well over two
months. She can 'breathe' through electrolytic 'gills' extracting oxygen
from seawater, thus obviating the need for a 'snort' tube which could
give away her position. There is no danger from radiation, exhaustive
tests having shown that radiation levels in nuclear submarines amount
to less than those experienced from the sun's cosmic rays. Periodical
monitoring is, however, carried out by the medical staff.

The *Dreadnought* commissioned for operational service in April
1963. Her commissioning was followed nine months later by the
launch of a second nuclear-powered submarine. Larger than the
Dreadnought and of a greater tonnage, she was named *Valiant* and
was the first all-British built nuclear submarine. Later came the
Warspite, Churchill, Conqueror and *Courageous* and, more recently
Swiftsure, Sovereign and *Superb*. The *Dreadnought* had cost just
under £20 million to build; her sisters were to cost even more.

In listing the technical equipment of the *Dreadnought,* mention
has been made of the Ship's Inertial Navigation System. Since from
a naval point of view this device constitutes one of the most significant
advances made in post-war maritime electronics, it is worth describing
in some detail. For inertial navigation is not only essential for missile-
carrying submarines, but for surface ships as well in view of its con-

tribution to survival at sea in time of war in this missile age. As well as providing positional accuracy impossible of interference by an enemy, it is also a first-class stabilisation reference for most modern weapon systems.

In order to pinpoint their position at sea navigators of the past had to rely on the visual observation of heavenly bodies. But when a 'fix', or observed position, could not be obtained, the prime means of maintaining the ship's track was by log and compass. To transform a position so achieved into a geographical position required allowances to be made for current, wind and tide. As these could only be estimated, positional errors were bound to occur, and the longer the time intervals between fixes the greater the accrued errors became.

By harnessing the principles of inertia, 'SINS' provides the seaman with a continuous and up-to-date ship's track over the surface of the earth so that in between fixes he may proceed with safety. And if a continuous up-to-date geographical position is provided at all times, then by comparison of these positions a read-out of course and speed made good can be obtained. 'SINS' supplies this.

The heart of the equipment comprises a stable platform and an electronic computer. The platform carries a sensitive two-axis accelerometer and three high-precision, single-axis integrating gyroscopes mounted with their sensitive axes mutually at right angles. The platform is thus always maintained in a true north-south direction and truly horizontal to the earth's surface, irrespective of the ship's motion, so that a line vertical to the horizontal plane of the platform is a true vertical to the centre of the earth. One of the stabilising gyros has its axis parallel to that of the earth, and angles between the true vertical and this meridian gyro axis automatically gives the angle of latitude.

The accelerometer, which is in effect a sensitive pendulum mounted on the platform in such a way that it can be rotated relative to the ship, provides electrical signals proportional to accelerations in two directions at right angles : viz., fore and aft, and athwartships. It is in fact a cylinder mounted horizontally and orientated either north-south or east-west, containing a weight which is free to move along its length. The weight is retained in the mid position by springs, unless accelerative or decelerative force is applied, when it moves to one side or other of the mid position. This movement is detected electrically and a signal transmitted to the computer, integrated with time, and the actual north-south or east-west movement over the earth's surface computed.

In 'SINS' it is desired to know the position of the ship on the surface of the earth, and therefore the equipment is corrected to compensate for the rotation of the earth as well as the motions of the ship in yaw, pitch and roll. To achieve this it is necessary to establish a true vertical from which all reference is made. The accelerometer and gyros are inter-connected through electrical servo circuits so that equilibrium will only be established when the axes of the platform are parallel to the axis of the earth, thus giving a true vertical. Measurement of the angle between the true vertical and the axis parallel to the earth's axis gives the latitude of the equipment.

Having established 'steady state' conditions, any movement of the ship over the earth's surface will disturb the accelerometer, and by measuring the output in the north-south plane and integrating, the velocity can be determined. This in turn can be used to rotate the pendulum support to restore the original position, thus continuously measuring the latitude angle. Similarly, a movement in the east-west plane will mean that the east-west velocity can be measured by integrating the east-west acceleration output and, knowing latitude, this can be connected to the rate of change of longitude. The combined north-south and east-west velocities give speed over the ground, and the total distance run is obtained as a by-product.

Although the principles of inertia have long been known, their application to the science of navigation was first put to practical use in the United States with the development of atomic power for submarines. In April 1958 the first experimental inertial navigation system, which had been produced for the US Air Force, was borrowed by the Navy and installed in the nuclear submarine *Nautilus* for her epoch-making voyage under the North Pole.

Having taken his last fix on the Pacific side of the Arctic Ocean on the morning of 1st August that year, the navigator of the submarine took the second when she surfaced in the Greenland Sea after passing beneath the Pole, in the morning of 5th August. The position by 'SINS' and the estimated position computed from gyro compass and log were both within ten miles of the fix. Since then 'SINS' has been fully developed in Britain, and fitted in aircraft carriers and missile ships as well as nuclear submarines.

Prior to the conversion of the *Bulwark* and *Albion* to the role of Commando ships, Royal Marine Commandos and their equipment were usually conveyed to the operational area in which they were required by the small force of ships which comprised the Amphibious Warfare Squadron.

Formed in 1951 as the result of experience gained during the war, the squadron consisted of the River class frigate *Meon* as directing vessel, three tank landing ships of 5,000 tons each, three tank landing craft able to beach in shallow water, and a number of assault landing craft of post-war design and construction.

The *Meon* carried the senior officer of the force, and was equipped as a headquarters ship with communications facilities for controlling a brigade group and its air and surface gunfire support. The personnel of the ships were drawn from the Navy in the usual way and possessed no particular specialist qualifications. The squadron could transport a complete army battalion or a Marine Commando and its heavy equipment, and when not so employed came under the aegis of the Joint Services Amphibious Warfare Centre.

In pursuance of the policy of increasing the Navy's amphibious capability and independence of overseas bases, it was decided to replace this small and ageing squadron with an entirely new type of assault ship. Designs were drawn up, and early in 1961 an order was placed with Messrs Harland and Wolff of Belfast for a vessel of between 10,000 and 15,000 tons displacement. She was laid down in the following July and launched in December 1963.

Named *Fearless*, the vessel is virtually a streamlined floating dock, able to carry four large landing craft in a special compartment aft. By taking in ballast to lower the ship in the water, the pre-loaded vessels can simply be floated out. In addition, four personnel-carrying landing craft are stowed on special davits. The ship's interior comprises a three-storey stowage space for vehicles, surrounded by accommodation for the ship's company and military personnel, and surmounted by a flight deck. From the latter all types of helicopters of any of the three Services, including the largest troop-carrying machines, can be operated by day or night.

The *Fearless* was designed to carry heavy tanks and equipment, including self-propelled guns, and troops of an infantry battalion or Royal Marine Commandos. But perhaps the most important aspect of her role is as headquarters ship from which the commanders of amphibious operations can exercise overall control of the forces engaged. Thus accommodation is provided in the main superstructure of the vessel for the Naval Amphibious Group Commander and the Military Force Commander and their staffs. From a Combined Services operations room—the nerve centre during any landings—

close liaison can be maintained with the higher command in London or elsewhere, and with supporting ships, aircraft, army units, and all the landing craft concerned in the operation.

When completed, the displacement of the new assault ship amounted to some 12,000 tons. Overall length is 520 feet and beam 80 feet, and her main machinery consists of steam turbines in two self-contained units, each driving one shaft to give a speed in excess of 20 knots. Adding to the peculiarity of her outline is that her two funnels are sited *en echelon.*

She carries a service complement of 42 officers, including Royal Marines and Army officers, and 410 ratings. In addition, 80 Royal Marines and 40 soldiers also form part of the ship's company. The latter are drawn from the Royal Engineers, Royal Corps of Transport, Royal Electrical and Mechanical Engineers, Royal Army Pay Corps, and the Army Catering Corps. Armament consists of four Seacat missile systems and two 40-mm Bofors guns.

Costing some £11 million, the *Fearless* commissioned for service in November 1965. She was followed sixteen months later by a sister ship, built by John Brown's of Clydebank and named *Intrepid* after the famous Zeebrugge blockship. Between them the two vessels, which took over the duties of the former Amphibious Warfare Squadron, are considered to be capable of dealing with any operation of 'brush fire' magnitude which can be visualised in the foreseeable future.

While the pattern of the Fleet of the future was thus steadily emerging, fresh changes were made in the entry regulations and training of officers and men to meet the requirements of the swiftly developing nuclear and electronic age. By and large these regulations continue to hold good.

Educational entry standards for Dartmouth cadets were raised to five GCE passes, including two at advanced level; one annual entry only at age 18 substituted for the former three entries a year; and the training syllabus reorganised, with the result that midshipmen again appeared in the seagoing fleet. Degree courses in electrical and mechanical engineering were instituted for engineering and electrical specialists, and the two branches amalgamated into a single engineering specialisation.

Commencing with the September 1961 entry, all General List cadets were to undergo a two-year period of common training. The first year would consist of three terms at the Britannia Royal Naval College, covering basic naval training and introductory courses, with one term of practical application in the Dartmouth Training Squadron. They would then be promoted to midshipman and go to sea for twelve months in the Fleet.

Successful completion of sea service would bring promotion to acting sub-lieutenant and mark the end of the period of common training. Thereafter Seaman and Supply & Secretariat specialists would return to Dartmouth for a year of academic studies, to be followed by a further twelve months at various technical training schools to sub-specialise in either aviation, submarines, gunnery, torpedo and anti-submarine, navigation and direction, or hydrographic surveying. During their fourth year Supply & Secretariat specialists would also receive instruction designed to fit them to take on the duties of Operations Officer and Officer of the Watch. At the end of the final year of training the successful would be confirmed as sub-lieutenants.

Instead of returning to Dartmouth with their Seaman and Supply & Secretariat colleagues, most engineering specialists would go on to the Naval Engineering College at Manadon, near Plymouth, for a three-year course to read for external B.Sc. (Engineering) degree London University, or a course leading to graduate membership of the Institutes of Mechanical, Electrical, Aeronautical or Marine Engineers. At the same time a limited number possessing high academic ability and appropriate qualifications could read for the Mechanical Science Tripos at Cambridge University. Subsequently all would be required to sub-specialise in either marine engineering, weapons and electrical engineering, air engineering, or submarine engineering.

A new system of short service commissions in the Seaman specialisation was also introduced. Aimed at attracting young men, including serving ratings, some RNR officers, and boys who lacked the full academic qualifications for the General List, service would be for ten years followed by four on the Reserve, with the option of leaving with a reduced gratuity after five years. Successful candidates would enter as cadets, and on completion of initial training at Dartmouth be promoted to midshipman for twelve months training at sea. Further promotion would follow according to age and progress during training.

A proportion of these short-service officers could qualify for permanent commissions on the Supplementary List after eight years' service, and, exceptionally, to the General List. In the main they would be employed on general seaman duties in all classes of ships, including submarines. There would also be opportunities of becoming Aircraft Direction Officers, Hydrographic Surveyors, or of specialising in other branches.

Short-service commissions were also made available in the Fleet Air Arm as fixed wing pilots and observers, or as helicopter pilots only. The former would serve for twelve years on the Supplementary List, and the latter for five years, followed by four years on the Emergency List. After eight years' service, fixed wing pilots and observers could be selected for permanent commissions on the Supplementary List.

To meet the growing need for qualified technical officers, a direct graduate entry scheme into the engineering specialisation was introduced in 1961. Under this scheme university graduates up to the age of 25 years with suitable engineering degrees or their equivalent could qualify for General List commissions. As with the Dartmouth entries, they would serve within the new single engineering specialisation and sub-specialise in one of the four branches.

Entries in the rank of acting sub-lieutenant would be made once a year, and after a short introductory course and sea training, candidates would go to various specialist naval schools for professional application courses lasting from twelve to eighteen months. The successful would be confirmed as sub-lieutenant after ten months, and promotion to acting lieutenant attained eighteen months after joining the Navy.

The increasing complexity of new warships coming into service and planned for the future meant that more electrical officers would be needed. In many new ships the electrical and electronic equipment accounted for up to 50 per cent of their total cost, and this was reflected in the number of Electrical Officers carried. In guided missile destroyers, for instance, between six and eight were included in their complement. Accordingly new entry regulations for electrical and electronic specialists were introduced for qualified men between 21 and 39 years of age.

Under the new scheme, which came into force in 1963, candidates were required to have one of three basic qualifications: a degree or its equivalent in electrical engineering—or in science with suitable engineering subjects; graduate membership of the Institute of Electrical Engineers or of the British Institution of Radio Engineers; or possession of a Higher National Diploma or equivalent in electrical subjects.

Entrants would be given seniority 'credits' up to a maximum of eight years on entry based on previous experience in outside industry, and additional seniority for academic qualifications. Thus a man with no special 'credits' on entry would enter as sub-lieutenant and serve as such for eighteen months. But an officer who qualified on entry for the maximum 'credits' would enter as a lieutenant with six and a half years' seniority. Before joining the Fleet all would do up to twelve months training at naval electrical schools.

They could serve for either five years (short-service commission), or a sixteen-year pensionable commission. There would also be opportunities to transfer to the Supplementary List and, for the best qualified, to the General List.

Similar educational standards to those for cadetships at Dartmouth were also required for entry into the Royal Marines, who had a similar scholarship scheme. Successful candidates would be entered as second lieutenant in the Officers' Wing of the Royal Marine Infantry Training Centre at Lympstone, in Devon, to undergo eight weeks' initial training—to include riding a horse, thus confounding those who think that 'Horse Marines' are only a myth! This would be followed by eight months' military training, a spell in the Amphibious Warfare Unit learning to handle landing craft and canoes, and another at Dartmouth for two weeks at the College and ten in the Training Squadron. Lastly came a Commando course, with promotion to lieutenant at the end of two and a half years' training.

Subsequently graduate entry for both full and short service careers was introduced for the Seaman and Supply & Secretariat specialisations and the Royal Marines, and for short service careers in the Instructor, Medical and Dental branches.

Mention was made in an earlier chapter of the Upper Yardman scheme for the promotion of Lower Deck ratings to commissioned rank. Originally introduced in 1944, the first post-war establishment for training Upper Yardmen was opened in August 1946 at Exbury House, near Southampton, under the ship name HMS *Hawke*. At this school special courses were held to enable outstanding ratings to attain the necessary educational and professional standards to fit them to take their place as commissioned officers.

On completion of the professional examination, candidates appeared before a final selection board which could recommend either promotion to acting sub-lieutenant, rating up to petty officer and placing on the roster for Warrant (later Branch) rank, or being sent back to sea as petty officer, according to ability.

At the end of 1950 HMS *Hawke* was moved to Dartmouth where

the candidates were housed in the ship's company block, but trained apart from the general entry cadets. Five years later, in order to provide additional accommodation at the College, the establishment was moved to South Queensferry where it became a separate unit of the local shore depot and the ship name changed to HMS *Temeraire*. The training courses remained much the same, successful candidates passing out as acting sub-lieutenants.

In 1960 Upper Yardman training returned to the Britannia Royal Naval College and HMS *Temeraire* was closed down. At Dartmouth the Upper Yardmen initially formed a separate Division, living in separate quarters in the college grounds, but within two years they had become fully integrated in the main college. At first they wore white shoulder flashes in place of the cadet's distinctive lapel twist until the end of their first term at the college. But as democratisation proceeded, this arrangement was altered so that the Upper Yardman was promoted to cadet before entry into the college, and the white flashes disappeared.

Successful candidates emerged as General List officers, their training at Dartmouth having been chiefly concentrated on acquiring the educational qualification required of direct entry General List cadets. Thereafter technical training and promotion followed the same pattern.*

In 1966 the prospects of Lower Deck promotion to commissioned rank were further enhanced by the introduction of a scheme whereby Upper Yardmen could qualify for entry on the Supplementary List. The new naval officer structure introduced ten years earlier had reduced cadet entries on the General List, the intention being to make good deficiencies by expanding the Special Duties List and instituting the Supplementary List. But these still fell short of requirements.

Under the new scheme, promising ratings could be selected at an early age to receive, if necessary, assistance to bring them up to the educational standard required for promotion to the Supplementary List. Thus, after recommendation by their commanding officer and vetting by a preliminary selection board, selected candidates would undergo a full time educational course lasting for one or two years. After obtaining four GCE 'O' level passes and appearing before an Admiralty Interview Board, successful candidates would be promoted

---

* *As a result of a review of officer entry and training undertaken in 1971 the rank of cadet, first approved for use in 1843, was abolished. All young officers other than graduate and university entrants join the Britannia Royal Naval College as midshipmen.*

to cadet and move on to Dartmouth. Thereafter their training would be the same as for direct entry Supplementary List officers. The scheme was to apply chiefly to Seaman specialists, but would also include a small number of Supply & Secretariat and Engineering specialisations.

At the same time a new zone of promotion was introduced for Special Duties List officers, lowering by twelve months the average time spent in the rank of sub-lieutenant. These officers were also required to be more knowledgeable in a wider field of activities than hitherto. In order to fulfil this requirement a special school under the eventual ship name of HMS *St. George* was set up in Portsmouth in 1963, in which all Seaman Special Duties List candidates could undertake a pre-qualifying course.

This lasted approximately eight months, the syllabus being both academic and vocational. The former covered a wide variety of subjects, including journal and essay writing, mathematics and mechanics. The vocational side covered a working knowledge of the regulations and other publications applicable to Divisional Officers, duties and responsibilities of the Officer of the Watch and navigation, with a brief spell afloat to put this to practical use.

Within four years of its inception more than 300 candidates had passed through the school, which in due course instituted its own Sword of Honour for the best pupil similar to Dartmouth. Since then a number of necessary changes have been made in the syllabus, such as the substitution of 'Science and the Arts' for mechanics.

The technical developments reflected in the new ships and weapons coming into service also had a considerable effect on rating training and the whole of the Fleet's manpower organisation. To meet these changing needs existing rating categories were adapted to fresh skills, and new categories created to meet new requirements. Among the latter are those of 'Weapon Mechanician' and 'Control Artificer', both of which stem directly from the Navy's growing involvement with guided weapons. Pre-war the number of rating categories in the Royal Navy totalled eighteen and included the Nelsonic crafts of sailmaker and ship's carpenter. By the dawn of the nineteen-sixties the number had risen to thirty-nine, more than half of them technical.

Royal Marines, too, are no longer simply 'sea soldiers', but have added considerably to their traditional versatility. As well as being trained Commandos, they now include such specialist qualifications as assault engineers, weapon technicians, landing craft crews, parachutists, light aircraft pilots and observers, drivers, radio technicians,

Arctic warfare specialists, frogmen and canoeists. Following a scheme introduced in 1961, Royal Marine Commandos now have their own helicopter pilots. Previously all Commando helicopters had been flown by naval pilots. Selected Royal Marine officers undergo twelve months flying training before joining Commando helicopter squadrons for two years' service. NCOs trained by the Army Air Corps pilot the Commandos' light reconnaissance helicopters.

Thus have been borne out still further the words of Prince Philip, their Captain-General, that 'there is nothing the Marines cannot do'.

In the spring of 1960 the Commander-in-Chief, Home Fleet, last of the Navy's Commanders-in-Chief to fly his flag afloat, moved permanently ashore. Since he also held the NATO appointment of Commander-in-Chief, Eastern Atlantic (CINCEASTLANT) it was only fitting that his new headquarters should be set up alongside the NATO Headquarters for the Eastern Atlantic area, which had been established at Northwood, just outside London, from which his important NATO duties could be more efficiently discharged.

Since 1937 when a large house which had once been a locally notorious night club was taken over by the Royal Air Force as an officers' mess, Northwood had been the headquarters of Coastal Command. It was this link and the need for close co-operation with maritime air control which led to the establishment of NATO's Eastern Atlantic naval headquarters at Northwood and the enlargement of existing facilities on the site. Prior to 1960 the Commander-in-Chief, Home Fleet, had to leave his flagship in order to conduct NATO exercises and proceed to Northwood with his staff wearing his 'other hat' as Commander-in-Chief, Eastern Atlantic.

The new Home Fleet Headquarters, later to be considerably expanded, was given the ship name HMS *Warrior*. Thus was established within twenty miles of Whitehall the staffs of the Air Officer Commanding-in-Chief and his NATO staff as COMAIREAST-LANT, and of the Commander-in-Chief, Home Fleet and his staff as CINCEASTLANT. Effective control of the Home Fleet was retained through the Flag Officer Flotillas (Home), the Commander-in-Chief's deputy, the C-in-C selecting an appropriate vessel in which to fly his flag when exercising or cruising with the fleet and visiting foreign ports.

Six years later a further change came about when the NATO Council decided that the British admiral occupying the post of CINCEASTLANT should also assume the post of NATO Commander-in-Chief, Channel (CINCCHAN) previously held by the Commander-in-Chief, Home Station, and the NATO staff of that command moved up from Portsmouth to Northwood. The Commander-in-Chief, Home Fleet, became Commander-in-Chief of the newly titled Western Fleet, adding to his NATO responsibility in wartime the security of an area of home waters stretching from the south-west approaches to the Wash.

Prior to his move ashore at Northwood, the Commander-in-Chief, Home Fleet, had been flying his flag in the destroyer depot ship *Tyne*, which by then was more than twenty years old. The other ships in the Home Fleet at this time were the carriers *Victorious* and *Albion*, the fast minelayer *Apollo* built in 1944, seventeen destroyers and frigates and sixteen submarines, including vessels under trials and training.

New ships under construction included an aircraft carrier; 2 cruisers—*Lion* and *Blake* which had not yet come into service; the first 4 guided missile destroyers; 17 frigates; 5 submarines; 2 minesweepers, a fast patrol boat and a boom defence vessel. In reserve or undergoing long refit, modernisation and conversion were 3 aircraft carriers; 5 cruisers; 29 destroyers; 2 fast minelayers; 19 submarines, including several 'midget' or X-craft; 152 minesweepers, ocean, coastal and inshore; more than a score of coastal craft, and a number of miscellaneous vessels.

The two remaining seagoing fleets of any size were stationed in the Mediterranean and Far East, both of whose Commanders-in-Chief had since the war continued to fly their flags on shore. Thus in the Mediterranean were two cruisers, nine destroyers and frigates of mixed types, five submarines, and a small minesweeping squadron. The term 'squadron' in this connection had been adopted in 1952 when a standard nomenclature for the various naval forces of NATO countries was introduced to facilitate communications. Thus small formations of any type of warship, whether aircraft carriers, submarines, coastal forces, etc., are today known as squadrons; while two or more squadrons of destroyers or smaller types grouped together form a flotilla.

On the Far East station were the light fleet carrier *Centaur* and the cruiser *Belfast*, ten mixed destroyers and frigates, two minesweeping squadrons, and three submarines with their own depot ship.

An important change in the command structure here too was about to be made. In May 1962 it was announced that Admiral Sir David

Luce, Commander-in-Chief Far East Fleet, was to become the first unified Commander-in-Chief Far East. This meant that he would assume command of all British forces in the Far East covering an area of some 18 million square miles. To mark the change of responsibilities the title of the new naval commander in the Far East was accordingly altered to Flag Officer Commanding-in-Chief, Far East Fleet. The revised arrangement was brought into operation in November of that year.

This unified command system under which supreme command of an area could be held by a single officer of any of the three Services was not new, having earlier been set up in the Middle East.

The Commander-in-Chief, South Atlantic and South America station, flying his flag ashore at Wynberg in Cape Province, had only two frigates and the Antarctic 'ice patrol' ship *Protector* under his command, one of the frigates being permanently stationed in the West Indies.

In the Persian Gulf, now designated the 'Arabian Seas and Persian Gulf station' under the command of a commodore ashore at Bahrain, were four Loch class frigates of 1944 vintage.

The home commands included the Commander-in-Chief Home Station at Portsmouth, the Commander-in-Chief Plymouth, and the Flag Officer Scotland and Northern Ireland. The two latter also held NATO appointments as Commander Central Sub-Area, and Commander Northern Sub-Area, Eastern Atlantic respectively. As mentioned in the last chapter, the appointment of Commander-in-Chief The Nore was about to lapse and this historic command to close down as part of the 'Way Ahead' economies.

The former Royal Marine barracks and the Naval Gunwharf at Chatham had been sold in 1959 to a private firm, but the dockyard itself would continue in operation. In addition to housing the Royal Naval Supply School for training officers and men of the Supply & Secretariat specialisation, the naval barracks would continue to provide accommodation for the crews of ships refitting at Chatham. Seven years later the port acquired fresh importance when the construction of new complex technical facilities conferred upon the dockyard the ability to service and refuel nuclear submarines.

The closing ceremony of the Nore Command took place on 24th March 1961, when the Queen's Colour of the Command was formally laid up in the presence of a large assembly. They included in addition to members of the Admiralty Board, several former Commanders-in-Chief and various civil and military dignatories, and the Commander-in-Chief of the Netherlands Home Station flying his flag in the new Dutch destroyer *Limburg* who had been invited to attend. In such fashion was commemorated an occasion in June 1667 when a Dutch squadron under Admiral de Ruyter sailed up the Medway and burnt the English fleet as it lay at anchor below Upnor Castle.

The foundation of the Nore Command had been laid as far back as 1547, when a storehouse was acquired at Gillingham for naval purposes at a rent of thirteen shillings and fourpence a year, and Drake's father was ministering as a village parson and chaplain to the Fleet in the Medway. In the next three years other storehouses were acquired in Rochester and Gillingham. Chatham dockyard was begun in 1567 and a grounding, or 'graving', place constructed in 1584, by which time most of the Navy's warships were being sent round from Portsmouth to be grounded for hull cleaning, and Chatham was receiving the lion's share of the funds allocated to the four naval building yards; the others being at Woolwich, Deptford and Portsmouth. During the seventeenth century wars with the Dutch the Medway grew in importance. Nelson's *Victory* was built at Chatham in 1759, and it was to Chatham that he came as a boy of twelve to join his first ship.

The earliest record of the appointment of a Commander-in-Chief The Nore was in 1752 when Isaac Townsend, Admiral of the Blue, was appointed 'Commander-in-Chief of HM Ships and Naval Vessels in the Rivers Thames and Medway and at the Buoy of the Nore'. From 1778 onwards the list of Commanders-in-Chief The Nore continued unbroken until sunset on 31st March 1961, when the flag of Admiral Sir Robin Durnford Slater was hauled down for the last time.

The Nore Command invariably bore the brunt of the seaborne attacks and threats of invasion of England that have taken place over the years. The east coast in particular has been the scene of a considerable amount of enemy raiding activity, chiefly by John Paul Jones in 1779 during the American War of Independence, by German warships in 1914, and by the Germans again during the Second World War when they made the east coast convoy routes the focus for all forms of seaborne and air attack.

It was also in that war that the Nore Command came into its own at two crucial moments in history: first at the time of Dunkirk

when an armada of little ships, the majority setting forth from Sheerness, snatched the British Expeditionary Force from seeming disaster;
and in 1945 when from ports of the Nore Command the tremendous
task of sustaining the Allied armies in Europe was carried on.

As from 1st April the area and remaining establishments of the
Nore Command were divided between the Commander-in-Chief
Portsmouth and the Flag Officer Scotland and Northern Ireland, the
demarcation line being fixed roughly at the Wash. For the purpose of
administration, however, the Admiral Superintendent Chatham
assumed the additional title of Flag Officer Medway.

A few months later the centuries-old Upnor Castle, built during
the reign of Queen Elizabeth I, which had been used as a Navy and
Army armament and gunpowder store since the end of the seventeenth
century and later solely as a naval armament depot, was handed
over to the Ministry of Works. Today it has become a place of historic
interest to visitors to the Medway towns.

Nearer London another link with naval history was snapped when
in June 1961 the Royal Victoria Victualling Yard at Deptford was
closed down in pursuance of the policy of economising in the Navy's
shore support.

It was early in the eighteenth century that the senior Commissioner
of Victualling reported to King George II that the Navy's victualling
yard, then situated on Tower Hill, was no longer large enough 'for
the needs of the Fleet. There was not 'room sufficient to lay in a
store of hoops, twiggs and flags', wrote the Commissioner, 'neither
is there sufficient and convenient room for the well and sweet
slaughtering, cutting, saving and keeping of the beef and porke that
is required'.

As a result the King issued an Order in Council establishing a new
victualling yard for the Navy on 11 acres of land which had once
formed part of the leafy grounds of the mansion of Sayes Court at
Deptford. The house had at one time belonged to John Evelyn, the
diarist, who leased part of the estate to the East India Company.

The old victualling yard at Tower Hill was finally closed in 1785,
by which time most of its functions had been transferred to Deptford. Among the fittings and equipment moved down was an enormous oaken rum vat with a capacity of no less than 32,817 gallons.
During the blitz on London in 1940 this massive veteran was all but
destroyed by bombs.

While the adjacent Royal dockyard at Deptford, created by Henry

VIII in 1513, continued to form the principal repository for the Fleet's cordage, sailcloth, hammocks, bedding, clothing, pitch, tar, resin and anchors, the victualling yard housed the Fleet's main stock of comestibles. These included salt meat, hard tack, rum, cocoa, pepper and mustard, also soap and candles. Later the yard was enlarged until it covered a total of 35 acres. A brewery was built, a cooperage, a butchery and slaughterhouses, and a bakery and flour mill. During the salting season some 500 beasts a week were slaughtered to provide the Fleet with salt junk.

By the middle of the nineteenth century the Deptford victualling yard was responsible for the production of a large proportion of the chief items in the sailor's diet. It also stocked in addition to biscuit and cocoa, soap, candles and tobacco, special provisions for the sick, which included port wine, preserved chicken and jellies. Stores for various expeditions to the Arctic and elsewhere were manufactured at Deptford, and the yard supplied the bulk of the provisions used by our forces in the Ashanti, Zulu and Boer Wars. In 1871 1,500 tons of provisions were despatched from Deptford to feed the starving citizens of Paris when the Franco-Prussian War came to an end. Following a visit by the Queen in 1858 the yard was renamed the Royal Victoria Yard.

By the end of the Second World War the yard had become less and less of a storehouse, the functions of its staff being chiefly confined to inspecting and checking the quality of the extensive variety of victualling stores needed by the modern Navy, all of which are today supplied by commercial firms under contract arrangements. Certain quantities of dry and refrigerated provisions continued however to be held in stock, together with materials and uniform clothing, flying clothing and special cold-weather kit. At the final closure these were transferred to the victualling depots at Portsmouth and Plymouth, and the yard handed over to the GLC for re-development. A commemorative plaque remains today to mark Deptford's long connection with naval history.

The first twelve months of the nineteen-sixties passed quietly from an operational point of view for the Royal Navy although there was trouble enough in the world. In fulfilment of their traditional role the ships of its reduced overseas squadrons took on a number of disaster relief, salvage and other humanitarian tasks in various parts of the globe. But in the summer of 1961 the Navy was called upon to give a practical demonstration of the part it would play in a limited war.

In June that year an agreement which had been signed back in 1899 between Britain and the Middle Eastern State of Kuwait was abrogated and replaced by a new agreement of close friendship, and an announcement of Kuwait's intention to apply for membership of the United Nations. The agreement also included a clause promising that Britain would come to the aid of Kuwait if its government should request such assistance. This oil-rich little State from which Britain was obtaining some 40 per cent of her needs of that vital commodity is bounded by Iraq to the north and Saudi Arabia to the south.

Less than a week after the signing of the agreement, Major-General Abdul Kassem, head of a military junta which had seized power in Iraq when the Royal Family was assassinated and the British Embassy in Baghdad sacked and destroyed, broadcast a claim to sovereignty over Kuwait as being an integral part of Iraq. He based his claim on the fact that Kuwait had formed part of the province of Basra in the old Ottoman Empire, and as such had been acknowledged by the British prior to the 1899 Treaty. 'Iraq', he declared aggressively, did not recognise the 'forged treaty imposed by Imperialists'.

Following reports of Iraqi troop movements towards the border between the two countries, the Ruler of Kuwait formally requested assistance from the British and from Saudi Arabia, while his country prepared to defend itself against attack. The British Government was quick to respond, and the Commander-in-Chief Middle East was instructed to begin landing troops in Kuwait on 1st July.

Already at Bahrain on 27th June were the frigate *Loch Alvie* and the amphibious warfare squadron, the tank landing ship *Striker* having half a squadron of Centurion tanks embarked. In dock at Karachi was another Persian Gulf frigate, the *Loch Fyne*, while a third, *Loch Ruthven*, was paying a visit to Mombasa.

HMS *Bulwark* with 42 Commando embarked was on her way to pay a call at Karachi before going on to the Persian Gulf for hot weather trials. She was promptly directed to Bahrain. The *Loch Ruthven* was also ordered back to the Persian Gulf, while the *Loch Fyne* cut short her docking and sailed from Karachi on 1st July.

Farther east the aircraft carrier *Victorious*, which was *en route* to join the Far East station, with the destroyer *Cassandra* and the frigate *Lincoln* in company were nearing Hong Kong. The three ships

Sea King helicopter

Two of the Navy's newest warships: HMS *Amazon* (Type 21) (foreground) and HMS *Sheffield* (Type 42)

The Type 21 class frigate *Amazon*

Guided missile destroyers in line ahead.

were turned round and routed to the trouble spot with all speed. Two
other frigates from the Far East station were sailed to join the
Victorious, together with replenishment ships. From Gibraltar the light
fleet carrier *Centaur* of the Home Fleet and three destroyers and a
Royal Fleet Auxiliary were sailed for the Persian Gulf, also a minesweeping squadron from Malta.

Meanwhile in a copybook operation, 42 Commando had been
flown into Kuwait from the *Bulwark* within twenty-four hours of
the Ruler's request for help. In temperatures reaching 124 degrees and
never falling to less than 90, and amid incessant sandstorms which
reduced visibility to a few hundred yards, the Commandos secured
Kuwait airfield and other key positions and proceeded to dig themselves in. On the following day 45 Commando was flown in from
Aden to join them. Supported by naval helicopters, they continued
to remain on the defensive in the forward area until relieved by an
Army battalion.

Subsequently a balanced force of nearly 6,000 men, with Centurion tanks and Hunter jets, was rapidly built up which, along with
a small number of troops from Saudi Arabia, established a defence
line 60 miles long close to the border with Iraq. A noteworthy feature
of the operation was that on her arrival the *Victorious* assumed full
air responsibility, controlling both her own aircraft and the RAF
fighters from Bahrain. This was the first time that her Type 984
radar had been used operationally.

In the event hostilities did not develop, this prompt show of strength
having effectively curbed the Iraqui leader's aggressive ambitions.
When Kuwait's complaint of the unfriendly attitude of her northern
neighbour was debated in the United Nations assembly the Russians,
as expected, sided with Kassem and declared that the presence of
British forces in Kuwait constituted a threat to peace. A British
resolution calling on all States to respect the independence and integrity of Kuwait was defeated by a Soviet veto. But the rest of the
Arab States and the Arab League did not support Iraq.

By September the emergency had passed except for some vague
threats by Kassem to 'liberate' Kuwait, and the bulk of the British
forces was withdrawn. Their place was taken by an Arab League
force to continue to maintain the defence of Kuwait's territorial
integrity.

This first operation in which a Commando carrier was employed
amply demonstrated the ability of the Royal Navy to concentrate
forces speedily, unobtrusively and effectively. In an editorial, one

prominent British newspaper summed up the affair by observing that 'If anybody thinks that the day of navies is over, Kuwait should make him change his opinion. For this police operation has been launched mainly by means of a sea-lift.'

There were to be more such operations in the not too distant future.

CHAPTER NINE

Run-up

The 1962 explanatory statement on defence outlined the further evolution of Britain's defence policy. Future basic objectives were set out rather more simply than hitherto as (a) maintenance of the country's security; (b) fulfilment of Britain's obligations for the protection of her territories overseas and those to whom special duties were owed by treaty or otherwise; and (c) to make contribution to the defence of the free world and the prevention of war in accordance with the arrangements made with individual countries and under collective security treaties.

Since Britain was simultaneously contributing to three collective security alliances, NATO, CENTO and SEATO, she must be able to maintain forces in three areas of the world. While the prevention of war continued to be vital, carefully balanced forces would have to be maintained to deter every form of aggression and military threat. Fitting the cost of defence into a general study of public expenditure in relation to prospective resources for the first time, a figure of 7 per cent of the gross national product (GNP), or some £1,721 million, was allocated to the defence budget for the coming financial year. Of this sum, £442 million was earmarked for the Royal Navy.

The statement went on:

> During the next ten years or so we may expect the Navy to be based on the present balanced Fleet, with a turnover to nuclear power for submarines, and further emphasis on afloat support to supplement shore bases and increase flexibility.

It also mentioned that as the existing aircraft carriers would be coming to the end of their lives in about 1970, and that it required no less than nine years to plan, build and work up a carrier, the necessary design work for a new vessel to replace the *Victorious* was to be put in hand. Four years later, however, with a new government in office there came a drastic change of heart.

Operational fleet strength comprised a total of 140 ships ranging from aircraft carriers to minesweepers; 37 vessels were engaged on trials and training, and a further 296 vessels were undergoing long refit, modernisation, conversion etc., or in reserve, half of them minesweepers. There were no fewer than 71 support ships and auxiliaries. Thus the policy of placing increasing emphasis on afloat support and lessening dependence on overseas bases was being progressively implemented.

The ships forming this modern development of the wartime 'Fleet Train' were now divided into three categories: Front Line Support, comprising replenishment tankers, fleet repair ships, stores support ships and armament supply ships; Forward Base Support, which included submarine depot ships, repair ships, escort maintenance ships, and minesweeper maintenance and support ships; and Freighting Support, consisting of tankers and solid freighters.

Front Line Support Ships transfer fuel, ammunition and stores to fighting ships under way so that they can remain independent of shore facilities for long periods, helicopters being used to transfer lighter loads. All are manned by officers and men of the Royal Fleet Auxiliary Service. The task of Freighting Support Vessels is to carry bulk supplies and replenish the Front Line Support Ships and Forward Base Support Ships. These are also manned by the Royal Fleet Auxiliary. Forward Base Support Ships are in effect mobile bases manned by naval technical specialists under the White Ensign.

Thus submarine depot ships are equipped with workshops to support a squadron or more of submarines; they also carry reserve torpedoes, a plant to charge submarine batteries, and provide accommodation for submarine crews. Repair ships provide mobile repair facilities. Escort maintenance ships equipped with all necessary maintenance facilities support destroyers and frigates, while minesweeper support and maintenance ships do the same job for coastal and inshore minesweepers.

In 1962 the existing replenishment tankers were vessels of some 13,000 gross tons, backed up by a number of smaller ships of from 3,400 to 8,400 tons. Fleet replenishment ships were converted merchantmen of between 8,000 and 10,000 tons, and the stores support ships of 7,200 tons. Armament supply ships were of similar size. The tankers which comprised the Freighting Support were all of one class of 12,300-ton vessels, and the solid freighters 7,250 tons.

But all were ageing and of inferior performance. In view of the growing complexity of modern warships, calling for more skilled maintenance and the increased necessity for them to achieve maximum sea time, it was decided to modernise the afloat support fleet by replacing the older vessels and those converted from merchantmen with new, purpose-built ships designed to operate with maximum efficiency at minimum cost. An extensive building programme was accordingly put in hand, and by the end of the nineteen-sixties the metamorphosed Royal Fleet Auxiliary comprised a fleet of some forty vessels totalling 300,000 tons, all of the latest design, construction, technical equipment and habitability, with a manpower strength of 1,600 officers and 3,000 ratings.

The principal ships of the fleet include nine super-tankers ranging from 17,400 tons deadweight to 22,350 tons, with a service speed of 19 knots, backed up by two mobile reserve tankers of 35,642 and 42,500 tons respectively; and five small fleet tankers of 7,060 dead-weight tons. The larger vessels can issue five different oil products and fresh water simultaneously to three warships while steaming at sea, at the same time transferring oil drums by helicopter.

There are three stores support ships of 16,500 tons each with a service speed of 17 knots, which carry a range of 80,000 items of general naval and aircraft stores, and sufficient food and canteen stores to support 5,000 men for a month. The stores are carried in four holds, all with varying degrees of environmental control to ensure their condition. The ships are so equipped that replenishment can proceed at four points simultaneously to two vessels steaming one at either side, while a third can be supplied by helicopter.

As well as a number of smaller specialist logistic vessels and oilers, a new addition to the fleet was an 8,000-ton helicopter support ship. Specially designed to meet naval training requirements in the flying, handling and maintenance of helicopters, the vessel is fully capable of training pilots and the control team of a frigate, thereby saving valuable time during work-up periods. Except for the training crews and maintenance personnel, the ship is manned and operated by the Royal Fleet Auxiliary Service.

In 1970 the remainder of the Navy's ocean-going support and auxiliary ships other than those of the RFA were amalgamated into a new organisation known as the 'Royal Maritime Auxiliary Service' (RMAS). Under the administration of the Director of Marine Services (Naval), this comprises research and development ships used by the Navy, the ocean towing fleet, mooring and salvage vessels, and cable ships. Totalling some fifty in number, RMAS ships have black hulls and boot topping with grey funnel and upperworks, and wear a Blue

Ensign defaced in the fly by a yellow horizontal anchor with two wavy yellow lines beneath it to denote their seagoing character.

Ever since the *Truculent* disaster in 1950 the Royal Navy's Submarine Command continued to investigate new methods of escaping from a sunken submarine, particularly in view of the advent of nuclear-propelled submarines.

In September 1962 a team of specialists belonging to the escape training staff at submarine headquarters in HMS *Dolphin* began a series of trials in the Mediterranean of a promising new technique of 'free ascent' escaping from a dived submarine. Each 'guinea pig', wearing an immersion suit, made two ascents from a depth of 260 feet. One was by 'free ascent' with buoyancy, the only additional equipment being a lifebelt; in the second a hood made of rubberised fabric was worn. This hood allowed the wearer to breathe 'trapped' air on his way to the surface.

The trials proved completely successful, and were followed by a further series of exhaustive tests carried out in Loch Fyne, and subsequently in the Mediterranean from depths as great as 500 feet. Dressed in a suit incorporating a cotton fabric hood with a plastic facepiece covering head and shoulders, the escaper entered a one-man cylinder inside the submarine, which was flooded up until the pressure equalled that of the surrounding sea. The cylinder's outside hatch was then opened from inside the submarine, no action being necessary on the part of the escaper.

One advantage of this method was that pressurisation essential for escaping from depth was activated rapidly, the escaper being subjected to this condition for the minimum period before leaving the submarine. It also obviated the possibility of contracting the 'bends'. While inside the flooded cylinder the escaper breathed air supplied through an air pipe from the submarine itself. On his way to the surface he used the air trapped in his hood.

Another advantage of the new system over previous escape methods was that it was unnecessary to flood the compartment in which survivors might be trapped until the air pressure equalled that of the water outside. Formerly this meant that survivors might have to wait for a long period in icy water and pitch darkness before attempting to escape.

After further tests in all conditions had proved its efficacy, escapes even being successfully accomplished from a moving submarine, the system was adopted for use in all British nuclear and conventional patrol submarines.

In its present form it consists of two escape towers, or small chambers, each to accommodate one man, running from the pressure hull to the inside of the submarine, fitted one forward and one aft. The chambers can be flooded up from the sea and blown down (emptied) after use by means of a control valve inside the submarine. Flooding can also be achieved by means of a valve inside the chamber itself for use by the last man to escape. An exterior escape hatch lifts automatically when pressure inside the chamber equals that of the sea outside.

Wearing an immersion suit fitted with built-in buoyancy life-jacket and water-activated light, and over his head and shoulders the special triple-skinned, plastic-faced hood, the escaper enters the chamber and plugs his lifejacket into the fitted air outlet. This supplies pure air from the submarine's air storage cylinders. When life-jacket and hood are fully inflated, the escaper signals to his companions inside the submarine who open a valve to flood the chamber. When pressure is equalised and the exterior hatch opens, the escaper shoots to the surface.

As soon as he has gone the escape hatch is closed from inside the submarine and the chamber blown down by compressed air from the vessel's normal supply. The next man then enters, and the cycle is repeated.

The new system, entirely pioneered by the Royal Navy and considered to be almost completely foolproof, allowing men with very little experience to escape safely from depths up to 600 feet, has since been introduced into many NATO navies.

Towards the end of 1962, because the weapon had proved disappointing in flight tests and was considered no longer to justify its eventual strategic value, the Americans decided to scrap the Skybolt air-launched missile they had been developing for the joint use of the US and British air forces.

This meant that the RAF's deterrent V-bomber force, which was to have been equipped with Skybolt in place of Britain's own Blue Streak long-range ballistic missile abandoned in 1960 because it could only be launched from a fixed site, would end their useful life in 1965 as no efficient stand-off missile would be available to succeed Blue Steel, the existing V-bomb. The American decision was to prove fateful for the Royal Navy.

Following Russia's explosion of her H-bomb in 1954, the Americans began to consider a new submarine missile system. Within two years they had developed a ballistic missile for launching from nuclear submarines. Originally called 'Jupiter', it was evolved from captured V.2 rockets used by the Germans in the Second World War. Renamed 'Polaris' in its fully developed stage, the weapon was a solid fuel, two-stage intermediate range missile with an initial range of 1,500 miles, capable of being fired from a submarine either submerged or on the surface.

Polaris was successfully tested in 1958, and within four years a proportion of the US Navy's rapidly growing fleet of nuclear submarines was equipped with the latest A.3 version of the missile, which had been given an increased range of 2,500 nautical miles. In May 1962 the United States decided to commit all Polaris submarines in their Atlantic Fleet to NATO and to make this weapon the NATO nuclear deterrent. By arrangement with the British Government the first US Polaris submarine squadron, with its own depot ship for servicing them, was based at Holy Loch, in Scotland.

In December President Kennedy and the British Prime Minister, then Mr. Harold Macmillan, met at Nassau, in the Bahamas, to discuss an American offer to supply Polaris missiles in place of Skybolt. As a result it was agreed that to succeed the V-bombers the Royal Navy should create and operate a force of Polaris-equipped nuclear submarines which would become Britain's independent contribution to the long-range strategic deterrent forces of the Western Alliance. America would supply the missiles without warheads, Britain to design and build the submarines and supply her own nuclear warheads. She would also retain the right to operate these missiles independently should supreme national interests be at stake.

One month after the signing of the Nassau Agreement the decision was taken to build a force of up to five nuclear-powered Polaris submarines for the Royal Navy, each to carry sixteen of the new A.3 missiles, the first to be operational by 1968. Rear-Admiral H. S. Mackenzie, a submarine specialist and the then Flag Officer Submarines, was appointed Chief Polaris Executive to maintain liaison between the Admiralty and the Ministry of Aviation in respect of the Polaris project; and Rear-Admiral F. Dossor, an electrical engineering and guided weapons expert, as Project Officer in the Ministry itself.

The Defence Estimates for 1964 increased the Naval Vote by some £55 million to meet the initial cost of the Polaris programme and for naval manpower to be expanded by 3,000. The orders for four nuclear submarines were placed in May 1963, and the intention to have a fifth confirmed nine months later. But in 1965, for economic reasons, the Labour Government dropped the plan to have five Polaris submarines, using the money thus saved to continue with the nuclear Fleet submarine building programme.

Once the Polaris project was decided upon little time was lost. The 'keel' of the first of the new vessels—a prefabricated circular section weighing over 100 tons—was positioned on the slipway in Vickers Armstrong's yard on 26th February 1964. It was announced that she was to be named *Resolution*, and her three sisters *Renown*, *Repulse* and *Revenge* respectively. These were all names held in recent memory as belonging to big-gunned capital ships, an indication of the growing importance of the nuclear submarine.

The keel of the *Renown* was laid at Cammell Laird's Birkenhead yard in June 1964; that of the *Repulse* at Vickers in March 1965; and the *Revenge* at Cammell Laird's in May 1965. By March 1968 all four had been launched.

Their construction involved the co-ordination of effort by hundreds of firms, both British and American. To achieve this, special project-team type organisations were set up to drive the project through. The complete task was spread over a nine-year period at a total cost of £353 million for the four vessels, and also included the provision of a base, workshops, training school, armament depot, married quarters and recreational facilities for 2,000 personnel sited at Faslane, on the Clyde, from which the submarines would operate. Each vessel would have two crews, known as 'Port' and 'Starboard', one on patrol and the other taking leave or carrying out refresher training. Patrols would last for eight weeks at a time.

Twice the size of the *Dreadnought* in order to accommodate the missile compartment and displacing over 7,000 tons, with a length of 425 feet and beam of 33 feet, Polaris submarines are powered by a similar form of nuclear propulsion.

The missile section, sited amidships, contains sixteen launching tubes, each 7 feet in diameter and 33 feet high, housing a 31-foot long Type A.3 missile with British warhead, maintained in readiness to fire but with an elaborate system of safeguards. The submarine's highly sophisticated fire control system includes eleven computers, and each missile also contains one. Armed with information about the target and from the ship's inertial navigation installation (SINS), the system calculates the missile flight path and passes the information to the individual weapons, so that at the moment of firing each has precise instructions where to go.

Basically this information consists of the submarine's launching position, sea state, the start point of the flight path and the latter's end, which is the geographical position of the target. Should the missile be moved off course, the guidance system computes the new course and puts the missile on to it. This system also maintains the stability of the missile in pitch, yaw and roll. At the precise instant that the guidance system shuts off the rocket motors, it triggers separation of the re-entry body which then follows a ballistic trajectory to the target.

The re-entry body, fitted at the fore end of the missile, is an assembly consisting of the nuclear warhead, fuzing and arming devices, all enclosed to meet the conditions of passage through the earth's atmosphere. On board the submarine the only sensation at the moment of firing is a quiet hiss as high pressure gas is discharged into the missile tube to start the weapon on its way, and a slight vibration. In addition to the Polaris missiles each submarine carries six 21-inch torpedo tubes for conventional homing torpedoes.

The living accommodation for the 13 officers and 130 ratings who form the complement of each boat was designed, like that of the nuclear-powered Fleet submarines, to be of the highest standard, with unlimited fresh water for showers, cooking and laundry. A large comprehensive galley serves a wide choice of meals on the cafeteria system. There are refrigerators, infra-red grills, and even ice cream-making machines. For recreation there is a cinema equipment with a large selection of modern films, a library, facilities for language and correspondence courses, and piped music. Junior ratings have their own recreational area and dining hall, senior ratings a lounge and coffee bar in addition. There is a daily newspaper at sea, and each crew member can receive messages from home. A sophisticated network of communications and control systems is used for transmitting information, directing remote services and round-the-clock monitoring of conditions throughout the vessel.

Navigation and underwater detection equipment is the most modern devised. Messages can be sent by radio and navigational information received when submerged. Air-conditioning machinery provides a constant supply of pure air; electrolysers extract oxygen from the sea water, and other machinery removes dust and carbon dioxide from the atmosphere. As in nuclear Fleet submarines, the control room resembles that of an aircraft or space ship, and at high underwater speeds, despite its huge size and dimensions, the submarine behaves and handles like an aircraft. Powered columns work rudders and hydroplanes, and the vessel can bank and dive underwater. Course and depth can be set by automatic pilot.

Since nowhere on earth is more than 2,500 miles from the sea, and Polaris submarines are able to range the oceans with little fear of detection, each vessel represents a greater deterrent than a whole squadron of pre-war battleships. But they, too, are primarily peacekeepers.

As each of the quartette of British Polaris submarines commissioned, a month of her initial shakedown cruise was spent at Port Canaveral, part of the Cape Kennedy complex in Florida, carrying out test firings of her missiles on the Atlantic range. In June 1968, just four years after being laid down, HMS *Resolution* set out on her first operational patrol, a remarkable achievement by any standard.

Meanwhile the new base for the Navy's growing nuclear submarine fleet had been constructed at Faslane, on the Gareloch. Commissioned in 1967 as HMS *Neptune*, the base can handle four Polaris submarines and a full squadron of Fleet and patrol submarines at one time. The operational area includes a specially designed jetty for alongside berthing of nuclear submarines, a floating dock, and a Polaris school for training crews on a round-the-clock shift system.

Within its 70,000 square feet of workshops and computerised stores every piece of submarine equipment can be repaired or replaced. Besides first-class accommodation and messing for submarine crews whose vessels are refitting, extensive married quarters have been provided, and nearly 1,000 houses at Faslane and nearby Helensburgh built to accommodate the base staff and their families. Thus a unique close-knit naval community has come into being at Faslane, with its own centre, educational, recreational and welfare facilities.

A special armament depot for storage of the missiles and other armament stores was also constructed at Coulport, on the eastern shore of Loch Long a few miles from Faslane. In June 1967 a Nuclear Refuelling Station was completed in Rosyth dockyard as part of an extensive modernisation programme for that yard; and, as mentioned earlier, a Nuclear Facilities Base opened at Chatham dockyard in the following year.

In July 1971 the Queen authorised the issue of a distinctive badge to personnel of the Royal Navy's Submarine Command to indicate their specialist role in the Service. Taking the form of a gold metal brooch to be worn above or in the position of medal ribbons, the badge depicts two dolphins supporting a crown over a fouled anchor. Qualification for award requires a submariner to complete three different parts of submarine training: submarine theory, the specialist application to his particular trade, and practical work in a submarine at sea.

Although recognising their importance, the badge does not indicate that submariners form a private Navy, but brings them into line with aircrew, parachutists and other specialists. In fact, its introduction fulfilled an earlier Admiralty intention, for in 1958 an arm badge was produced for submarine ratings but never issued.

In the spring of 1963 a momentous change was foreshadowed in the control and direction of the Navy, which had remained almost unaltered since the days of Pepys. The Government announced that in order to centralise the administration of Britain's armed forces and improve control of defence policy, an integrated Ministry of Defence was to be set up and authority and responsibility vested in a single Secretary of State for Defence. The necessary legislation would be introduced during the coming autumn and the new Ministry established on 1st April 1964.

Because of the increasing interdependence in action of the three Services the move, long urged by many, followed logically on the creation sixteen years earlier of a single Defence Minister. Each Service was however to continue to keep its own separate identity, the traditional role of the Navy remaining unaffected.

Accordingly the offices of First Lord of the Admiralty and of the Secretaries of State for War and Air were abolished, together with the Board of Admiralty and the Army and Air Councils. In place of the latter there would be three Ministers of State for Defence (Royal Navy, Army and Royal Air Force), each assisted by a Parliamentary Under-Secretary of State to discharge whatever responsibilities were delegated to them from time to time by the Secretary of State over the whole of the defence field.

A Defence Council was to be established under the Secretary of State to exercise the powers of command and administrative control previously exercised by the Board of Admiralty and the Army and Air Councils. Replacing the Defence Board set up in 1958, the new Council would consist of:

The Secretary of State for Defence;

The Ministers of State for the Royal Navy, Army and Royal Air
    Force;
The Chief of the Defence Staff;
The Chief of the Naval Staff;
The Chief of the General Staff;
The Chief of the Air Staff;
The Chief Scientific Adviser to the Secretary of State for Defence;
The Permanent Under-Secretary of State.

(Subsequently the three Ministerial posts were abolished, and two
new posts created : Minister of Defence (Administration) and Minister
of Defence (Equipment), assisted by small teams of high-level advisers
on Personnel and Logistics, Projects, and Studies, the Boards of the
three Services coming under their respective Parliamentary Under-
Secretaries. Thus the revised Defence Council comprised the two
Ministers, the three Parliamentary Under-Secretaries, the Chief of the
Defence Staff, the three Chiefs of Staff, the Chief Adviser on Projects,
and the Permanent Under-Secretary; chaired as before by the
Secretary of State himself. The tasks of the new Ministers would be
chiefly concerned with organisation and procurement, while those of
the Under-Secretaries primarily with the efficient execution of policy
decisions.)

The Council would deal mainly with major defence policy, management being delegated to Navy, Army and Air Force Boards of
the Defence Council, of each of which the Secretary of State would
be chairman. Judicial and quasi-judicial powers for the review of
disciplinary awards, the redress of grievances and the like would be
vested in these Boards. But all regulations, orders and instructions
hitherto issued by the Board of Admiralty and by the Army and
Air Councils would be issued under the authority of the Defence
Council.

Within the Ministry the organisation would comprise the Defence
Staff, including the Naval, General and Air Staffs, under the Chief
of the Defence Staff and the Chiefs of Staff Committee; the Defence
Scientific Staff under the Chief Scientific Adviser; the Defence
Secretariat under the Permanent Under-Secretary of State; the staffs
of the principal personnel and administrative officers of the three
Services; the staff of the Controller of the Navy; the staff of the
Master General of the Ordnance, and the staffs of the Second Perma-
nent Under-Secretaries of State of the three Services.

In future the Secretary of State for Defence would present to

Parliament a single set of Defence Estimates, although the latter would continue to be debated separately each year.

Replacing the old-time Board of Admiralty, which had formerly consisted of nine members—two of them, the First Lord and the Civil Lord, political appointments—six naval officers known as Sea Lords, and the Permanent Secretary, would be a new Board consisting of the Chief of the Naval Staff and First Sea Lord; Vice and Deputy Chiefs of the Naval Staff; the Chief of Naval Personnel and Second Sea Lord; the Controller of the Navy, and the Chief of Naval Supplies and Transport and Vice-Controller. It was at first proposed that this new naval governing body should be known as the 'Navy Board', a reversion to the days of Henry VIII. But after a lively debate Parliament decided that their title should be 'Admiralty Board'.

The new Defence Ministry was to be housed under one roof in a building in Whitehall Gardens previously occupied by the Air Ministry and the Board of Trade. This meant therefore that the famous old Admiralty building at the top of Whitehall would no longer be the headquarters of Britain's Navy. On Thursday, 26th March 1964, the last meeting of the existing Board of Admiralty was held in the historic first floor Board Room, from which in the past Britain's sea affairs had been directed by such famous personalities as Admiral Lord St. Vincent and Sir Winston Churchill. The following statement by Earl Jellicoe, the First Lord, was recorded in the official minutes :

> We are now about to hold the last meeting of *this* Board in *this* room. It will be the last meeting of the Lords Commissioners for executing the Office of Lord High Admiral—a body which has been in being, with some interruptions—since 1628 and which has formed, and forms, part of our naval, indeed of our national tradition ... The next time we meet we shall be the Admiralty Board, not the Board of Admiralty. Whether the nature of our discussions will be changed or not is a thing that time will show. But in one way there will be no change. The Shop will remain open and the purpose of the Shop will remain the service of the Royal Navy, and through the Royal Navy, the nation.

Five days later, at sunset on 31st March, the crimson and gold anchor flag of the Lord High Admiral was hauled down in the presence of the Lords Commissioners and a naval guard and Royal Marines band playing *Auld Lang Syne* on Horse Guards Parade.

This flag had flown over the Admiralty building since the office of Lord High Admiral was first put into commission and only half-masted on the death of the Sovereign. From the 1st April onwards when the new Defence Ministry officially came into being it would be flown only by her Majesty the Queen, who now assumed the title of Lord High Admiral.

The nineteen-sixties marked the emergence into fully independent statehood of a large number of former British colonies and protectorates, twelve of them in the African continent alone. Not all accomplished the transition without 'birth pangs'. One of them involved Britain's armed forces, and particularly the Navy, in a prolonged 'brush fire' operation which lasted for several years.

Mention was made in Chapter 7 of the formation of the independent State of Malaysia, created by the federation of Malaya, Singapore, and the colonies of Sabah (British North Borneo) and Sarawak. The projected Federation was also to include the British-protected Sultanate of Brunei, whose ruler had accepted the plan in principle.

But on 8th December 1962 a large-scale revolt broke out in Brunei and the adjoining areas of Sarawak and North Borneo. The insurgents, who called themselves the 'North Borneo Liberation Army', were headed by the leader of the Brunei People's Party which was strongly opposed to Brunei's entry into the Federation. Styling himself 'Prime Minister of the Revolutionary State of North Kalimantan' (the Indonesian name for Borneo), he declared that he would fight Britain for independence even if it took twenty years, and ordered his forces to engage in general sabotage, particularly against the Shell oil installations in Brunei upon which the country's economy was almost entirely dependent.

To the Sultan's appeal for help British response was immediate. An advance party of 42 Royal Marine Commando was flown in from Singapore, other companies following by air and sea. Even before the complete unit had assembled in Brunei Town, one company of the Commando was despatched post-haste to Limbang where the Resident and five other Europeans, two of them women, were being held hostage by the rebels. After making a difficult ten-mile river approach in requisitioned lighters, the Marines stormed ashore on the night of 11th/12th December. They lost several killed and wounded in the initial landing, but drove off the rebels and rescued the hostages in the nick of time. Meanwhile other units of the Commando, using river boats and helicopters, took up pursuit of the fleeing rebels.

At the time of the outbreak HMS *Albion*, the Commando ship, with 40 Commando on board was away on exercises. Ordered back to Singapore at top speed, she embarked Headquarters 3 Commando Brigade and sailed for Labuan. 40 Commando were landed by helicopter and coastal craft at Kuching, in Sarawak, whence they were transported by air to Brunei to join up with 42 Commando on their jungle patrols. Other British warships, including the *Bulwark* and *Tiger*, destroyers and frigates, minesweepers and tank landing craft, were sent to the trouble spot by the Commander-in-Chief Far East, bringing more troops from Singapore and heavier fire support.

Within a week the main insurgent forces had been broken up and dispersed, but operations to round up those who had fled to jungle hideouts continued. While helicopters from the Commando ships supported the troops, supplying rations and other necessities and evacuating casualties and prisoners, coastal minesweepers maintained sea and river patrols, watching out for pirates, smugglers and illegal immigrants. When abnormally bad weather brought torrential rains which swept away houses and destroyed livestock and crops, food and supplies were taken to cut-off villagers by the sailors and troops.

By February 1963 all major towns in Sarawak and Brunei had been freed of rebel activities, and life was beginning to return to normal. British casualties in the operations had been seven killed, five of them Royal Marines, and twenty-eight wounded. Between sixty and seventy rebels had been killed and ten times that number captured. The Brunei People's Party was banned and several of its members arrested. Its leader fled to the Philippines.

Unfortunately this did not mark the end of the trouble. In September 1963 the new Federation of Malaysia was proclaimed, but without Brunei due to failure to reach agreement on the allocation of the Sultanate's oil revenues. The proclamation was met with violent reaction in Indonesia, whose President Sukarno had at the outset of the Brunei revolt declared his country's sympathy with the 'North Borneo Liberation Army' which he had surreptitiously supported. Now Sukarno not only refused to recognise the State of Malaysia, but threatened a 'terrible confrontation' with the new Federation. This was followed by widespread anti-British riots throughout Indonesia, during which the British Embassy in Jakarta and the homes of British nationals were sacked and burned by howling mobs. When Malaysia broke off diplomatic relations with Indonesia, Sukarno threatened to 'crush' her.

Guerrilla attacks were now stepped up all along the 970-mile frontier between Malaysian and Indonesian Borneo. British and Gurkha battalions and Royal Marine Commandos were engaged in extensive patrolling of the border against infiltration, and Royal Naval ships and coastal craft were sent in to back up the defensive operations of the Royal Malaysian Navy. To augment patrols around the Malayan coast, coastal minesweepers and seaward defence boats were brought out of local reserve at Singapore, and Australian and New Zealand warships joined in.

Naval helicopters created records for operational flying and maintenance over the steaming jungles of Borneo, transporting passengers and stores in all weathers. One of the most protracted policing operations undertaken by the Royal Navy, the Indonesian 'confrontation' lasted until mid-1966, when it was formally brought to an end by the signing of an agreement after President Sukarno had been ousted from power.

In addition to operating in Borneo itself, the Navy's primary task had been to guard the western coastline of Malaya against attempted infiltration by groups of Indonesian regulars, saboteurs and terrorists. This work was complicated by the barter trade which continued between the Indonesian islands, Malaya and Singapore, and the fishing craft swarming in the narrow waters of the Malacca and Singapore Straits. During the peak period of the emergency, British and Commonwealth warships were continuously on patrol in the Straits for over 700 days and nights, and intercepted 90 per cent of known attempts to infiltrate. The brunt of the patrols was borne by the little ships of the inshore flotillas which spent an average of twenty-one days a month at sea.

Commando ships filled a vast reinforcement role and were employed almost continuously ferrying battalions of Commonwealth troops and Army and RAF light aircraft to and from the operational area. From the opening stages of the 'confrontation' Royal Navy helicopters operated over near virgin jungle under extremely arduous conditions in support of the ground forces and largely pioneered special tactics and techniques of helicopter support during the campaign. Around the coast of Borneo warships and small armed motorboats manned by the Royal Navy kept up incessant patrols of offshore approaches and rivers vulnerable to infiltration by sea. Royal Marine Commandos, who had been the first to see action at the outset, were continuously on active service throughout the campaign. When British forces were finally withdrawn in September 1966, the last fighting unit to leave was, appropriately, 40 Commando.

Almost as long drawn out as the Indonesian 'confrontation' were the troubles which preceded the birth late in 1967 of the People's Democratic Republic of Yemen, which includes the former Aden Protectorate.

Early in 1963 Aden had joined the South Arabian Federation, a recently formed association of Arabian Amirates of the south. But there was considerable local opposition to the merger, some wanting union with neighbouring Yemen. This manifested itself in outbreaks of violence and terrorism, fomented and encouraged by the Yemen with Egyptian support. Backed up by British forces, which included Royal Marine Commandos and aircraft of the Royal Navy and RAF, the Federal Army tightened security along the border with Yemen and endeavoured to restore law and order.

Then in 1964 came an armed insurrection by tribesmen in the Radfan Mountains, north of Aden, actively supported by the Yemenis. Together with military reinforcements flown out from the United Kingdom, strong detachments from 45 Commando and the regular Federal Army operated for many months against the rebels in gruelling conditions up country. Naval helicopters working from the RAF station at Khormaksar helped to supply them with stores and equipment, water, food, ammunition and mail. Helicopters from the Commando ship *Albion* also aided security forces in Aden to combat terrorist outrages.

Two rival political factions were contending for power within the Federation: the Egyptian-sponsored 'National Front for Liberation of the Occupied South' (NLF), and the 'Front for the Liberation of Occupied South Yemen' (FLOSY), both of which also fought and harassed British forces and civilians. All attempts by the British Government to reach peaceful agreement on future independence for the Federation were frustrated, not least by the unhelpful intervention of the United Nations Colonialisation Committee.

Finally, when the Sultanates were overrun by the forces of the NLF and the Rulers were deposed, resigned or fled, the High Command of the Federal Army declared the NLF to be the only organisation representing the people of South Arabia. Accordingly power was ceded to its leaders, all British forces were withdrawn, and the country became an independent republic outside the Commonwealth on 30th November 1967.

No ceremony was held to mark the end of 129 years of British rule, but a special naval task force was assembled to cover the final stages of evacuation. Once again, Royal Marines were the last to leave.

They were the men of 45 Commando who had spent seven years in Aden, much of the time on active service, at a cost of six killed and sixty-two wounded.

Farther west the Royal Navy and Royal Marines were involved in more police actions when, early in 1964, mutinies broke out in the armies of newly independent Tanganyika (now Tanzania), Uganda and Kenya.

The troubles were sparked off when the government of the Sultan of Zanzibar was overthrown in January by a revolutionary party which seized power and proclaimed the establishment of a republic. The survey ship HMS *Owen*, which had been working off the Kenya coast, was ordered at full speed to Zanzibar to evacuate British subjects whose lives might be in danger. She was speedily joined by the frigate *Rhyl* from Aden.

A number of troops in the Tanganyikan Army then revolted, forced their British instructors to quit the country, and threatened and manhandled Europeans. When President Nyerere sought the assistance of the British Government, the *Rhyl* was ordered to Dar-es-Salaam from Zanzibar, while the aircraft carrier *Centaur* was despatched from Aden with units of 45 Commando. Landed by helicopter near the barracks occupied by the mutineers, they quickly overcame what resistance there was. Three African soldiers were killed and nine wounded without loss to the Marines.

With the situation restored, the Commando left at the end of the month and were replaced by 41 Commando which had been flown out from Britain to Nairobi following a request for help from the Kenya Government, which was also having trouble with mutinous troops.

Then unrest among men of the Uganda Rifles near Lake Victoria caused the President of that country to seek aid from the United Kingdom Government. A contingent of British troops was flown in from Nairobi, and reinforcements brought from Mombasa in the *Rhyl*. HMS *Owen* also remained at hand.

Two other former British protectorates in Africa which gained full independence in the nineteen-sixties were Nyasaland, which assumed self government in 1963 and became the independent State of Malawi in July 1966; and Northern Rhodesia which became the independent Republic of Zambia in October 1964. Prior to 1963 both countries had been united in a federation with Southern Rhodesia. But the break-up of the Federation was to bring a less happy outcome for the latter and involve the Navy in a long drawn-out and unpleasant duty.

In April 1964 and again the following year, discussions between Mr. Ian Smith, the Prime Minister of Southern Rhodesia, and successive British Governments failed to reach agreement on the form and constitution of independence for his country. Eventually, on 11th November 1965, Southern Rhodesia unilaterally and illegally declared itself independent, though at first remaining within the Commonweath. The United Nations Security Council called on all members to break off economic relations with Southern Rhodesia; only Portugal and South Africa refused to conform.

The United Nations called for an embargo on oil and petroleum products into Southern Rhodesia—subsequently full mandatory sanctions were imposed—and in pursuance of this resolution a naval blockade by British warships was begun early in 1966 off the port of Beira, in Mozambique. Since then British warships have been continually engaged on the 'Beira blockade'. Working in pairs, they usually spend up to six weeks at a stretch patrolling the Mozambique Channel in search of vessels seeking to break the blockade. Essential logistic support is provided by ships of the Royal Fleet Auxiliary.

On two occasions British warships provided the venue for meetings between British Government representatives and Mr. Smith in attempts to resolve the deadlock—in November 1966 on board the cruiser *Tiger* off Gibraltar, and two years later at Gibraltar in the assault ship *Fearless*. Both conferences failed to reach agreement. Meanwhile the Beira patrol continues, illustrating the Royal Navy's traditional capability of maintaining a military presence in an area far from its nearest base in support of Government policy.

On the other side of the Atlantic there was trouble in British Guiana during 1964 which arose from proposed constitutional changes, marked by strikes and terrorist activities. Since it proved impossible for the police to maintain law and order unsupported, the garrison was reinforced by troops flown out from the United Kingdom, and the Royal Marine detachment from the frigate *Whirlwind* was landed. Once again helicopters of all three Services made possible the rapid deployment of patrols to troubled areas.

Eventually the situation quietened down, elections were held for a National Assembly, and the new independent and renamed State of Guyana emerged in 1966. Four years later it became a republic within the Commonwealth.

With the ordering in 1964 of three oceanographical surveying ships of completely new design, a long overdue programme of modernisa-

tion of the Navy's ageing surveying fleet was put in hand. The programme also included four ships of a new class of coastal survey
craft to work on hydrographic surveying tasks overseas, and the
replacement of two old survey launches by the conversion of two
inshore minesweepers.

Not only was the existing surveying fleet becoming worn out; it
was stretched to the limit by a progressive expansion of effort
attributed to three main reasons reflecting the demands of this
modern age. First the growth in size and numbers of super-
tankers, necessitating more extensive knowledge of underwater
topography; second, the stimulation of interest in the continental
shelves due to the quest for untapped fuel resources beneath the sea:
and third, the requirements of deep-diving nuclear submarines.

Reconstituted soon after the end of the war, the Navy's surveying
fleet comprised eight ocean-going vessels, half employed in United
Kingdom waters and half overseas, and six wartime built harbour
defence motor launches for inshore work. Four of the larger vessels
were converted frigates of 1945 vintage, the others former fleet minesweepers which had begun their active lives as far back as the
nineteen-thirties. The only new additions had been the *Vidal*, mentioned earlier in connection with the formal annexation of the island
of Rockall, and three small 160-ton inshore survey craft which came
into service in 1959. Nevertheless, the volume of work performed by
these ships on a task that has no finality was truly immense.

Built with commendable speed, the first of the new larger ships
was commissioned for service in September 1965. Named *Hecla*, she
was quickly followed by the *Hecate* and *Hydra*, all names which have
old-time hydrographic connotations. Designed for world-wide operations and fitted with the most modern electronic and scientific equipment, the ships are 260 feet long, have a beam of 49 feet and displace
2,800 tons. Their hulls are all-welded and strengthened for navigating
in ice. Anti-roll tanks provide a stable platform for precise hydrographic work in varying sea conditions. Propulsion is diesel-electric,
and the ships have a bow thruster—a propeller built into a transverse
tunnel in the bow—to aid manoeuvrability. Their cruising speed is in
excess of 12 knots and they have an operational range of 12,000 miles.

The latest electronic navigation systems enable the ships to fix their
position accurately up to 200 miles off shore; sophisticated echo-
sounding gear can provide a picture of the seabed at any depth up to
five miles and its nature determined and photographed; while sample
cores can be drilled from the seabed at 33,000 feet. Continuous

underway records of the earth's magnetic gravity fields can be made. Cartographic work is carried on in special chartrooms, and laboratories are provided for scientific tasks. Each ship carries a Wasp helicopter, two 35-foot survey boats, and a Landrover for use in supporting survey parties ashore.

The ships, which have a complement of 13 officers and 104 ratings, including hydrographic specialists, are air-conditioned throughout and boast such previously unheard of amenities as a library, laundry and cinema. Accommodation includes cabins for senior ratings and fixed bunks for juniors, while a large single galley provides meals on the now customary cafeteria system. With capacious storerooms, electrical, engineering and shipwright workshops, these vessels, the first to be built on commercial lines without a supplementary naval function, can operate independently of shore support for long periods.

Deployed mainly in the deep oceans, they map the physical characteristics of these waters, their depths, currents, temperatures, salinities, densities, transparencies and acoustics, as well as the shape and composition of what lies beneath them. In due course they are to be joined by a fourth vessel of the same class, although slightly larger and incorporating various improvements.

The new coastal survey craft entered service in 1968, when the last of the older vessels was discarded. Named *Bulldog*, *Beagle*, *Fox* and *Fawn*, they, too, perpetuate earlier famous vessels in British hydrographical history.

With a length of 190 feet and a beam of 38 feet, they have a standard displacement of 1,030 tons. Diesel-propelled, their service cruising speed is 15 knots and endurance range 4,000 miles, enabling hydrographical survey work to be undertaken in coastal waters anywhere in the world. The ships have a complement of up to seven officers and thirty-six ratings, and are equipped with echo-sounders, fisherman's sonar (to search for and locate wrecks and underwater rock pinnacles), an electronic fixing system, precision ranging radar, and fibre-glass motor survey boats. Living conditions and accommodation are of a high standard of spaciousness and comfort.

In 1967 the Hydrographer introduced new-look, easier to read charts for the Royal Navy. The changes include the introduction of colour for land areas and inter-tidal zones, the adoption of modern symbolisation for traditional features, and the use of modern lettering and numerals. Perhaps an even more startling break with naval tradition was made when the Hydrographer announced that, following national policy towards the general adoption of the metric system, future Admiralty charts would show depths and heights in metres and decimetres instead of fathoms and feet. His announcement included the comment that 'the passing of the time-honoured fathom will no doubt occasion regret in some hearts, but its replacement by the metre should pose no problem to the mariner'. Nautical miles and cables were, however, retained, since the international nautical mile is in general use on the charts of nearly every nation.

In the following year the Hydrographic Department moved from Cricklewood in North London where the chart compilation offices had been located since 1946 to Taunton, in Somerset. Thus for the first time in almost 150 years the Department was reunited as a complete entity, except for small units in London and Hurstmonceux. It also included the Naval Weather Service which had earlier been merged back into the Department to form a new Oceanographical and Meteorological Services Division. The move from Cricklewood involved the transfer of several tons of historic documents, among them charts compiled by Captain Cook and earlier surveyors.

Some four and a half years after being taken in hand at Devonport dockyard for refitting and modernisation, the aircraft carrier *Eagle* finally emerged to rejoin the Fleet in May 1964. She was the second of the large fleet carriers to undergo major changes under the programme begun in the nineteen-fifties for the progressive improvement of carriers to maintain their ability to operate the most modern aircraft with their increasing weight and performance. With the exception of the *Victorious*, this was the biggest and certainly the most expensive modernisation project ever undertaken by a Royal dockyard. The bill came to £31 million, twice as much as the ship originally cost to build. Nevertheless money was saved thereby, since the cost of a new replacement for the *Eagle* and other fleet carriers would have been in excess of £50 million.

The alterations not only brought the vessel thoroughly up to date but were designed to extend her life well into the nineteen-seventies. Probably the most important of her new installations was 'ADA' (Action Data Automation), an automated system of handling tactical information received by her Type 984, or 3D, radar installation. 'ADA' could perform perfectly the duties which required no less than sixty men in the *Victorious* and *Hermes*.* Other examples of her electronic wizardry were an integrated and computer-assisted com-

* *Subsequently an even more versatile version of ADA was installed in the guided missile destroyers.*

munications system; and an all-round scanning sonar which could detect submarines and torpedoes from any direction and give sufficient warning to permit counter-action.

The carrier was also given a fully angled and extended flight deck, stouter flight deck armour, and a new 'island' superstructure incorporating equipment which cost approximately half the total amount spent on her modernisation. For close-range defence she deployed six Seacat guided missile systems, backed up by four twin 4.5-inch guns. Her two steam catapults were capable of launching the heaviest aircraft then in service and visualised for the future. She was also the first surface warship in the Royal Navy to be equipped with an inertial navigation system. These changes added some 8,000 tons to her original displacement of 36,800, giving a total of 50,000 tons at full load. But her active life after rejuvenation was to be comparatively brief.

While she was still in dockyard hands controversy arose over a proposal to replace the Navy's Sea Vixen day and night fighter by a supersonic vertical take-off (VTOL) strike fighter designated P.1154 which had been developed by Hawker Siddeley. Adoption of the P.1154 was to have been a joint venture between the Navy and the RAF, since the latter needed a replacement for their ground attack Hunter. But because agreement could not be reached over certain specialist requirements of the two Services, the high cost of development of the P.1154, and the fact that it would not be ready in time to serve as a replacement for the Hunter, the plan was dropped. Instead it was decided to purchase a number of McDonnell Phantom II aircraft from America, to be fitted with a British engine and other components, as a partial replacement for both Hunters and Sea Vixens.

The Phantom, a two-seat, all-weather strike fighter already in service with the US Navy, Air Force and Marines, had a top speed of 1,600 mph and could climb to 98,000 feet in just over six minutes. It fulfilled the requirements of the Royal Navy and would suit its air defence needs for many years. Accordingly twenty-eight of these aircraft were purchased, and the first Fleet Air Arm Phantom squadron formed for intensive flying trials in May 1968. Today the British version of the Phantom, powered by two Rolls-Royce Spey turbo-jet engines giving a speed of Mach 2 plus, and with an impressive attack capability, spearheads the striking force of the Fleet Air Arm along with the Buccaneer.

Among the miscellaneous small naval craft flying the White Ensign which from time to time patrolled the creeks and rivers of Sabah and Sarawak during the Indonesian 'confrontation' in 1964 were two strange looking objects which terrified the natives who beheld them for the first time. Even to more sophisticated Western eyes they resembled the 'flying saucers' of science fiction as they skimmed over mangrove swamps, beaches, mud flats and river surfaces with equal facility. They were in fact SRN.5 hovercraft, two of which were sent out by the Royal Navy to undergo extensive trials under active service conditions.

Ever since the first of these novel vehicles had been successfully tested in 1959, all three Services showed great interest in its military potential. In January 1962, by which time civilian hovercraft had entered commercial service as passenger and car ferries, the Admiralty set up the Inter-Services Hovercraft Trials Unit at HMS *Ariel*, Lee-on-Solent, with a mixed complement of sailors, soldiers and airmen to evaluate the uses of hovercraft in the anti-submarine, air-sea rescue and minehunting roles and logistic support of Army units.

Designed and built by the Saunders Roe Division of Westland Aircraft Ltd., in association with the National Research Development Corporation, to prove the working principles of air cushion vehicles devised by Mr. (now Sir) Christopher Cockerell, the SRN.1 was a 2-ton craft powered by a 435-hp engine, giving it a speed of 25 knots. The 1964 naval SRN.5 version was a 7-ton vehicle capable of speeds up to 70 knots. It could also operate over six-foot waves and in gale-force winds. The two craft sent out to Malaysia carried a radio and light machine-gun on service, and they could transport 15 fully equipped troops. Subjected to the most gruelling conditions for almost twelve months, they fully justified their existence as anti-infiltration patrols and amphibious transport vehicles.

In all, some four years were spent in thoroughly evaluating the performance of hovercraft under all sorts of conditions. Thus in addition to their work in Malaysia they were tested over pack ice in the North-West Territories of Canada and in the torrid deserts of the Middle East. They were also successfully tried out in the fishery protection role, the trials including poacher interception, navigational fixing, and boarding to make an arrest. In the event, the Army formed the world's first military hovercraft squadron early in 1967, to be followed in June of that year by the Royal Navy, which commissioned its own operational hovercraft unit under the title of Naval Party 8902'.

The unit consisted of two officers and eight ratings, and their craft was a civilian-type SRN.6 modified for Service use, including the installation of radar, fresh-water washing facilities to free the engine of salt deposits from spray during rough weather operations at sea, and comprehensive military communications equipment. Since its primary role was to be that of a fast amphibious communications craft capable of acting in support of Royal Marine units, it carried no armament. 48 feet long and 23 feet wide, and powered by a 900-hp Rolls-Royce Marine Gnome engine, it had a range of 200 miles and a speed of 50 knots, and could carry thirty fully equipped men or three tons of cargo. The unit's first overseas operational service was spent on further evaluation trials in the inhospitable waters around the Falkland Islands, and they subsequently successfully demonstrated their craft in several South American countries.

In 1970 the Inter-Services Hovercraft Unit took over the largest hovercraft thus far built for military service. Known as the BH.7, the vehicle is 78 feet long and 48 feet wide over the inflated skirt, and weights 40 tons. It is powered by a Marine Proteus gas turbine developing a maximum of 4,250 shp, giving a speed of over 70 knots in calm seas. With a normal crew of seven, short-term living and feeding accommodation is provided for ten people. Double bunk settees are fitted, with aircraft seats in rest areas. Storage for dry and frozen provisions is provided in a small galley, which is equipped with a microwave oven and radiant heat stove for cooking. Freight and vehicles can be embarked through a bow door when the craft is being used in the logistic support role.

Further developments visualised for this revolutionary addition to British naval strength are as fast patrol craft with speeds of up to 100 knots, armed with surface-to-surface missiles in addition to guns; as mine countermeasures craft, amphibious assault craft, and even ocean-going warships.

Following the setting up of NATO's command structure in 1949, units of the navies of member nations began regularly exercising together. At first these exercises were little more than attempts to practise communications and to give simple orders in a multi-national force. As the years went by they developed into large-scale fleet manoeuvres conducted under the direction of NATO flag officers of various nationalities and involving scores of ships and aircraft from many different countries. Gradually standards improved as lengthier and more sophisticated exercises were introduced.

But while for training purposes and in the event of war naval forces were earmarked by the oceanic NATO nations for assignment to the Supreme Allied Commander Atlantic, the latter had no permanent naval force attached to his command with which to demonstrate the will of the Alliance in an emergency. This somewhat anomalous situation was, at least partially, remedied after a novel experiment had been conducted in 1964. It followed on the late President Kennedy's promise to make a US warship available to demonstrate the concept of multi-national manning to interested countries within NATO.

Seven member nations, who included Britain, West Germany, Holland, Italy, Greece, Turkey* and the United States, agreed to provide contingents of officers and men to commission an American guided missile destroyer for a trial period. Under an American captain, the vessel was to spend several months at sea in European waters and the Mediterranean as a fully operational naval unit.

The experiment was a success in that it proved that officers and men from different countries and navies with widely varied technical and tactical practices could work together. But something more was needed. At the suggestion of Admiral Sir Charles Madden, then NATO Commander-in-Chief Eastern Atlantic, it was followed by the formation of a squadron of ships drawn from the navies of interested NATO countries to work and exercise together for a prolonged period.

Designated 'Matchmaker', the scheme was launched in March 1965. The original squadron was composed of four anti-submarine vessels, one each from Britain, the United States, Canada and the Netherlands. Initially under a British commander and with English as the common language, the Matchmaker squadron remained together for a period of five months, exercising operationally at sea, carrying out self maintenance in harbour and visiting the ports of other NATO countries.

Matchmaker was repeated over the next two years, with American and Dutch commanders taking over from the British. Its success was such that the feasibility of having a permanent NATO Navy became clearly apparent. Thus when reviewing strategy in December 1967, a Ministerial meeting of the Alliance in Brussels decided to turn Matchmaker into a permanent operational NATO force. Formally approved by the full NATO Council, it was inaugurated as 'Standing Naval Force Atlantic' (short title STANAVFORLANT) at Portland under a British commodore on 13th January 1968. Its aim was to

* *Turkey later withdrew from the experiment before the ship sailed.*

operate NATO naval units continuously as a single force to enhance the ability of the various navies to act together with the greatest effectiveness.

Four ships from Britain, the United States, the Netherlands and Norway comprised the force at first. Subsequently warships from every NATO country bordering on the sea have joined in, the vessels being sent on a rotational basis to stay for about five months at a time. Member nations take turns to provide the force commander and various staff officers each year, and its total strength is kept to a maximum of eight destroyers or frigates. Submarines and auxiliary vessels have also worked with it.

Operating under the overall command of the Supreme Allied Commander Atlantic, the Commander-in-Chief Eastern Atlantic controls the force when it operates in the eastern Atlantic area, administers the force, and is responsible for providing other services to assist it in its role. It is ready to proceed to any part of the Atlantic where its presence may be required as a visible deterrent. Because it is a NATO-led squadron, it provides a nucleus around which a more powerful NATO naval force can readily be assembled.

In 1973 a permanent NATO mine countermeasures force, composed of British, Dutch, Belgian and West German minesweepers and minehunters, was formed to take part in exercises and show the unity and common purpose of the Alliance. Known as the Standing Naval Force Channel (STANAVFORCHAN), it is commanded on a rotational basis by officers of the various navies of participating nations, and is the overall responsibility of the NATO Commander-in-Chief Channel Command.

CHAPTER TEN

The Navy of the Seventies

After more than twelve years continuously in office, the Conservative Government was replaced by a Labour Administration in the autumn of 1964. As might be expected, the change in government brought about changes in policy affecting the armed forces. Despite the inevitable criticisms, not all of them were perhaps for the worse.

Introducing their first defence budget, details of which were published early in 1965, the new Administration complained that it had inherited defence forces which were seriously overstretched and in some respects dangerously under-equipped. The past expenditure of many millions of pounds had failed to provide the necessary incentive for voluntary recruitment in some vital fields or produce all the weapons needed for current tasks. No real attempt had been made to match political commitments to military resources, nor defence resources to the economic circumstances of the nation.

Accordingly a series of studies on defence policy would be set in train to try to ascertain the means by which defence expenditure could be reduced over the next few years to roughly the present figure in real terms. The way estimates had been presented in the past defeated effective planning, having previously been divided into categories of expenditure which did not show the functions for which they were visualised.

As part of the reorganisation of the Ministry of Defence, a unified Operational Requirements Committee had been set up to make a closer examination of new requirements and the progress of research and development. The examination would include for the first time the 'cost effectiveness' of new equipment and obviate duplication with other equipment. A special department was also being created (Defence Operational Analysis Establishment) staffed by officers of the three Services, scientists, administrators and economists, to carry out cost-effective studies, the nature of future warfare, and the types of weapons required by the Services in the long term. These measures, together with a system of functional costings, would provide essential tools for producing more economical defence programmes, the aim being to obtain the most efficient fighting forces at the lowest cost.

The budget totalled just over £2,000 million, of which nearly one-quarter was to be spent on the Navy, but not on new construction which would have to await the findings of the defence review. Meanwhile the shortage of naval manpower had to be tackled. The age-old cry was repeated that too few men, particularly in skilled trades, were re-engaging for further service and, although the rate of recruitment was being maintained, the numbers fell short of requirements, especially in the seaman category, and would have to be stepped up. More important was the falling rate of re-engagement, the trend being largely attributable to the separation from home associated with naval service. In yet another attempt to remedy this, two new schemes were introduced.

All researches showed that the key to re-engagement problems was the sailor's family life. Aimed at inducing the more experienced men to stay on in the Service, the first of these schemes was to give them financial help to buy their own homes. Leading ratings and above and their Royal Marine counterparts who re-engaged, or had re-engaged to complete time for pension would therefore now be able to obtain a loan on favourable terms so as to bridge the gap between the price of a house and a normal building society mortgage.

The second scheme applied only to skilled and semi-skilled ratings in categories where shortages were particularly acute: engine-room, weapons, electrical and radio artificers and mechanicians, and electrical and radio mechanics. Ratings of these branches who signed on beyond their first engagement of nine or twelve years for twenty-two years' service would in future receive a taxable re-engagement grant. This would be £750 for all except engine-room artificers and mechanicians, who would receive £375, payment being confined to leading ratings and above. Ten per cent of the grant would be paid to those who qualified when they signed on for the new engagement, and the balance when they began their tenth or thirteenth year of service. (This had the desired effect for, the re-engagement position having improved, the scheme was ended in March 1969).

In the spring of the following year the Government published its promised defence review, the chief objectives of which were to relax the strain imposed on the nation's economy by the inherited defence programme, and to shape a new defence posture for the Seventies.

This declared that to continue spending 7 per cent of the gross national product on defence would be seriously damaging to Britain's economy at a time when a rapid increase in production was required, industry needed to be re-equipped and modernised to increase production for exports, and the country was running into a shortage of manpower. Defence expenditure was therefore to be brought down to a stable level of about 6 per cent of the gross national product by 1969–70, and a financial target of £2,000 million at 1964 prices was set to be reached in that year.

Outlining future policy, the Government emphasised that, while general disarmament remained a major aim, membership of the North Atlantic Alliance would continue as being vital to Britain's survival, but there would be limitations on her commitments outside Europe. Thus no major operations of war would be undertaken except in co-operation with allies; no obligation accepted to provide another country with military assistance unless the latter was prepared to provide the facilities needed to make such assistance effective in time; and no attempt made to maintain defence facilities in an independent country against its wishes.

Overseas, naval and other installations in Gibraltar would continue to be maintained and, although Britain had a defence agreement with Malta, economies would be made there over the next few years. Defence facilities would be withdrawn from Aden after South Arabia became independent in 1968 (as already described, this actually took place about a year earlier), but Britain's remaining obligations in the Middle East would be fulfilled by making a small increase in British forces stationed in the Persian Gulf. Military facilities in Malaysia, Singapore and Hong Kong would be retained, and British obligations to CENTO and SEATO fulfilled.

The role of the Navy was re-defined as being (a) to make a contribution in keeping the peace and furthering the trade and other interests of the country; (b) to be ready in emergency to safeguard use of the sea and to support the Army; and (c) to make an effective contribution to the naval forces of NATO, CENTO and SEATO.

Ships of the Fleet were now divided into two main categories: the 'Nuclear Strategic Force', consisting of the Polaris submarines; and the 'General Purpose Combat Elements', comprising amphibious forces; aircraft carriers and squadrons; Fleet and patrol submarines; cruisers; destroyers and frigates; mine countermeasures forces, and support and other auxiliaries. While naval stations as such had virtually disappeared, the 'Combat Elements' of the Fleet continued to be disposed under geographical heads. In emergency, all could be sent if required to other theatres, either to reinforce or undertake joint operations with the Army and RAF.

Thus there were the ships on Home Sea Service (Home Fleet), which included destroyers and frigates, submarines and coastal minesweepers, whose main tasks were to carry out training, trials and fishery protection (the frigate elements of the Fishery Protection Squadron became part of the Home Fleet in 1967); also certain NATO commitments. In addition there were always a certain number of General Service commission ships on the Home Station, mainly to refit and give crew leave. Operational Fleet Air Arm squadrons were also temporarily based in the United Kingdom while their parent carrier was being refitted.

In the Mediterranean and Near East were stationed destroyers, frigates and minesweepers, supplemented from time to time by other major units of the fleet. Aircraft carriers and Commando ships operated between the Middle and Far East commands to cover the seas east of Suez. In the Far East various types of smaller warships were maintained, also Royal Australian and Royal New Zealand naval ships attached to the command as part of the Commonwealth Strategic Reserve. A small force of frigates was stationed in the Caribbean and South Atlantic, and an ice patrol ship in the Falkland Islands and Antarctic.

The Reserves comprised two main elements : the regular Reserves, consisting of officers on the Emergency and Retired Lists, pensioner ratings, and the Royal Fleet Reserve; and the volunteer Reserves, consisting of the Royal Naval Reserve and associated women's Reserves, and the Royal Marine Forces Volunteer Reserve (renamed Royal Marines Reserve in 1966). There were eleven Royal Naval Reserve Divisions, each having a coastal minesweeper attached, which collectively formed the Tenth Mine Countermeasures Squadron. Thus a total of some 14,000 officers and 23,000 ratings could be mobilised in emergency, of which 5,000 officers and 5,500 ratings belonged to the volunteer Reserves.

Fleet strength showed four aircraft carriers in service and one in reserve; two Commando ships; two Assault ships; one cruiser in commission and four in reserve; six guided missile destroyers; nine destroyers—four of them of the obsolescent *Daring* class—and eleven in reserve; fifty-six frigates in commission, including seven Tribals, three anti-aircraft and three air-direction, plus fourteen in reserve; thirty-six submarines, including three nuclear, and ten in reserve; sixty-one minesweepers, coastal and inshore, and thirty-six others in reserve.

The Government's plans for 'the Navy of the Seventies' included conversion of the *Tiger* class cruisers to carry anti-submarine heli-copters, confirming a decision taken by the previous Administration in 1964; and a new type ship designed to succeed them. In the event only two of the three cruisers were actually converted due to shortage of manpower.

But the plans contained an unexpected blow for the Fleet Air Arm. In 1963 the Conservative Government had announced its intention to order a new aircraft carrier (designated CVA.01) to replace the *Victorious* which was expected to end her useful life in 1970. After the new Government came to power Mr. Mayhew, Minister of State for Defence (Navy), hinted publicly that since only the *Hermes* and the newly modernised *Eagle* could operate Phantom aircraft, the new carrier would certainly be built, and might be expected to be followed by others.

But before publishing the results of their defence review, the Government decided not to build CVA.01. Disagreeing profoundly with the Cabinet's revised defence plans, both Mr. Mayhew and the First Sea Lord, then Admiral Sir David Luce, resigned in protest. The former was replaced by Mr. Mallalieu, and Admiral Sir Varyl Begg took over as First Sea Lord.

Justifying their decision not to order a new carrier, the Government explained that experience and study had shown that only one type of operation existed for which carriers and carrier-borne aircraft would be indispensable : the landing or withdrawal of troops against sophisticated opposition outside the range of land-based air cover. Unaided by allies, Britain could not expect to undertake operations of this character in the nineteen-seventies, even if the country could afford a larger carrier force. The best that could be maintained in the future would be very small. The existing force of five carriers would reduce to three in a few years' time. Even if CVA.01 were to be built, the force would still be limited to three throughout the seventies at a cost of some £1,400 million over a ten-year period, which would give an insufficient operational return for money.

The tasks for which carrier-borne aircraft might be required in the later seventies could be more cheaply performed in other ways. Thus aircraft operating from land bases would take over the strike recon-naissance and air defence functions of the carrier on the reduced scale envisaged for British commitments after the mid-Seventies. Close anti-submarine protection of naval forces would be given by heli-copters operating from ships other than carriers.

But in order to give time to reshape the Navy and re-provide the necessary parts of the carrier's capability, the existing carrier force would continue as far as possible into the Seventies. The *Ark Royal** was therefore to be given a major refit, and the Fleet Air Arm gradually run down.

To counter-balance this unwelcome news was the announcement that the first of a new class of guided missile destroyers, designated 'Type 82', was to be ordered. Displacing about 6,000 tons, slightly larger than the existing County class, the ships were to be designed around a powerful new weapons system. Propelled by a combination of steam and gas turbines, they would be fitted with an Action Data Automation (ADA) system, new 3D radar and other sensors, and the latest radar and sonar to provide long-range information for the Sea Dart and Ikara weapons with which they were to be armed.

Sea Dart, a highly sophisticated missile developed to meet the air threat of the future, is a semi-active radar-homing weapon, smaller and lighter than the Seaslug but with a considerably improved surface-to-air performance, particularly at very high and very low levels. It has a quicker reaction time, considerably improved target-handling capacity, and effective anti-ship capability. All-British, the missile can be fitted in small ships, and meets NATO military requirements.

Ikara, an anti-submarine missile developed by the Royal Australian Navy, is designed to deliver a homing torpedo to a position where it can attack submarine targets. Propelled by a rocket motor providing it with long-range capability, the weapon is equipped with an all-weather rapid reaction system conferring considerable accuracy.

But only one of the Type 82 vessels was in fact to be built. Laid down in 1967, she was launched in mid-1969 and named *Bristol*. Chief among the various factors which combined to bring about cancellation of her three projected sisters was the conversion solely to gas turbine propulsion during 1966 of the Blackwood class frigate *Exmouth*, the first warship in the Western world to be so powered. The space and weight-saving advantages of this revolutionary development were so attractive that they prompted a fresh design for a missile-armed destroyer, smaller and more cost-effective than the Type 82. Two years later the policy of fitting gas turbine propulsion in all future ships of the Royal Navy was adopted, and a new design

---

* *Launched in 1950 and first commissioned in 1955, the* Ark Royal, *sister ship of the* Eagle, *underwent modernisation between 1966 and 1969 at a cost of £32 million which transformed her into the Navy's most powerful aircraft carrier.*

of guided missile destroyer known as the 'Type 42' was ordered. The first of these was launched in June 1971 and named *Sheffield*.

Barely had the criticism aroused by the Government's decisions regarding the future size and shape of Britain's armed forces begun to subside when it was revived by the publication in the following year of two further Defence White Papers. The second, a supplementary one, followed discussions by the NATO Defence Planning Committee on a possible revision of Alliance strategy, but in the event made no alteration to British naval commitments to NATO. These stated that the review of defence policy started in 1966 was a continuous exercise, and announced further decisions. As regards the Royal Navy they can be briefly summarised.

While continuing to play a leading part in the maritime forces of NATO, outside Europe the Navy would provide a peacekeeping capability in the Indo-Pacific area. Its roles, to which the Royal Marine Commandos in the amphibious ships would have a vital contribution to make, were therefore, as ever, far-ranging across the world.

Apart from the Polaris submarines, there would be a growing force of nuclear Fleet submarines with a virtually limitless potential. The surface fleet would be strengthened by the addition of more *Leander* type vessels, with a new small frigate as successor. (Known as Type 21 and designed as a collaborative venture by Yarrow and Vosper Thornycroft, the first of the latter, named *Amazon*, was launched in 1971. A total of eight are to be built.) The latter would be armed with a new close-range, surface-to-air missile to follow the Seacat,* a medium range gun, and a new general purpose helicopter to replace the Wasp.

The design of the Type 82 would be developed, firstly into a new class of (through-deck) cruisers to succeed the converted *Tiger* class; and secondly, scaled down, for the new class of smaller (Type 42) destroyers. The cruisers, which would provide command and control facilities for the naval forces, would be armed with the Sea Dart. They would each deploy a force of Sea King helicopters carrying not only anti-submarine weapons and sonar, but also an air-to-surface guided weapon. The new destroyers would carry a modified Sea Dart and a smaller helicopter. All future frigates would carry helicopters with the most effective capacity for submarine and surface ship attack that these aircraft can offer. Future alternative developments in mine

---

* *Called 'Sea Wolf', this confers greatly improved self defence capability against supersonic anti-ship missiles and aircraft.*

countermeasures and inshore patrol craft were being studied, and replacements for the Commando ships would be considered when the need arose. The aircraft carrier *Victorious* would be phased out in 1969 and the *Hermes* in 1970.

In manpower terms the task over the next seven to nine years was to tailor the numbers and specialisations of officers and ratings to the size and shape of the Fleet in the Seventies, and its afloat and shore support within the framework of improving Service conditions. The strength of the Navy and Marines, including WRNS and QARNNS, then standing at 97,000, was to be reduced to an estimated 88,400 by 1971. Although the reductions would be achieved chiefly by natural wastage and adjustment of entries over the next ten years, there would be some redundancies.

For officers these were not expected to exceed 500 out of a total of about 10,000. For ratings they were unlikely to affect artificers and mechanicians, supply and secretariat, medical, submarine ratings, radio operators, Royal Marines, and Wrens and Nurses. Non-continuous service engagements and engagements beyond twenty-two years ('Fifth' and 'Sixth Fives') would have to be reduced. No redundancies would, however, start until 1970–71. Compensation would take the form of tax-free lump sum payments and various retired pay or pension benefits for officers and men prematurely released.

As to overseas commitments, withdrawal from bases in Singapore and Malaysia would be effected by the mid-nineteen-seventies, though naval and amphibious forces would be left, and from Malta by the end of 1970.

Rundown of our naval forces in the Mediterranean had in fact begun when the naval dockyard in Malta was converted to commercial use. Ships on the station declined as those east of Suez increased. By the end of 1964 the Mediterranean Fleet was down to four frigates and six coastal minesweepers. Since then, on average, no more than fourteen British warships of all types had been present in the area during any one year, chiefly to take part in various NATO exercises.

By 1966 naval facilities in Malta had been reduced to the status of forward operating base, including a fleet maintenance unit to ensure that ships could be accepted for minor repairs, self refits, etc. But a larger scale organisation existed in embryo which could be activated to provide support for ships, including carriers, operating in the eastern Mediterranean in 'brush fire' wars. These were now to go, as also was the Mediterranean Station as such. But first another British naval station was to disappear.

In January 1967 the ten-year old agreement with South Africa for the continuing use of the Simonstown base was re-negotiated. At the same time, as part of the economy programme, it was decided to withdraw our Commander-in-Chief South Atlantic, whose 'fleet' had by now shrunk to two frigates, one of which was permanently in the West Indies, and for the South African Government to assume greater responsibility for that area in time of war. From 12th April therefore that part of the old station in which South Africa lies became the responsibility of the Commander-in-Chief Home Fleet, a commodore being appointed as his representative in South Africa to continue the existing liaison with the South African Navy, and as naval attaché on the staff of the British Ambassador.

On 11th April the flag of the Commander-in-Chief South Atlantic, Vice-Admiral J. M. D. Gray, was lowered for the last time. But the final act of closing the command took place seventeen days later when in a more impressive ceremony the Queen's Colour of the station was slow-marched through the dockyard and embarked in the last remaining frigate, which then sailed for home. Thus ended 170 years of British naval history at the Cape.

With further reductions being made in the base facilities in Malta, the decision was now taken to abolish the Mediterranean command to coincide with the expiration of the normal period of appointment of the Commander-in-Chief, Admiral Sir John Hamilton. When therefore the admiral struck his flag on 5th June 1967 the Royal Navy's Mediterranean Station ceased to exist. In his place a Rear-Admiral was appointed as Flag Officer Malta to administer the remaining naval installations in the island. Admiral Hamilton was thus the last of ninety British naval commanders-in-chief to fly their flags in the Mediterranean since 1711. Among these were numbered such illustrious names as Hood, St. Vincent, Nelson, Cunningham and Mountbatten.

The abolition of the British naval commander-in-chief in the Mediterranean necessitated certain changes in NATO naval commands in the area. Two new posts were created: that of Commander, Allied Forces Southern Europe, held by an Italian admiral with headquarters at Naples; and Commander, South-East Mediterranean Area, held by the Flag Officer Malta. Both came under the overall command of the NATO Commander-in-Chief, Allied Forces Southern Europe.

From 6th June 1967 control of all Royal Navy ships in the Mediterranean also passed to the Commander-in-Chief, Home Fleet, who now became responsible for all ships in the sea areas west of Suez. These areas were in future to be known as the Western Station, and his title was altered to Commander-in-Chief, Western Fleet. Stretching from Pole to Pole, his command included the west coast of Africa and round the Cape to a point roughly halfway between Capetown and Port Elizabeth. At the same time all Royal Navy ships east of Suez were designated Eastern Fleet and came under the control of the Commander Far East Fleet.

To round off this account of the re-structuring of commands in the Navy of the seventies, it is convenient here to record subsequent further changes which took place in the context of the new defence policy of unified commands and economy in administration.

In July 1969 the appointment of Commander-in-Chief, Portsmouth, lapsed and this officer now became Commander-in-Chief of a newly constituted Home Station, with responsibility for three of the four naval shore commands in the United Kingdom. Odd man out was the Flag Officer, Scotland and Northern Ireland, who retained his independent command except for shore training matters since these now came within the administration of the Home Station commander-in-chief.

Although the latter continued to retain responsibility for the Portsmouth area, the Admiral Superintendent, Portsmouth, was re-appointed as Flag Officer Spithead and Admiral Superintendent, responsible to the Commander-in-Chief for the fleet base and to the Ministry of Defence for the dockyard. At the same time the post of Flag Officer, Medway, and Admiral Superintendent Chatham was upgraded to full flag officer status and the boundaries of his command extended. The appointment of Commander-in-Chief, Plymouth was abolished in May 1969, being replaced by a Flag Officer, Plymouth.

Two years later when the appointment of Commander Far East Fleet was also abolished, the combined east and west of Suez naval forces of Britain became simply 'the Fleet', and the Commander-in-Chief Western Fleet was re-titled 'Commander-in-Chief Fleet'. This was not a new conception, but a reversion to an earlier century when the British Navy was deployed under a single commander-in-chief.

Under this arrangement two subordinate flag officers were appointed to exercise command at sea. Designated the Flag Officers, First and Second Flotillas respectively, each commanded a guided missile destroyer squadron and a number of frigate squadrons.

Additionally, responsibility for the Portland squadron came under the former, with Portsmouth as home port; while the latter, who also commanded the cruisers *Tiger* and *Blake*, was made responsible for the Dartmouth Training Squadron, with Devonport as home port. A third flag officer, with the title 'Flag Officer, Carriers and Amphibious Ships' (FOCAS) was appointed to spend part of his time at sea and part ashore.

Unaffected by these arrangements were the Flag Officer Submarines, the Hydrographer of the Navy, the Flag Officer Sea Training, the Senior Naval Officers, West Indies and South Africa, and the Captain, Minesweeping and Mine Countermeasures.

The changeover in the Navy's sea command whereby all warships now come under a single 'Supremo' brought little variation to the existing work of the Commander-in-Chief Fleet in his headquarters at Northwood. The network of communications established when the Western Fleet was formed was already world-wide. What had changed was responsibility. Should a war situation involving the Royal Navy develop anywhere in the world, strategic directions can be flashed across the globe from the underground nerve centre at Northwood, where all information from airborne early warning, surface ship radar, submarine reports, and intelligence is centralised, the tactical command of ships being left to the flag officer on the spot.

In September 1971 the Flag Officers and Admiral Superintendents of the Royal dockyards were re-styled 'Port Admirals' and dropped the title of Admiral Superintendent. This change reflected developments in the organisation and management of support facilities at the main bases. While the responsibility of the general managers of dockyards had increased, there was also a wider naval base concept than formerly, under which the Port Admiral was required to control and co-ordinate a wide range of base support activities, to include ship repair and fleet maintenance organisations, stores and transport establishments, operational support elements, and accommodation and other services for uniformed personnel.

Following closely on the Government's defence review, various economic troubles bedevilling the country necessitated further cuts in defence expenditure. It was aimed to secure these however without changing political commitments or the structure of the armed forces already settled; the major contribution to savings being sought in the field of hardware. This meant postponement and cancellation of building programmes, the rundown of stocks, and research and development expenditure. For the Navy these cancellations included the immediate phasing out of the aircraft carrier *Victorious*, and a reduction in the number of Buccaneer aircraft on order for the Fleet Air Arm.

The planned withdrawal of British forces in Malaysia, Singapore and the Persian Gulf was now to be advanced and completed by the end of 1971, the garrison and naval base at Hong Kong being retained, and no special capability maintained outside Europe after that date—although forces could be deployed overseas if circumstances demanded. The remaining carriers would then be phased out. There would also be some reduction in the rate of new construction. Naval manpower was to be further cut, the reductions being accelerated, and the original figure of 88,400 reduced to 79,000 by 1973.

As before, the redundancies were as far as possible to be volunteers, but if these were insufficient or unsuitable, officers and men would have to be detailed for premature release. Thus about 700 officers were to go, 3,750 ratings and 250 Royal Marines, but there would be no redundancies in the WRNS or QARNNS. Releases would be effected in two phases spread over a period of three years. Locally entered personnel from the Maltese, Singapore and Goan Divisions would be run down, but those from Hong Kong continued. Since fixed wing flying would cease with the phasing out of the carriers, the Fleet Air Arm was the Service area most affected.

No further drastic changes affecting the Navy were announced in the Labour Government's two succeeding defence budgets. But to stimulate recruiting in the seaman and electrical mechanic branches, whose numbers were seriously under strength and intake continuing to decline, a new type of engagement was introduced. Aimed at young men of 18 or over, the engagement was in effect for four years. Thus entrants under the scheme could sign on for nine years' service, followed by three years in the Reserve, with the option of shortening the engagement to four years followed by three in the Reserve. Men engaging with this option would receive a slightly reduced rate of pay from those committed to the nine-year engagement. But at any time after the first three months of service the option to leave at the four-year point could be renounced, and from then on they would become eligible for the full rates of pay.

A change of strategy affecting the Mediterranean was, however, necessitated by the spread of Russian influence in the area which was filling the naval vacuum left by the British withdrawal. After that station had been closed down it had been intended to retain the squadron of minesweepers which had been left behind in Malta only until the spring of 1969, backed up by two frigates which would be sent out on a rotational basis earmarked for NATO but not based on Malta. But in view of increasing Russian naval and maritime air activity in the Mediterranean, the decision was taken in 1968 to strengthen Britain's contribution to NATO's southern flank by stationing an aircraft carrier, or a Commando or assault ship, and a guided missile destroyer almost continuously in the area, supported by Royal Fleet Auxiliary ships.

Farther east, in pursuance of the policy of phased withdrawal from that part of the world, Singapore dockyard was in the process of being handed over to be managed by a British firm on behalf of the Singapore Government (Singapore had left Malaysia in 1965 to become an independent Republic). But for some time the Royal Navy continued to be its main client, the Far East Fleet still comprising more than thirty vessels, including a Commando ship and submarines. Also attached were frigates from the two Commonwealth navies. At Hong Kong was a mine countermeasures squadron.

In the early summer of 1970 a general election once more returned a Conservative Government to power. Notwithstanding criticisms of the general defence policy of their predecessors while in opposition, the decision to withdraw from Malaysia and Singapore was not rescinded by the new Administration. But, believing that a continuing British presence would help to preserve confidence in the area, withdrawal was not now to be total. After consulting with the Governments of Australia, New Zealand, Singapore and Malaysia regarding the defence of south-east Asia, it was agreed that a Commonwealth Naval Task Force should be formed and based on Singapore. Known as the ANZUK Force, this would consist of a number of frigates or destroyers provided by the Royal Navy, the Royal Australian and Royal New Zealand navies. A submarine would also be attached to the Force, and other British warships, including major units, would pay regular visits to the area for maritime exercises and training.

The Five-Power Agreement was duly signed in April 1971 and, four months later, on the last day of October, the flag of Rear-Admiral J. A. R. Troup, Commander Far East Fleet, was lowered over the Singapore naval base and his command ceased to exist. He was the last of sixty-nine British flag officers to exercise command in the Far East since the first was appointed in 1816. In his place

Rear-Admiral D. Wells of the Royal Australian Navy hoisted his flag as the first Commander of the ANZUK Force, its naval component being commanded by a British commodore.

Only one other British overseas naval command now remained, and this, too, was closed down when on 4th November 1971 the broad pennant of Commodore Sir Peter Anson, Commander Naval Forces Gulf, was hauled down over HMS *Jufair*, the shore base on Bahrain Island. Its closure followed discussions with local rulers in the Persian Gulf as to how best Britain could contribute to the maintenance of peace and stability in the area, with no final settlement being reached. It was therefore decided to withdraw our remaining naval forces, leaving behind only a small military presence. Regular visits to the Gulf would continue to be made, however, by one or more of the six frigates to be stationed east of Suez.

The squadron of minehunters based on Hong Kong for maritime policing duties remained unaffected. Subsequently they were reinforced by a frigate sent out to act as permanent guardship at Hong Kong.

In 1972, following discussions with the Malta Government, a military agreement was signed giving Britain the right in peace and war to station forces and use facilities in Malta for the defence purposes of the United Kingdom and of NATO. These included port and harbour facilities, naval and air headquarters, barrack accommodation, and the use of an airfield. Following the signing of this agreement, units of all three Services returned to the island. But the Mediterranean Fleet as such was not to be revived.

In a supplementary White Paper on defence policy the new Administration also announced that because the plan to phase out the fixed wing carriers would have created a serious gap in the capability of the Fleet, the *Ark Royal* would remain in commission until the late nineteen-seventies. By then improved weapons systems would be coming into service, and the new cruisers capable of operating V/STOL Harrier aircraft and advanced helicopters becoming available. The *Eagle* would not however be retained, nor would the *Ark Royal* be replaced by another fixed wing carrier. Some adjustment would be made to the rundown of Fleet Air Arm officers and ratings, but recruitment for fixed wing flying would not be re-opened.

By 1973 the *Eagle* had been reduced to a hulk, and at the same time the ageing Commando ship *Albion* was discarded, her place being taken by the *Hermes* which had been newly converted to the role. In that year also the first of the new through-deck cruisers was ordered and given the name *Invincible*.

The continuing rundown of Britain's overseas bases meant that gaps could be created in the Navy's communications network, which was dependent on high frequency radio links.

Since radio frequency bands were becoming saturated, British scientists had for some years been researching into the potentialities of satellite communications for defence purposes. The Americans were also experimenting in this field, and in the early sixties a collaborative effort was begun when the Anglo-American Interim Defence Communications Satellite Project (IDCSP) was set up to test the efficacy of global communications in the military sphere, using artificial satellites as active repeaters in the microwave range of frequencies.

Briefly, the system requires the positioning into geo-stationary orbit of transmitting satellites whose operating functions and position in the sky are controlled from an earth station. Signals are transmitted to the satellites and re-transmitted so that they can be picked up by any station within coverage of the satellites. These signals are received through a ground terminal which consists of a parabolic dish aerial directed at the satellite through an auto-tracking system.

The advantages of such a communications system are flexibility, independence of relay stations, higher quality unaffected by variations in ionospheric conditions, and longer transmissions. Communication can be established over a third of the earth's surface from a single site. Many simultaneous channels of communication can be handled, and telegraphy, voice and facsimile traffic accommodated.

The first of three British ground stations, interoperable with US stations, was set up early in 1966 and manned by Royal Navy communications specialists. Using satellites launched by the Americans, the system was successfully proved. In the following year a smaller British terminal was set up in the trials frigate *Wakeful* to explore the problems of a shipborne system and, in particular, the communications traffic capacity of a small terminal, the operational procedures necessary to provide an effective mobile communications system, and the techniques for acquiring and maintaining communications in a ship environment of motion and radio interference. Whereas a 40-foot diameter dish aerial was used on shore, that fitted in the *Wakeful* was only 6 feet in diameter.

Two years later, profiting from the experience gained in the earlier experiments with IDCSP, and using satellites procured from and launched by the Americans, but controlled by telemetry and command stations built in the United Kingdom, an all-British satellite communications system known as 'Skynet' was brought into operation. The first shipborne terminals were fitted in the assault ships *Intrepid* and *Fearless*, being subsequently transferred to the *Ark Royal* and *Hermes*. Since then a new 3½-foot lightweight terminal has been produced for fitting in smaller ships. Skynet is complementary to and interoperable with IDCSP.

Representing an important milestone in naval signalling history, which dates back more than six centuries, Skynet provides an operational communications capability of far more flexibility and greater capacity than ever before. The majority of British warships are to be fitted with the system, when they will be able to send and receive messages (SATCOMS) by space relay with complete security and freedom from the interference encountered with conventional radio traffic.

As part of the various satellite programmes then current, the US Navy launched 'Project Transit', subsequently to become firmly established as the 'Navy's Navigation Satellite system' (NAVSAT), to provide data by means of which the position of ships and submersibles anywhere in the world can be accurately fixed on an all-weather basis.

The principle of the system is to enable a ship to determine her position by measuring the doppler shift of signals received from one or more of the system's special satellites. 'Doppler' is a term well known to sonar operators, and denotes the change in the tone of a 'ping' depending on whether the range between a surface ship and a submarine she is hunting is opening or closing; or, more simply, the change of sound frequency when the source of it is moving towards or away from the observer.

Similarly with radio waves. When a ship receives transmissions from a satellite passing overhead, these are heard in rising frequency as the satellite approaches. For a brief period the note remains constant, then begins to diminish in frequency as the satellite recedes. This change in frequency depends directly on the position of the ship in relation to the orbiting satellite. Therefore, if the path of the latter is known to a receiving ship it is possible to compute her position.

To provide the ship with details of this path four satellites are used, continually circling the earth and transmitting all the time. Four ground stations receive these transmissions and measure the doppler shift. Since the position of the ground stations is fixed they are thus able to determine the position of the satellites. This information is fed at frequent intervals into a computer which calculates in advance the orbital paths of the satellites and passes the details to an injection station. From thence they are transmitted to the satellites themselves, each of which receives and stores them in its memory.

At successive two-minute intervals throughout their orbits the satellites broadcast their own path parameters, or constants, for two minutes at a time, together with some past and future parameters. Ships fitted with the NAVSAT system receive these transmissions, and also the satellite's standard frequency to enable the doppler shift to be measured, which are fed into a special computer on board. The latter is also fed with the measurement of the doppler shift, time, and the ship's own course and speed, and it then finally displays to the navigator his position in latitude and longitude to a high degree of accuracy from a single satellite pass. Normally with four satellites in orbit it is possible for a ship's navigator to obtain an acceptable 'fix' every two hours.

Satellite navigation can be integrated with other navigational devices such as the inertial system, and with various other navigational components to provide, if required, a completely automatic means of navigating a ship throughout all the various stages of her voyages, even to final berthing. The system is particularly valuable in oceanographical work, and the Royal Navy's larger surveying ships are fitted with NAVSAT.

The Grigg Committee in the late nineteen-fifties recommended a biennial review of Service pay, and this recommendation had been accepted. But by the time the 1966 review was due to come into effect a Prices and Incomes Board had been set up by the Government to deal with wage claims in industry and price rises generally. The question of Service pay increases was therefore referred to the Board, with resultant sweeping reforms in the pay structure of the armed forces.

The Grigg Committee had recommended that future Service pay reviews should take into account changes in average earnings and wages in manufacturing and certain other industries. Revised pay rates for officers should be governed by relative changes in the pay of comparable grades in the Home Civil Service.

After a job evaluation survey had been carried out by special tri-Service teams, each accompanied by an official of the PIB, to compare Service conditions with the civilian sector, the Board, which had found the existing pay structures of the armed forces extremely complicated and giving rise to many disparities, recommended the creation of a comprehensive 'Military Salary'. This would consist of one basic rate for each rank and trade, subject to tax in the normal way, and out of which Service men and women would pay for food, lodging and clothing (excluding uniform). For the Navy, charges for accommodation and food would not be applicable while on board ship.

It was also proposed that because of the special conditions of their employment the Services should receive an additional emolument known as the 'X-factor'. Amounting to 5 per cent of the basic salary, the 'X-factor' was to compensate financially for a man's commitment to his Service, the code of discipline to which he was subject, liability to be exposed to danger, and the upheaval and uncertainty caused by the need for mobility.

The resultant pay increases, which were considerable, should apply also to the Reserves and, as a step towards equal pay for women, the rates for Servicewomen increased to 90 per cent of the corresponding scales for men. (Subsequently these were further increased to 95 per cent, but lacking the X-factor paid to men.)

The Board's recommendations were accepted, and the military salary duly came into force from 1st April 1970. As before, it was to be reviewed biennially, and for this purpose an independent Armed Forces Pay Review Body was set up.

Up to and for some years after the war naval pay had been calculated on a daily rate basis—later weekly—that for ratings including additions for specialist and professional qualifications, or non-substantive rates, length of service increments, good conduct badges, charge pay, trade pay, watchkeeping certificate allowances for engine-room artificers, kit upkeep allowance, and, where applicable, grog money at the rate of threepence a day paid quarterly to those who did not take up the rum ration. Except for kit upkeep allowance, all these were now swept away—although compensated for—including pay for good conduct badges; but length of service increments were retained and in some cases increased. Flying pay, submarine pay, diving pay and parachute pay were also retained and increased.

The issue of duty-free tobacco in the Navy, a privilege enjoyed by sailors for many years, was not taken into account by the Prices and Incomes Board when assessing the new naval emoluments. Nor was rum, but in the not too distant future the fate of the sailor's 'tot' was to be sealed.

The introduction of the military salary had a concomitant effect upon a long-standing feature of naval life—the fortnightly pay muster. For, unless they opt to receive their pay in cash, ratings as well as officers may now (and are indeed encouraged to) have their pay credited directly into their personal bank accounts on a monthly basis, cashing cheques as required with the ship's Supply Officer.

The Navy man of the Seventies has thus come a very long way indeed from the bad old days of his forebears, when the 'wooden wall' sailor was issued at the end of a commission, which often lasted for years on end, with a 'pay ticket' which could only be cashed at the Navy Pay Office in London. Nor could he be sure that this would be honoured, even if he managed to arrive there without being robbed or swindled on the way!

The advent of computers as a feature of everyday life was to bring about a revolutionary change in the Navy's pay accounting system. Up until the Sixties this was run on lines not greatly dissimilar from that in force in Nelsonic days. The old-time 'Muster' and 'Description' books kept on board warships by the Purser and his Clerk had gradually evolved into hand-written ledgers upon which all officers and ratings serving in ships were borne. The ledgers were large sheets of specially printed paper ruled into headed columns which were roughly sewn up into book form at the beginning of each quarter. They were kept in duplicate by Writer ratings, one copy for each completed period being sent to the Admiralty, and the other retained for two years or until a ship paid off. After the end of the Second World War the accounting periods were changed to three a year, and the duplicate ledger replaced by a special form given to each officer and rating for retention.

By 1964 computers were being increasingly used in the commercial world to take the drudgery out of clerical work in business and science, and had been introduced into the Navy's research and development establishments, the naval dockyards and store depots. In that year the Admiralty Board set up a mixed team of naval and civilian personnel known as the 'Naval Pay and Records Computer Project Team' and directed them to devise a 'detailed plan for a centralised organisation embodying a computer which will be capable of calculating the pay and maintaining the Service records of all personnel in the Fleet'.

As a result of their efforts, a large four-storey office block with attached computer building was erected near Fort Rowner, Gosport. In October 1970 the new establishment was formally 'commissioned' under the ship name HMS *Centurion*, with a commodore in charge of a mixed complement of naval and Civil Service personnel. Some of the latter were drawn from the Department of Navy Accounts, itself to be absorbed into an all-Service Accounts Directorate under the Ministry of Defence policy of simplification and economy in various fields of administration, notably logistics and the pooling of certain supply services.

All drafting authorities were duly transferred to the new establishment, and pay accounts gradually built up in the computer, first from shore establishments and later individual ships. By the beginning of 1973 all officers and men of the Royal Navy, Royal Marines, and personnel of the WRNS and QARNNS had been taken on, together with their pensions, drafting, advancement, and associated records. The old ships' ledgers were finally banished, their place being taken by a computerised and periodically renewed pay entitlement record, from which shipborne accounting staff can make cash payments as required.

Thus automation snapped another link with the old-time Navy when, prior to revision of the Naval Discipline Act in 1957, no officer or rating was considered to have any official naval existence unless he was 'borne on ship's books'.

Coincident almost with the introduction of the military salary, the Admiralty Board created a new top level for ratings : the Warrant Officer. Highest rung of the Lower Deck advancement ladder, the new rate—to be called 'Fleet Chief Petty Officer', and the equivalent of the Warrant Officer Grade I (Regimental Sergeant-Major) in the Army and Warrant Officer in the Royal Air Force—was open to both male ratings and Wrens. Formerly no naval equivalent of these grades had existed.

The new rate was not a reversion to the former rank of Warrant Officer which ceased to exist in 1949, since its holders would continue to be ratings rather than officers. Messing in ships and shore establishments along with other chief petty officers, Fleet Chiefs would wear the same uniform but with a more elaborate cap badge, and a cuff insignia incorporating the Royal Arms. They were to be employed principally on managerial tasks in billets which required the performance of duties of a particularly high standard, with the prospect of having to shoulder yet higher and wider responsibilities under the Navy's developing management system. Privileges appropriate to their position would include being addressed as 'Mr.' by their superiors and 'Sir' by subordinates. For Wrens the mode of address would be either 'Miss' or 'Mrs' according to marital state, and 'Ma'am' by juniors.

Fleet Chief Petty Officers would have to serve for five years longer than the normal maximum for ratings of twenty-two years from the age of 18, and would receive higher rates of pay and pension. To qualify for the rate, the introduction of which was one of the recommendations of a Ministry of Defence 'Advancement Working Party', candidates would be required to have served for three years in the Chief Petty Officer or Chief Wren ratings. Promotion would be via selection boards which would be looking for ability not seniority.

The creation of this new top-level rating with its enhanced status was warmly received by the Fleet, whose senior ratings had long considered that they lagged unfairly behind their sister Services in this respect.

The story of the Royal Navy is a continuing one. For, as an island nation dependent upon seaborne supplies for survival and for defence against invasion, Britain's need for her Navy remains as great as ever it did throughout the past centuries.

Those centuries have wrought many changes in its ships, weapons and equipment—even some of its customs and traditions. Only one factor has remained constant : the quality of its sailors. It may not be entirely inappropriate, therefore, to end this record of nearly thirty years of naval history which have followed the end of the Second World War with a brief reference to the abolition at the threshold of a new decade of a custom, grown into a tradition, whose origin mirrors the harsher days of the past, and abolition their transformation to the more enlightened ones of the present.

On 31st July 1970 the rum ration, first made official in the Royal Navy some 240 years earlier, was issued for the last time. In decreeing its end the Admiralty Board explained that 'in the light of the conditions of the modern Navy the rum issue is no longer compatible with the high standards of efficiency required now that the individual's tasks in ships are concerned with complex and often delicate machinery and systems, on the correct functioning of which people's lives may depend'. (In compensation, a capital sum of over £2 million was paid into a special amenities fund for the benefit of sailors and marines.)

Even so, tradition refuses to be banished entirely. For rum is still to be available in the Navy of the Seventies and beyond for those special occasions when the signal is made to 'Splice the Mainbrace'.

First Sea Lords Since the End of the Second World War

Date of appointment

Admiral of the Fleet Sir Andrew B. Cunningham	15th October 1943
Admiral Sir John H. D. Cunningham	10th June 1946
Admiral Lord Fraser of North Cape	6th September 1948
Admiral Sir Rhoderick R. McGrigor	20th December 1951
Admiral the Earl Mountbatten of Burma	18th April 1955
Admiral Sir Charles E. Lambe	23rd May 1959
Admiral Sir Caspar John	23rd May 1960
Admiral Sir John D. Luce	6th August 1963
Admiral Sir Varyl C. Begg	28th February 1965
Admiral Sir Michael Le Fanu	August 1968
Admiral Sir Peter Hill-Norton	June 1970
Admiral Sir Michael Pollock	12th March 1971
Admiral Sir Edward Ashmore	March 1974

The Navies of the Commonwealth

Since the end of the Second World War the navies of the older countries of the Commonwealth have also undergone changes along similar lines to the Royal Navy. Matching increased responsibilities and commitments, they have grown in size and strength, and today consist of versatile modern ships with advanced weapons and equipment, backed where necessary by maritime air power. Newer and smaller member nations with a coastline to defend have instituted their own naval forces.

In 1939 the Royal Australian Navy, then the largest of the old-time 'Dominion' navies, comprised six cruisers, four ageing destroyers, two escort vessels, one depot ship and a surveying vessel. When the war ended its manpower strength had risen to 33,000 officers and men and the active fleet, which had fought in every theatre of the sea war, totalled well over 100 warships ranging from cruisers to minesweepers.

With the emergence of the submarine threat in the nineteen-fifties Australia decided to expand her anti-submarine forces along similar lines to the Royal Navy and, having earlier established her own Fleet Air Arm, to build her future fleet around a core of aircraft carriers. Gradually more modern vessels were added, including guided missile ships, frigates and submarines. In 1967 a new naval ensign was adopted instead of the White Ensign of the Royal Navy which had been flown since the formation of the Royal Australian Navy in 1911. On it the red cross of St. George was replaced by six blue stars representing the Southern Cross.

Today the Royal Australian Navy includes an aircraft carrier, modernised and converted to the anti-submarine role; three US-built 4,600-ton guided missile destroyers; three *Daring* class destroyers; four 'O' class submarines; six modern frigates armed with Seacat and Ikara weapons systems; minehunters, minesweepers, patrol boats, support ships and landing craft, and four survey ships. The Fleet Air Arm is equipped with American Skyhawk fighter bombers and Tracker anti submarine aircraft; also British Wessex helicopters.

*   *   *

Officially established in 1910 with two ageing British cruisers and a handful of small Customs craft, the Royal Canadian Navy entered the Second World War with six old destroyers and a manpower strength of under 2,000 officers and men. During hostilities the Canadian Navy expanded 52-fold and, as well as playing a major part in the Battle of the Atlantic—sinking seventeen U-boats and assisting in the destruction of ten more—its ships took part in the D-Day landings, and formed part of the British Pacific Fleet. Along with warships from Australia and New Zealand, Canadian warships joined those of the Royal Navy in the Korean war.

Following rapid post-war manpower and fleet reductions, the Canadians began in the nineteen-fifties to build up their naval strength, particularly in anti-submarine vessels, and for the first time introduced submarines. Ten years later a more extensive building and modernisation programme was put in hand, concentrating on the anti-submarine role in all its aspects. In 1964 the Canadian Navy Board was dissolved and Naval Headquarters integrated with Canadian Forces Headquarters. In 1968 the Canadian Forces Re-organisation Act unified all three Services. A new naval Jack was adopted, the White Ensign having earlier been replaced by the Canadian national flag.

Today the combat fleet strength of Canada's Maritime Command, which has the longest coastline in the world to defend, comprises four gas turbine-propelled guided missile destroyers armed with Seasparrow and homing torpedoes and carrying Sea King helicopters; eighteen modern 2,400-ton anti-submarine frigates; three 'O' class submarines and one US-built submarine; backed up by maintenance and replenishment ships, tankers and research vessels.

Originally the New Zealand Division of the Royal Navy, this small 'Dominion' naval force was re-titled the Royal New Zealand Navy in September 1941. In 1939 its strength comprised two cruisers, two escort vessels and a minesweeping trawler. Within three months of the outbreak of war the New Zealand-manned cruiser *Achilles* earned renown by taking part in the River Plate battle.

At the end of the war, in addition to two cruisers, the Royal New Zealand Navy had acquired a number of corvettes and minesweeping trawlers. In the late nineteen-fifties a programme of modernisation was begun with the building of *Leander* class frigates in the United Kingdom and the acquisition of a number of patrol craft. Today, with a manpower strength of just over 3,000 officers and men, the

Royal New Zealand Navy comprises four modern frigates armed, in addition to guns, with the Seacat weapon system and the Limbo anti-submarine mortar; escort minesweepers, seaward patrol craft, a survey ship and an Antarctic support vessel.

The birth of the Indian Navy can be traced back to the days of the first Queen Elizabeth. Originally the Honourable East India Company's Marine, this naval force has borne the titles over the years of Bombay Marine, Indian Navy, HM Indian Marine, Royal Indian Marine and Royal Indian Navy, reverting to the present title in 1950 when India became an independent republic.

In 1939, with a British admiral as its commander-in-chief, the Royal Indian Navy consisted of five escort vessels, one patrol vessel, one survey ship and a trawler. By 1945 its strength had grown to thirty-four frigates, corvettes, sloops and fleet minesweepers, and a large number of trawlers, manned by 30,000 officers and men.

Three years later the Indian Navy acquired its first cruiser (the famous *Achilles*, renamed *Delhi*), and a number of ex-British destroyers converted to fast anti-submarine frigates. In 1952 the Tudor crown and Star of India were dropped from the badges and crests of all Indian warships and naval establishments, and the first Indian admiral took over as Flag Officer Indian Flotilla.

During the nineteen-fifties and nineteen-sixties the Indian Navy began to build up its strength with the purchase of a fully modernised aircraft carrier from Britain and the acquisition of British-built *Leander* class frigates, Russian-built escort frigates, submarines and other warships. Today the fleet includes in addition to the aircraft carrier, two modernised cruisers; three destroyers; twenty-eight frigates; four patrol submarines; eight fast attack craft armed with surface-to-surface missiles; eight minesweepers; seventeen coastal patrol craft; four survey ships, and various miscellaneous vessels and support ships. In addition to the two main naval commands—West based on Bombay, and East based on Vishakapatnam on the Bay of Bengal—a naval base has also been set up in the Andaman Islands. India is now building her own submarines and larger surface vessels.

In 1948 a small naval force was raised, paid for and administered by the Singapore Government. Consisting of ten minor war vessels lent by the Royal Navy, its manpower strength totalled 900, largely Malayan personnel with British officers. Four years later the title of Royal Malayan Navy was bestowed on the force. In 1958 when the

Federation of Malaya came into being, the Royal Malayan Navy became part of the Federation's armed forces, and subsequently of the independent State of Malaysia which succeeded it.

Since then this Commonwealth navy has grown both in manpower and number of ships. Modelled on the Royal Navy, efficient, well trained and well led, it consists of some fifty vessels, which include frigates, coastal and inshore minesweepers, and a large number of fast modern patrol boats. Some of the latter are armed with surface-to-surface missiles, and others can be adapted to the torpedo, gunboat and mine-laying roles.

Three years after leaving the Federation in 1965, the independent State of Singapore instituted its own unified defence force on the Canadian model. Today its maritime strength includes three missile boats, ten fast patrol craft, and two seaward defence boats.

Other Commonwealth naval forces which have come into being since the war are the Royal Ghana Navy, first instituted in 1959 with two inshore minesweepers purchased from Britain. Today it totals eight ships which include a modern corvette, two seaward defence boats and two Russian-built patrol boats. The Nigerian Navy, which also started life in 1959, today has twelve ships. These include a general purpose frigate, two corvettes, six seaward defence boats and three fast patrol boats. Nigeria also has two surveying ships. Total manpower strength is 200 officers and 2,100 ratings.

In 1958 Tanganyika (Tanzania), Kenya and Uganda combined to form the Royal East African Navy with a fleet minesweeper lent from the Royal Navy. Four years later the force was disbanded. Subsequently Tanzania acquired her own small fleet of six fast patrol boats; and Kenya, whose navy was inaugurated in 1964 on the first anniversary of the country's independence, has three British-built fast patrol boats, and a manpower strength of 300 officers and men. Sri Lanka's navy, formerly the Royal Ceylon Navy, comprises some thirty vessels, which include two frigates and a large number of patrol boats.

Although South Africa is no longer a Commonwealth country, she has always looked on the Royal Navy as her *alma mater*, and is regarded as the natural protector of the sea routes round the Cape. Her naval strength is therefore of importance both to Britain and the NATO countries. Since 1957 when the Simonstown base was transferred, South Africa has expanded and modernised her naval forces, which were minimal in 1939. She now possesses some thirty major units, which include destroyers, modified *Leander* class anti-submarine frigates built in the United Kingdom; submarines; coastal mine-sweepers and patrol craft; a survey ship; fleet replenishment ship, and various miscellaneous vessels. Manpower strength totals 475 officers, 2,320 ratings and 1,400 National Servicemen.

A Select Bibliography

How They Won the War in the Pacific, S. P. Hoyt
Task Force 57, P. Smith (Kimber, 1969)
Naval Policy Between the Wars, S. W. Roskill (Collins, 1965)
The Eagle Spreads His Claws, L. Gardiner (Blackwood, 1966)
The Royal Navy Today and *British Sea Power*, B. B. Schofield
NATO And The Defence of the West, Lowenstein & Zuhlsdorff, (Deutsch, 1963)
Maritime Strategy, P. Gretton (Cassell, 1965)
Yangtse Incident, L. Earl (Harrap, 1950)
Escape of the 'Amethyst', C. E. Lucas-Philips (Heinemann, 1957)
The Day Before Yesterday (Sidgwick & Jackson, 1971).
Brassey's Annual
Post War Mine Clearance, Reports by the International Central Board
Keesings Contemporary Archives
White Papers on Defence, HMSO
Grigg Committee Report, HMSO Cmd. 545
Annual Register
Admiralty Monthly News Summaries

Index